HEINZ
WALKS
—FOR—
WILDLIFE

W0008501

HEINZ
WALKS
FOR
WILDLIFE

WITH AN INTRODUCTION BY

Dr. Nick Middleton

on behalf of the World Wide Fund for Nature

EBURY PRESS LONDON

Published by Ebury Press
an imprint of Century Hutchinson Ltd.
Brookmount House
62–65 Chandos Place
Covent Garden
London WC2N 4NW

First impression 1989

British Library Cataloguing in Publication Data
Walks for wildlife.
1. Great Britain. Nature trails
I. World Wildlife Fund
508.41

ISBN 0 85223 753 7

Edited by Helen Southall
Illustrations and maps by Kate Simunek

Typeset by Textype Typesetters, Cambridge
Printed and bound at The Bath Press, Avon

CONTENTS

Foreword by Bill Oddie

Introduction by Dr. Nick Middleton   1

SOUTH-WEST ENGLAND   34
Avon, Cornwall, Devon, Dorset, Somerset

SOUTH-EAST ENGLAND   64
Kent, London, Surrey, Sussex, Wiltshire

WALES   88
Clwyd, Dyfed, Glamorgan, Gwent, Gwynedd, Powys

CENTRAL ENGLAND   114
*Bedfordshire, Berkshire, Buckinghamshire, Cheshire,
Derbyshire, Gloucestershire, Hereford and Worcester,
Leicestershire, Lincolnshire, Manchester (South),
Merseyside (South), Nottinghamshire, Oxfordshire,
Shropshire, Staffordshire, Warwickshire, West Midlands*

EAST ANGLIA AND REGIONS   160
Cambridgeshire, Essex, Hertfordshire, Norfolk, Suffolk

NORTHERN ENGLAND   186
*Cleveland, Cumbria, Durham, Humberside (North),
Lancashire, Manchester (North), Northumberland,
Tyne & Wear, Yorkshire*

SCOTLAND   216
*Borders, Central, Dumfries and Galloway, Grampian,
Highland, Strathclyde, Tayside*

NORTHERN IRELAND   230

The Wildlife Trusts   239

WWF – World Wide Fund for Nature is an international conservation organisation devoted to the wise use of natural resources. WWF is probably best known for its work to save endangered species of animals and plants, such as the tiger and Arabian oryx. However, the scope of WWF's work includes the conservation of nature in all its forms: soil, water and clean air, as well as complete ecosystems ranging from tropical rainforests, coral reefs and mountains to wetlands and savannas. WWF was founded in 1961 and is now the world's largest voluntary conservation organisation with offices in 24 countries around the world.

For further details of the World Wide Fund for Nature please write to WWF – UK, Panda House, Weyside Park, Cotteshall Lane, Godalming, Surrey GU7 1XR.

Heinz Guardians of the Countryside is a major British conservation programme sponsored by Heinz in conjunction with the World Wide Fund for Nature. Its objective is to help protect those UK wildlife species and habitats in greatest danger, thus safeguarding them for future generations.

The programme has achieved a number of successes. It has saved the Trehane Barns in Cornwall, a vital breeding site for a large colony of the rare greater horseshoe bat; provided protection for the Helford River, which has now become a designated voluntary marine conservation area, and helped to safeguard rare orchid seeds by funding wardens thorughout the flowering season in five counties. This was undertaken in collaboration with the Royal Society for Nature Conservation's local wildlife trusts.

In Somerset, the programme provided experimental nestboxes for dormice while in Shetland, a study was carried out on otters. A further study was carried out on dolphins in British waters to establish their ecological needs.

The biggest undertaking was to purchase Cape Cornwall, England's only Cape, whose deeds were given to the National Trust. The programme also helped to buy Coaley Wood in Gloucestershire, Trigon heathland near Wareham in Dorset and Asham Meads, an ancient meadow in Oxfordshire.

Guardians of the Countryside has also published many educational booklets including the "Species Alert" series of leaflets, and sponsored two editions of "The Good Beach Guide" with the Marine Conservation Society. Last year, Heinz also sponsored Walk for Wildlife, the World Wide Fund for Nature's annual fundraising walk.

FOREWORD
by Bill Oddie

Every infant school has a nature table; every young child loves going on nature rambles. Nature study is almost invariably a standard lesson at primary schools. The undeniable fact is that young people have – to coin a phrase – a natural fascination for wildlife, and this is surely the beginning of a concern for our environment. But what happens as they get older? At secondary school there are no nature lessons, and in the adult world nature study is relegated to the status of a hobby or pastime. So does this mean that concern for the environment is something we grow out of? Does it follow that conservation is a topic we need only consider in our spare time? Well, look around at the state of our world. It seems to me that mankind *is* guilty of just such a false and dangerous maturity. The present dire condition of our earth, oceans and atmosphere is the work of grown-ups.

The truth is that if we don't have time for nature, we don't have time for ourselves. I fervently believe that the more people there are who are enthusiastic about plants, flowers, trees, birds, insects, animals, pond life and so on, the better, healthier and safer place this world will be.

Please make sure that YOU are one of those people. You've made a pretty good start by buying this book! You will find it an excellent teacher. Now get out into the countryside, and open your eyes wide...as wide as a child's.

London 1989

INTRODUCTION

This book contains more than 270 wildlife walks specially chosen because they provide the public with an opportunity to enjoy the countryside and see some of the many plants and animals that live there. The UK has a rich variety of countryside packed into a small space which is arguably unparalleled anywhere else in the world. The landscapes and wildlife we see today are the result of an evolution that combines plants, animals, soils, the climate and the history of human habitation.

The walks in this book cover the wide diversity of countryside and landscape found in the UK. The types of woodland walks included range from ancient woodlands in the Cheddar Gorge on the Long Wood Nature Trail, or the broadleaved trees of Priory Wood in Gwent with its abundant wild cherry, to the pinewoods and wetland willows of Doune Ponds, near Stirling in Central Scotland. The wet meadowland of Lagan Meadows in Belfast contrasts with the fenland and broads of Upton Fen in Norfolk, and the open grassland of Taf Fechan in Glamorgan is a very different landscape from the moorland of Bridestones Moor in North Yorkshire. A walk over the sand dunes at the Umbra Nature Reserve in Co. Down, Northern Ireland, reveals a distinctive coastline different from the tidal mudflats and saltmarshes of the Fal-Ruan Estuary in Cornwall or the cliff walks of Dyfed's Cemaes Head.

These walks have been chosen so that you can see the conservation of our wildlife being practised. The description of each walk gives an indication of the sort of countryside and wildlife you can expect to see. An Ordnance Survey map reference is given along with details of how to obtain further information about the walk. For some walks, a guide can be arranged who will take you round and point out sites of interest, so helping you to get more out of your walk for wildlife. You may like to use this book to plan a day in the country, or as a reference source for school trips to see examples of nature conservation, or as a guide to help you plan your exploration of the countryside.

The efforts to conserve our countryside heritage are particularly important today because many parts of our landscape are under threat from a range of dangers, such as pollution, urban development and the spread of intensive farming and forestry. The main threats to the wellbeing of our countryside are outlined in the following pages. On some of the walks, these threats are all too visible and are listed in the Under Threat sections.

Our Countryside

The table below lists the main types of vegetation and habitat currently existing in the UK. Each habitat, eg. woodland, fen, sand dune or mudflat, supports its own 'ecosystem', or collection of plants and animals. The following paragraphs describe the nature of each habitat, its eco-system, and the particular plants and animals that may be seen living there. Although these habitats are divided here to make description easier, many of the walks in this book pass through a number of different types which may merge into one another.

Commonly used names for the main types of vegetation in the UK

Main Growth Form	*Ground Conditions*	
	Dry	Wet
trees	woodland	carr
shrubs	scrub	carr
dwarf shrubs	heath	moor
tall grasses, herbs, sedges, rushes	meadow	fen
grasses, herbs, sedges	pasture	marsh
mosses	moss heath	bog (moss)
bare ground	dune, shingle arable	mudflat

Forest and woodland

Oak is the traditional tree of England, and there is little doubt that many of Britain's lowland areas were once covered by oak forests. Through the ages, oak wood has been used for charcoal, shipbuilding, church pews, panelling and floorboards.

In much of southern and central England you will see oakwoods that have a few large (standard) oak trees surrounded by 'coppice' or 'copse': trees of other species, such as hazel, ash or birch, which have been cut to use as fence posts, etc. Recently cut coppice woods are often carpeted with masses of glorious bluebells or primroses.

Many insects live on the oak, attracting birds such as woodpeckers and wood warblers. High in the trees, grey squirrels feed on the acorns in autumn and winter. Tawny owls may nest in holes in the trunks of rotting oaks, eating field voles and shrews which live in the dead leaves and litter on the forest floor.

The oakwoods of the western coast of Britain and Northern Ireland usually grow in boulder-strewn dells with little fertile soil. These oaks are often stunted and festooned with ferns, brackens, lichens and mosses.

Birch is a very hardy tree, common in the harsh northern territories of Lapland, Russia and Siberia. In the Highlands of Scotland, birchwoods are often found on valley sides where they provide valuable winter shelter for sheep, cattle and deer. The birch is easily recognised by its white bark and it is often popularly called 'silver birch'. The tree never grows very tall, 24 metres (80 feet) is a good height, and as it matures, the bark becomes covered in dark patches. Many old birch trees are attacked by wood-rotting fungi which weaken the trees by inner decay, eventually killing them. Between August and November you will often see the fungus, fly agaric, beneath birch trees. The bright red- and white-capped toadstool is poisonous to humans, but does not harm the tree.

Birch forests predominate in the north west of the Scottish Highlands and Islands where rowan, blaeberry, wood sorrel, violets and ferns also grow. The winter snows record the tracks of rabbit, hare, mouse, vole, red deer, fox, badger, wild cat, otter, weasel and ermine.

Beech trees are typical of the chalk landscapes of England: the North and South Downs, the Chilterns and parts of the Cotswolds. For most of the year, a beechwood is a dark, quiet place, since the heavy foliage prevents most of the sunlight from penetrating the canopy, and the ground is covered by a thick, rust-coloured blanket of fallen leaves and twigs under which few green plants can grow. Often the only plants to be seen are pale green cushions of moss, the bird's-nest orchid which lives amongst the decaying leaves, and the strange-looking arum lily, sometimes called cuckoo-pint or lords-and-ladies.

The leafy floor of a beechwood is home to many leaf-eating creatures, such as leaf-mining moths and weevils, aphids and spiders, lacewings and ladybirds, which in turn form the prey of titmice and other small birds. Squirrels, badgers and black voles are among the larger creatures of the beechwood.

Sometimes yew, holly and rowan are found below beech trees, with bracken, heather and bilberry forming the otherwise sparse ground cover. In woodlands where beech is mixed with ash, a rich plant life develops: dog's mercury, herb paris, yellow archangel, nettle-leaved bellflower and most of Britain's woodland orchids are to be found in beech-ash woods of the southern limestone scarps.

Ash dominated woods are also common to limestone areas, but more typical of the north and west of England in the limestone dales of Yorkshire and Derbyshire, and in the Mendips. These woodlands have a wide variety of other plants below the thin ash canopy. Shrubs include dogwood and spindle, while columbine, celandine, Solomon's-seal, wild garlic and dog's mercury can also often be seen.

Alder and **willow** trees are typical of wet soils and are to be found on the banks of rivers, lakes and marshes. Alder, willow and ash commonly make up the woodland, or 'carr', of boggy ground. A tangle of under-shrubs often grows in fen woodlands, including buckthorn, blackcurrant, redcurrant, gooseberry and bog myrtle. Sedges and tall herbs, such as angelica and marsh marigold, are also common in alderwoods, as are stinging nettle, hogweed and elder.

Conifers, or cone-bearing trees, make up about half Britain's woodland. Most of the conifers you see are species that have been introduced from abroad, since only the Scots pine, yew and juniper are native to the British Isles. In Scotland, pinewoods once covered large parts of the broad valleys, or 'straths', of the Highlands and the glens, but much of this original Caledonian forest has been cut down. Fragments still remain, such as the Black Wood of Rannoch, Rothiemurchus and Glen Affric.

Most of today's coniferous woodland has been planted for the timber industry. Beneath the conifers, few other plants can grow as, with the exception of larches, conifers are evergreen and cast a heavy shadow all year round. You may see some ferns and mosses on the needle-covered forest floor, and in areas where trees have been felled, brambles, foxgloves and willow herb can grow.

Many coniferous woodlands also offer shelter to larger animals from the surrounding countryside. These include deer, hares and foxes. Conifers are also the preferred home of the red squirrel. This animal has become more common in Britain as the number of conifer plantations has increased, after being greatly reduced in numbers by disease and competition from the grey squirrel in the mid-1800s.

Heathland, moorland and grassland

Heathland is now largely covered by ling and heather, although almost all heathland in the UK was once covered by forest. It was cleared centuries ago for agriculture but was found to be too infertile to allow the development of real pasture or the cultivation of arable crops. Grazing by deer, cattle, sheep and goats kept trees from recolonising heaths and now and again the heaths were burnt to encourage new grasses to grow. Heaths are not invaded by trees today because of a hard layer or 'pan' in the soil that prevents the roots of trees from penetrating deep enough.

The classic heathlands are the lowland dry heaths of southern England which are dominated by a variety of heathers, often with gorse and bracken. These heaths are very rich in insects which attract birds such as the nightjar, hobby (a small falcon), Dartford warbler (one of the UK's rarest breeding birds) and the occasional kestrel. Heathlands are also an important habitat for many of our dragonflies and several species of butterfly and moth, including the emperor moth. The six reptiles native to the British Isles are all found on heathland: the slow-worm, common lizard, sand lizard, adder, grass snake and smooth snake.

Heaths are also found in the sandy areas of Norfolk and Suffolk and on parts of Exmoor and Dartmoor. In Yorkshire, the name 'moor' is often used for areas of true heathland where, unlike in the south of the country, bilberry and mosses become dominant over large areas. The name 'moor' is often used in the Highlands of Scotland, too, to describe areas covered in ling or bell heather and roamed by red deer and grouse.

Normally heather is a plant that dislikes lime, but areas of 'limestone heath' and 'chalk heath' occur under special circumstances where non-limey soils overlay the calcium carbonate rocks. Areas of the north Pennines combine heather, bell heather, heath grass and betony with species normally found in limestone grassland (see below).

Moorland includes a number of different types of vegetation and animals, although the vegetation is essentially that of peaty soil. This soil is often deep, almost pure peat, but in some areas there may be only a shallow layer of surface peat mixed with other rock fragments. This results in a natural transition from heathland to moorland, as in the 'moors' of the North Riding of Yorkshire.

A broad division can be made between lowland moors, such as the areas known as 'mosses' in Lancashire, and upland moors. If you visit a lowland moor you will be walking on green carpets of sphagnum moss, with here and there an expanse of cotton grass. You may see bog myrtle, cloud berries or the spoon–shaped leaves of the sundew which survives by eating insects. Cotton grass moors are the most common upland moors and they are widely distributed on the summit plateau of the Pennines. Where the peaty ground is wet, the pink flowers of cross-leaved heath grow among the heather in the summer. In areas where the peat is thicker and wetter, the heather gives way to sedges and grasses which in turn yield to bog. The animals you may see on treeless upland moors include adders, the common lizard, deer, grouse and hares.

Moorland is different from fenland in that its peaty soils are acid rather than alkaline. When drained, fens leave a dark-coloured, very rich soil, whereas a drained moorland is difficult to cultivate because the soil that remains is so acid.

Limestone grasslands are well known for their springy turf, in most cases made up of the grasses known as red fescue and sheep's fescue. The grasslands of southern England's chalk are known as the 'Downs'. Similar grassland is found on the Jurassic limestone of the Cotswolds.

The Downs support a rich variety of flowering plants and many insects. You can see some plants on every down, including ribwort plantain, birdsfoot trefoil, wild thyme, salad burnet and cowslip. Many rare species, including most of our wild orchids, can only be seen on limestone grasslands. They include the bee orchid (whose flower looks like a large bumble bee busily sucking nectar), the monkey orchid and the military orchid as well as the less rare fragrant orchid and pyramidal orchid. The bushes and shrubs you will see on downland walks include traveller's-joy, whose feathery autumn plumes have caused it to be given the popular name of old man's beard. Juniper used to be common to limestone pastures, but is now rare in lowland Britain.

The wide variety of flowering plants growing amid limestone grasses supports a diverse range of wildlife. The chalk-hill blue butterfly, for example, which is on the wing from mid-July to September, only feeds on the small golden flowers of the horseshoe vetch. Since the vetch is only found on limestone grasslands, so is the butterfly. The adonis blue, silver-spotted skipper, tortoiseshell and peacock butterflies may also be seen. Snails and glow-worms are common to limestone lands, as are slow worms, common lizards and many small mammals, though these are less easy to see. Limestone grasslands are also important for the adder and kestrel which prey on them. Other typical birds include the skylark, meadow pipit and cuckoo.

Acid grasslands are found in the uplands of the north and west of the British Isles, where rocks yield acid peaty soils under conditions of heavy rainfall. This type of grassland probably covers a greater area than any other in the UK, the typical grasses being bent grasses and sheep's fescue. These grasslands are relatively poor both in other plant species and animals. Typical flowering plants you may see include mat grass, purple moor-grass, sweet vernal grass, heath rush and tormentil. If grazing is not too heavy, these acidic grasslands can be dominated by heather and can eventually become heathland or moorland. The birds commonly found on acid grasslands are meadow pipits and wheatears. Adders are also quite common.

Neutral grasslands are those existing on soils that are neither very acid nor very calcareous (chalky, rich and alkaline). These grasslands are usually the most fertile so there are few areas in the UK today that are not intensively used by farmers. Neutral grasslands range from regularly flooded areas next to rivers, and wet grasslands in clay vales, to dry unenclosed grasslands on infertile soils.

Vigorous grasses, such as Yorkshire fog and meadow foxtail, are common in lush lowland valleys. Sedges and rushes are typical of the wetter neutral grasses which are often also rich in orchids, especially marsh and spotted orchids. Buttercups and clover are also found, as are cowslips in the drier grasslands, and fen species, such as meadowsweet, in the wet. The typical breeding birds of meadow grasslands include lapwing and yellow wagtail. In wet meadows, redshank and snipe may be seen, and where ponds are to be found the surrounding grasses are home to amphibians such as the common frog and newts. These species are fed on by the olive brown grass snake (though this non-poisonous species of snake is not found in Northern Ireland).

Wetlands and coastlands

Fenland is essentially waterlogged land with reeds and other plants growing in patches of standing water. Much of the area known as the Fens in East Anglia has in fact been drained, so that true fens are now only found in a few isolated places, such as the Nature Reserves of Wicken, Holme and Woodwalton Fens. Other parts of the UK where fens are found include the shores of Lough Neagh in Northern Ireland, the head of Esthwaite Water in the Lake District and round the Norfolk Broads.

The peat of fen country is full of lime, so that its vegetation is very different from the lime-deficient peat of boglands (see below). Tall herbs, including meadowsweet, hemp agrimony and yellow flag, are typical. Reed grasses (which are cut and used for thatching and basketry), bulrushes and sedges invade open water, while along the verges of drainage channels green-winged orchids, water violets, alders and willows grow. Over 70 species of molluscs and 215 different kinds of spider have been recorded in Wicken Fen. Heron, black-tailed godwit, reed warbler, lapwing and redshank are just a few of the many types of birds that can be seen. The Fenland of East Anglia is the only place where you might see the rare yellow and black swallowtail butterfly.

Peat bogs dominate large parts of the landscape of Northern Ireland, Scotland, Wales, the Pennines and the south west of England. The wet and spongy peat soil of bogland is made up of many generations of dead moss and other plants. Bogs form in areas where drainage is poor and the water lacks calcium to neutralise the acids of dead plants. When bog plants die they do not completely decompose because a lack of oxygen prevents bacteria from acting on them. Thus, large amounts of dead plant material build up, adding to the peaty soil.

Generally, peat bogs do not support a wide variety of plant species. They are dominated by sphagnum moss (the main peat-forming plant), though cross-leaved heath, cotton grass, the insect-eating sundew, cranberry and sedges are also common. Pools contain water boatmen, water beetles and dragonfly larvae. There may be a few birds such as curlews and skylarks. Dragonflies, moths and butterflies, such as the large heath, are common, and the air is often thick with biting midges.

Peat bogs may be found in a number of different situations. 'Valley bogs' occur in small depressions in wet heathlands, such as in the New Forest or the west Surrey heaths. 'Raised bogs' develop on top of valley bogs or over fens as a floating mat of moss peat. This is how 'quaking bogs', or quagmires, such as Dartmoor's Fox Tor Mires, originate. They are very deep and dangerous as they can swallow up people and animals. Areas that are completely covered with bog moss are described as 'blanket bogs'. They form where the amount of rainfall is high, such as on upland plateaus and in most parts of western Ireland.

Estuaries are where large rivers meet the sea, so that the wildlife reflects both the fresh water of the river and the salt water of the ocean. The water in the estuary itself is often layered, with fresh water at the surface flowing towards the sea and heavier salt water at depth, flowing upstream with the tides. The few species that can withstand the daily changes in salt of the brackish water in between include shore crabs, lugworms, grey mullet, flounder and some types of prawn.

The sediments brought downstream by rivers often form mudflats in estuaries. These may seem barren but are in fact teeming with life: lugworms, ragworms, polychaete worms, snails and other molluscs, which in turn form the food of fish for which mudflats are important feeding and breeding grounds. Huge bird populations include waders, such as knots, curlews, oystercatchers and godwits, and wildfowl such as teal, pintail and mallard.

When mudflats build up to the level at which they are only occasionally covered by tidal sea water, land plants may start to invade and a saltmarsh develop. The succulent green jointed stems of the glasswort are often seen in saltmarshes; other common plants include cord grass, sea aster, seapoa grass and sea plantain. There is often a gradual change in plant types with distance from the sea, so that a middle marsh area may be dominated by thrift and sea lavender with their masses of pink and purple blossoms in summer. The highest levels of saltmarsh are sometimes coloured yellow-green by the dominating sea purslane.

Sand dunes are usually found behind broad beaches or sand flats around the coastline of the UK. These coastal dunes are often colonised by hard, wiry grasses, particularly the sea couch and marram grasses. In areas where there is a series of dunes, a transition can be seen from active dunes nearest the sea to progressively more vegetated dunes inland. Away from the beach, dune surfaces start to become colonised by red fescue, ragwort and sand sedge, and mosses and lichens may carpet the sand surface. Since many coastal dunes contain large amounts of broken sea shells they are often rich in calcium, so that some plants found on them, such as lady's bedstraw and several types of orchid, are similar to those found on chalk grassland.

Coastal dunes often form in more or less parallel ridges, and the depressions between these ridges are marshy areas, usually of fresh water but sometimes of salt, where the remains of a saltmarsh have been trapped by moving dunes. The rare natterjack toad lives in these marshy dune environments.

Cliffs and **rocky coasts** do not have a particularly distinctive vegetation of their own. Rocky coasts often exhibit very diverse wildlife in that the plants and animals to be seen on an exposed cliff are often very different from those of a sheltered cove or gully. The fringe of spray-washed rocks above the tidal zone is often coloured by grey, black and orange lichens, and a few plants such as rock samphire, sea belt, sea campion and thrift can be seen on most rocky coastlines. Otherwise, the vegetation of a particular cliff is usually that of the nearby landscape.

Sea cliffs are naturally the place to observe seabirds. Many of the cliff faces and tops of the UK coastline support large breeding colonies of guillemot, kittiwake, razorbill, cormorant, shag and puffin. The rare rock dove and the eider duck are more or less confined to the rocky coasts of Northern Ireland and Scotland.

The Countryside Under Threat

The countryside is made up of many different elements: rocks, soil, plants and animals. All these elements are related to each other and affect each other, and are in turn affected by the weather and by people. On the largest scale, the nature of our countryside is dictated by our climate: we do not see arctic tundra, hot desert or tropical forest here. On a smaller scale, we have seen how particular types of ecosystem are found in particular conditions: alder and willow trees are typically found on wet ground, for example, and grassy downs and beechwoods are very characteristic of chalklands. However, the various sets of conditions that lead to the development of typical ecosystems are subject to change. The landscape we see today is the result of such changes brought about by a number of influences, including the climate and human action, and it is still changing.

By far the oldest constituents of our landscape are the rocks, some of which are hundreds of millions of years old. The living bits of our countryside are, of course, much younger, the longest living being the trees which mostly live for a few hundred years, although the oldest tree in the UK (a yew in Perthshire) is probably over 3,000 years old. However, the species of wildlife we see today are the modern representatives of plants and animals that date back through time. Some of today's ferns, for example, are still very much the same as their ancestors which grew 300 million years ago. The remains of these 'ancestors' now make up some of our coal reserves.

The context in which these landscape parts operate consists of the weather and the climate. The weather may change from day to day, and the climate itself changes on a longer timescale. Indeed, although the geological framework of today's countryside is dated in millions of years, many of the land shapes, plants and animals that we see can be traced back only 10,000 years, to the end of the last Ice Age. At that time, the severe disruptions caused by the Ice Age were over, the ice which covered most of the British Isles had retreated, the climate was more or less as it is today and the plants and animals were growing in roughly the same places as they are now. This is not to say that the UK countryside has been static for the last 10,000 years – far from it. What we *can* say is that the basic ingredients of the countryside have changed little over that period of time, save for one important influence – the actions and very existence of human beings.

Superimposed upon the natural set of conditions that make up a landscape are the influences of people, and in the last few thousand years human action has had a very significant impact. The first forest clearances were probably carried out by Neolithic peoples, and since then the landscape has been subject to continual human interference and transformation. Today there are very few parts of the UK countryside that do not owe some aspect of their character to human influence; from the cutting of trees and the digging of ditches to the ploughing of fields. Today, however, many people consider that our countryside is under much greater threat than ever before. Let us examine these threats to see how they work, why they are happening and to what extent they risk our natural heritage.

Farming

At first it may seem a little odd to begin a catalogue of threats to the countryside with farming. Farmers are traditionally thought of as protectors of the countryside, the few remaining members of our society who are still familiar with the rhythms of nature, in contrast with the large majority who live in towns and cities. Indeed, can the farmers' threat to the countryside be a serious one since farming has taken place and left its mark on the landscape for well over 1,000 years?

Unfortunately, the answer is yes, and the reason lies in the fact that since World War II farming in the UK has become much more of an industry than it used to be. Modern farming is intensive farming, with a heavy reliance on machines and chemicals. This new 'agri-business' presents several real threats to the countryside. The immediate effects are the destruction of landscape and habitats: by uprooting hedgerows, draining wetlands and ploughing up heathlands. Less immediate is the impact upon the countryside of pervasive threats such as soil erosion and the long-term use of chemicals.

The revolution in British agriculture dates from World War II when German U-boats played havoc with food imports to the UK and highlighted our reliance on imports of foreign food, particularly from Europe. Indeed, our agriculture had been gradually declining since the mid-18th century so that by 1939 more than two-thirds of our food came from overseas. Since the war years, successive governments have encouraged farmers to produce more food at home. This increase in farmers' productivity has been achieved in two main ways. Firstly, by increasing the actual area of land used to produce food, often referred to as 'extensification', and secondly by getting more out of the land, or 'intensification'. Intensification has led to a rapid rise in the use of machinery on the farm, along with an increased use of chemicals to control pests and weeds, and fertilizers to make crops grow faster and produce more food, thereby increasing the 'yield' from an average hectare.

Destruction of habitats Many parts of the countryside have suffered from the national drive to increase food production by cultivating more land. The speed with which farmers ploughed up and converted natural habitats increased following the UK's entry into the European Community in 1973/4 when additional subsidies from the Common Agricultural Policy encouraged farmers to grow more at almost any cost. There were rapid losses of hedgerows, moorland, meadows and rough grasslands throughout the late 1960s and 1970s.

A government drive to make the UK a cereal-surplus nation was a further spur to this countryside conversion. Large areas of coastal marshes were drained and ploughed for cereals in the 1970s and 1980s. In the north Kent marshes, for example, nearly 15,000 hectares of saltmarsh and freshwater grazing marsh were lost in the fifty years to 1983, virtually all to agricultural expansion.

Hedgerows The effects of modern farming methods have been particularly noticeable on British hedgerows. Since World War II, the rural landscape has been transformed from the traditional patchwork of small fields to one more reminiscent of the North American Prairies. Hedgerows, it has been argued, take up valuable land that might otherwise be used to grow crops, and make ploughing with new, bigger machines more difficult. Their removal increases the area of land producing food and makes the use of machinery more efficient, saving both time and energy.

The counties of south and south-east England have been worst affected. In Huntingdonshire, the average size of field was more than doubled from less than 8 hectares (20 acres) in 1945 to 18 hectares (44 acres) in 1972 as four-fifths of the county's hedgerows were torn up. In Cambridgeshire in 1947 you could have seen an average of 39 hedgerow trees on each 40 hectares (100 acres) of farmland. By 1972 this had fallen to just five. Over 100,000 hectares (250,000 acres) of arable land has been put into production since 1950 by hedgerow removal.

Although the effect on the countryside is obvious to the casual observer – a spoiling and homogenising of the landscape – there are also sound conservation arguments against the destruction of hedgerows, quite apart from its deleterious effect on what we can see and enjoy. Hedges provide shelter for both crops and livestock. By reducing wind speeds, hedges improve yields and reduce soil erosion by storm water and wind. Although hedgerows do harbour some insects and fungi that harm crops, such as wheat rust and the bean aphid, many hedgerow animals are the friends of farmers. Bumble bees, for example, are vitally important in pollinating flowering crops, and many of the bird species living in hedgerows prey on insects and other pests that would otherwise harm crops. If these species are reduced by hedgerow removal, it becomes necessary to control such natural pests and insects with greater applications of chemicals, which in their own way harm the environment (see below).

Wetlands Drainage, largely for agriculture, has been responsible for massive losses of British wetlands. Drainage in postwar Britain has completely transformed over 80 per cent of lowland meadows, 60 per cent of lowland bogs and 50 per cent of lowland marshes. Widespread field drainage in Northern Ireland has removed most of the suitable wetland breeding grounds for populations of wading birds such as the dunlin and curlew.

Heathland Most of the heaths in the UK were at one time covered by forests and are themselves the result of tree felling for agriculture at various times through history. Most of this land has in the past proved to be too infertile to allow cultivation of good pasture or arable crops, but since World War II, heaths have been put to the plough once more, and can be used productively if enough chemical fertilizers are applied. In Dorset, for example, three-quarters of the heathland has disappeared in the last 50 years, and in Fife 76 per cent has been lost since the mid-1950s.

One example of a victim of habitat destruction is the large blue butterfly whose specialised life cycle depended on undisturbed grasslands. Fifty years ago naturalists thought that the large blue may be heading for extinction as 90 known sites declined to 30 by the mid-1950s, in the Cotswolds, Somerset, Devon and Cornwall. By 1967 just three sites remained as the old grasslands continued to be ploughed up. In 1979 the last large blue butterflies died and the species vanished from our countryside. Subsequently, a project to reintroduce a new large blue to Britain has been sponsored by WWF. A Swedish sub-species of our large blue is being established in a small reserve in the West Country, where its specialised habitat is intensively managed.

Use of chemicals The destruction of these various types of natural landscape, whether heathland, grassland, meadow, wetland or hedgerow, is all the result of the intensive farming methods designed to produce more food, and it has been noted that this destruction endangers plants and animals and changes the face of our countryside. In most parts of the rural landscape the trend has been towards converting non-agricultural land and extending farmed areas to plant more of the same types of crops. This intensive agriculture often results in whole regions being planted with just one crop, a practice known as 'monoculture'. This practice presents problems in itself, the modern solutions to which also pose threats to the countryside. The problems come from pests and diseases which feed off crops, so reducing yields. The modern solutions are chemical pesticides, fungicides and herbicides.

Agriculture has always been prone to pests and diseases, but in traditional landscapes a range of crops and their varieties were grown so that an area would contain some resistant plants and some vulnerable plants. Monoculture tends to homogenise landscapes, so that a pest or disease that feeds on the one crop can have a veritable banquet in a monocultural landscape.

The modern answer is to apply chemicals to kill pests and diseases. One problem with this is that some forms of wildlife may also be affected, the peregrine falcon being an excellent example. Before World War II, the peregrine bred in many parts of Scotland, northern England, the Isle of Man, Wales and south-west England. After the 1950s the British peregrine suffered from the use of persistent pesticides such as DDT and dieldrin. The result was a huge decline in numbers, mainly through the thinning and consequent breakage of egg shells. Although both chemicals are tightly controlled today, the peregrine has largely disappeared from south-west England, Wales and the Isle of Man. Although peregrines are now recovering in the north and west, they are not spreading back into the areas they formerly inhabited which are now intensively farmed.

Conservation groups have highlighted the deaths of many different animals caused by pesticides: the disastrous decline of British hares has been linked to the use of paraquat to clear stubble; pesticides used to destroy rodents have been deemed responsible for the widespread deaths of barn owls and in some areas pheasants; the fact that the grey partridge faces possible extinction is largely blamed upon pesticides; insects of all kinds are directly killed by pesticides and indirectly if herbicides destroy the plants they live on. Wild plants are also affected, of course, in areas where sprayed chemicals are carried in the wind. These problems should not be surprising, however, since pesticides, herbicides and fungicides are specifically designed to kill wildlife.

Erosion Erosion, or the loss of soil from land caused by water and wind, is a further problem of agriculture. Soil erosion is a natural process, but it often operates faster on the farmer's field. The loss of soil reduces fertility which, of course, affects the ability of plants to grow. The effects of soil erosion on crop yields in the UK have been masked by the widespread and growing use of fertilizers. Indeed, until quite recently, soil erosion was not thought to be a problem in our type of climate. Consequently, it has not been studied in very much detail, but the results of investigations in the last ten years or so have shown that it is a significant threat to agriculture.

Some of the practices of modern agriculture tend to make erosion worse. These include compaction of soil by machinery, planting crops that are not suited to certain soils and the removal of hedgerows. It is not just agriculture that promotes erosion, however. When you enjoy one of the walks in this book, look at the path you follow. Trampling feet do the same as tractor tyres, they compact soil and prevent plant growth, and plant cover is the best protection against soil loss. Footpath erosion is becoming a serious problem in some of our National Parks.

Forestry

Commercial forestry is a controversial land use in our countryside. It is not the planting of trees that worries conservationists, but the methods and objectives of commercial forestry.

The growing, management and sale of timber in the UK is carried out by the Forestry Commission both on its own estates and by regulating private forest land. The Forestry Commission is a government body that was set up in 1919 in response to Britain's strategic disadvantage during World War I. The poor state of the nation's forests, which had been declining since the late Middle Ages, was revealed, and the Forestry Commission's brief was to grow new ones. However, before any of the newly-planted forests had reached maturity, World War II made even further demands on the UK's sparse stocks. After World War II there was a second drive to plant more trees, with a target of 2 million hectares (5 million acres) by the turn of the century. It now seems unlikely that this target will be met, and the original strategic arguments for increasing forest stocks are no longer valid. Nevertheless, since the Forestry Commission came into being, over 800,000 hectares (2 million acres) of new forest have been planted, causing one of the largest ever changes in the natural landscape of the UK.

The visual impact of this change has been cause for some concern. Modern forestry is a business, requiring quick returns on investment and a uniform product for the timber processing industries. The result is that it uses a few species of fast-growing trees, the most widely used being the Sitka spruce and the lodgepole pine. Since the business also needs to make the most of every available square metre of land, the result is plantations of conifer monoculture, growing in geometrically shaped blocks. Complaints against the dark green conifer blocks plastered on the countryside have been countered to some extent in recent years. The Forestry Commission has employed landscape consultants to improve its planting patterns and is now using screens of deciduous species around its large conifer belts.

Destruction of habitats The most dramatic aspect of the Forestry Commission's afforestation programme has been in the postwar period which has seen an unprecedented destruction of ancient woodlands and other natural landscapes. Between 1947 and 1980, 50 per cent of our ancient woodland was lost, mostly to conifer plantations, the rest to arable farmland. In Lincolnshire, for example, over half the ancient woodlands that were present in 1920 have now been converted to commercial plantation. These ancient woodlands are the last fragments of forests that have survived, more or less undisturbed, for several thousand years.

Heathland has also suffered widely from the effects of conifer plantations. The upland heaths are rapidly being afforested, with 90 per cent being lost in Dumfries and Galloway since the mid-1950s. The loss of the Welsh upland, Llanbrynmair Moors, internationally important for its birds and plants, is still mourned by conservationists.

Effects on wildlife As these former habitats are destroyed, so their plants and animals die with them. The new conifer plantations offer new habitats, and the number of bird species to be seen in young plantations increases rapidly for the first few years after planting and continues to rise slowly as the trees mature. Unfortunately, however, plantations are never left long enough to develop enough diversity to attract the variety of birds found in a natural woodland. Upland forestry also has the effect of replacing birds, such as the dunlin, golden plover and greenshank, with more common woodland and farmland species.

Birds of prey may thrive while plantations are young, preying on the many small mammals in the grasses, but as the trees mature, the grasses, mammals and birds of prey disappear. The replacement of hill sheep farming by large-scale afforestation in the Scottish Highlands is the most serious threat to the golden eagle.

Conversely, the spread of conifer plantations has been beneficial for other species, such as the polecat, although the less adaptable pine marten appears to be declining.

It could be said, however, that in recent years, nature's beasts have been hitting back at the UK's foresters. Almost all the commercial plantation conifers have been introduced to this country from abroad, and some have fallen prey to pests, such as the pine beauty moth. Formerly thought to be confined to the native Scots pine, this pest has now started to feed on the lodgepole pine, introduced for commercial forestry from North America. The moth is controlled by aerial spraying of pesticides, which also endangers other animal species. Some Sitka spruce plantations are threatened by the great spruce bark beetle, a recent introduction to Britain.

Other effects of afforestation The effects on soils of long-term conversion to plantation conifers is not well understood. Lodgepole pine dries peat soils irreversibly, which may cause losses in soil strength, while on lowlands, conifer plantations tend to make soils more acidic. In some areas, the streams draining plantations have been seen to become more acidic, adding to problems largely put down to 'acid rain' from industry (see below).

Plantations also have other effects on rain water that runs off the land into streams and, in many cases, the planting of trees reduces the amount of water reaching streams. This can be beneficial for people who live in flood-prone areas, but the reduced flows also affect the life of the stream. Soil erosion from forested parts of the River Severn, for example, has been greater than from nearby grassland on the River Wye. This is thought to be due to drainage ditches dug 40 years before when the area was being prepared for planting. When plantations are felled, it is highly likely that the bare ground will allow much greater amounts of rainfall to enter rivers, carrying much of the topsoil with it.

It should be remembered that the felling of our woodlands has been carried out for as long as perhaps 4,000 years. Nevertheless, the picture of the UK in the 11th century, given to us by the Domesday Book and other sources, is one of predominant forest, pock-marked here and there with clearings, marshes or moorlands. In the 900 years or so since then, the countryside has been transformed as woodlands have been put to the axe. In this light, it could be argued that the efforts of the Forestry Commission should be applauded as they attempt to reverse 4,000 years of destruction. There may be some value in this suggestion, but the speed with which their attempts have been made, coupled with the adoption of a small number of foreign species that were not selected for their ecological value, the overriding commercial drive and the general disregard for environmental concerns and aesthetic values sheds a rather different light on the 'progress' that has been made and is still being pushed forward.

Acid rain

'Acid rain' is a rather misleading term used to refer to the acidity of deposition from the air. This includes wet deposition, such as rain, snow, fog, sleet, hail, mist and dew (all forms of what is termed 'precipitation'), and dry deposits such as gases and solid particles like ash and soot.

Acidity is measured in pH units. The pH scale ranges from 0 (the most acid), through 7 (neutral), to 14 (the most alkaline). With each unit on the scale there is a ten-fold increase in acidity, so that pH5 is ten times more acidic than pH6 and pH4 is one hundred times more acidic than pH6. Some common liquids on the scale include lemon juice (pH2), apple juice (pH3) and sea water (pH8).

Rainwater is naturally acidic because it combines with carbon dioxide in the atmosphere to form a weak carbonic acid. However, the burning of fossil fuels, such as coal, oil and natural gas, produces waste gases of sulphur dioxide and oxides of nitrogen that are released into the atmosphere. These gases are converted in the air to produce sulphuric acid and nitric acid. In this way the acidity of precipitation is increased. Much of the offending gas is produced by power stations and other industrial processes, such as metal smelting. Nitrogen oxides are also released from motor vehicle exhausts.

Acid rain is not a new phenomenon, since the acidity of precipitation can be increased by such natural events as volcanic eruptions or forest fires. The phrase was first coined by an English chemist in the 1850s who found a relationship between the sooty skies of Manchester and the acidity of rainfall. Throughout this century, however, the quantities of fossil fuels burnt in power stations and the number of motor vehicles on the nation's roads have increased.

The geographical areas under threat from acid rain have also been enlarged in recent decades. Ironically, this has come about partly as a result of laws that were passed to try to lessen the effects of this atmospheric pollution. The answer to the problem in the immediate areas around heavy industry was to build much higher smokestacks for power plants. The effect has been to widen the polluted areas so that today acid rain is a problem for much of the UK's countryside and is even 'exported' from Britain in the westerly winds to fall on Scandinavia and other parts of northern Europe.

The ecological effects of acid rain remain a subject of some debate and, like agriculture and forestry, it is one that raises emotions and has important political and economic connotations. It can affect vegetation, soils, rivers and lakes, as well as the many types of wildlife found in all these environments.

Trees As long ago as the 1930s, conifer plantations were abandoned in the Pennines because of the high pollution levels of sulphur dioxide which killed trees. Despite this, the effects of acid rain on vegetation and other forms of wildlife have been largely ignored until recent years. In part, this has been due to lack of research and because of the difficulties of identifying one cause for any particular effect.

In the case of trees, damage to leaves, pine needles, and young shoots can be due to natural causes such as disease, fungi, insects and the weather, but acid rain is also important. Different surveys have reached different conclusions. One in southern England, carried out by Greenpeace in 1988, showed that three-quarters of the yew trees, half the oaks and a third of beeches are sick or dying. Air pollution was thought to be a major culprit.

Surveys by the Forestry Commission in recent years have been more dismissive of acid rain as a cause of tree problems. Nevertheless, a few weeks after the Greenpeace report was published in November 1988, the Forestry Commission produced the results of its own survey which concluded that Britain's trees were showing some of the worst symptoms of ill health in Europe. A combination of climate, air pollution, insect attack and fungi was blamed. The ancient Scots pine is showing signs of rapid decline and the Sitka spruce is also badly affected. These, and some other conifer species, are showing similar damage to those in West Germany's Black Forest which has been ravaged by a combination of acid rain and ozone pollution from car exhausts.

Crops The effects of acid rain, in conjunction with other atmospheric pollutants, are also thought to damage crops. Sulphur dioxide, oxides of nitrogen and ozone originate from acid rain and motor vehicle exhausts. They combine to make cocktails of pollutants that reduce yields, increase certain insect infestations and damage foliage. Barley, peas, lettuces and beans are amongst the crops that are thought to have been damaged by this type of air pollution.

Soils The soils on which acid rain falls are also affected. On some soils that are high in calcium, the acids are neutralised, but in others the acidic water can remove valuable nutrients from the soil, thus making them less available for plant growth. The solubility of some toxic substances in soil, such as aluminium, increases with rising acidity and can be released from soil structures to be taken up by plants or flushed out into rivers where they may cause major physiological stress to some aquatic organisms.

Rivers and lakes The impact of acid rain on our rivers and lakes can be severe. Many of the lochs of Galloway in south-west Scotland have lost their fish stocks as the water's acidity has increased. In some cases the losses date from the 1930s. Investigation of the skeletons of tiny algae in loch beds has shown that the acidity has increased since the mid-19th century. Particles of soot in among the skeletons in the sediment confirm that air pollution played an important role in the lake's acidification.

Perhaps a more serious problem for fish is caused by a sudden pulse of acidity brought on by melting snow or heavy rains following drought. In these cases, large amounts of acid may enter fresh water, releasing aluminium into the water. Aluminium can be deposited on fish gills and can cause death.

Acid waters and declining fish stocks have also been recorded in the rivers and lochs of the Isle of Arran, the rivers of north Argyll and the lochs on the island of Islay. Concern is growing that the waters of the Cairngorms may face a similar threat. Acidification of lakes and rivers in the Lake District and southern Pennines is probably due, at least in part, to acid rain. Many Pennine bogs have become too acidic even for sphagnum moss to grow. Declines in the brown trout and salmon populations of Welsh upland rivers have also been blamed on acid rain. In the River Wye, acid waters seem to be responsible for declines in dipper birds since the insect larvae on which they feed do not thrive in acid waters. In Northern Ireland, acid waters have been found in the Mourne Mountains and other vulnerable areas.

Some parts of southern England have also been affected. Brown trout have been lost from acid streams in the Ashdown Forest, newts are becoming scarce in Hampshire's New Forest and the rare natterjack toad, which does not breed well in waters with a pH below 6, has disappeared from many parts of east and south-east England. Acid rain is implicated in all cases.

Hopeful signs Since 1980, however, emissions of sulphur dioxide in Britain have been reduced. Monitoring of waters in some Yorkshire reservoirs has shown that acid levels have fallen over this period. This is a hopeful sign for the countryside and its wildlife, but the effects of acid rain and how these effects work are still not fully understood. It appears that some of these effects operate on long timescales of decades or more, so that we may not yet have seen the full realisation of the acid rain threat. In the case of water pollution, the addition of lime to neutralise acid waters has been widely practised in Scandinavia and in parts of the UK. It is a costly business, especially since it appears to be necessary to keep up regular doses to maintain the beneficial effects. Meanwhile, significant steps towards solving this widespread environmental problem could be accomplished if the output of offending gases from fossil-fuel-burning power stations, the major culprits, was limited.

Power generation

We have already seen how coal, oil and natural gas-fired power stations produce waste gases that are having a severe impact on the countryside. The UK produces nearly one-fifth of its energy from nuclear power plants and this form of energy production also has its effects upon the environment.

Nuclear power The fuel that drives nuclear power plants (uranium), and the waste produced by the reactors, is radioactive. Radioactive substances decay or break down by giving off radioactivity as particles and rays. We live in a naturally radioactive world with most of the radioactivity we are exposed to coming from the earth itself and from outer space. The dangers arise when large quantities of radiation are released in small spaces, as with nuclear waste, when release may be accidental or deliberate. High doses of radioactivity can harm, mutilate or destroy living cells and tissue.

The disposal of waste from nuclear power plants is a problem. High level waste remains dangerous to living things for tens of thousands of years. At present it is stored at Sellafield in Cumbria, a nuclear complex that collects and reprocesses spent fuel from power stations in the UK.

Discharge of low level waste from land occurs from Sellafield into the Irish Sea, and concern has been expressed about the effects of this on the marine ecosystem because radioactive substances, like many other pollutants, tend to build up in the tissues of living organisms. As smaller organisms are eaten by larger ones, the build-up increases, and so on up the food chain, ultimately in some cases to human eaters of seafood.

Most of the dangers from radioactive waste in the UK are centred on Sellafield. Like all nuclear installations, Sellafield is built to be as safe as humanly possible. But accidents do happen. The threat of a major nuclear accident is one that looms constantly over our countryside and the whole globe. Although such disasters are statistically very unlikely, their potential for damage is very great indeed. Because of the scale of the impact, the incident does not have to take place at a nuclear plant in the UK. Like so many pollution problems in the modern world, the threat of nuclear disaster is no respecter of international boundaries.

Just after midday on Saturday, 26th April 1986 an explosion destroyed one of the four nuclear reactors at Chernobyl, a small town in the Ukraine of the Soviet Union. A few days later much of Europe was recording the highest levels of radioactive fallout it had ever experienced. Within two weeks minor radioactivity was detected in Washington, Tokyo and throughout the northern hemisphere. The radioactive cloud from Chernobyl spread over most of the UK and heavy rains over north Wales, Cumbria and Scotland washed down considerable quantities of radioactive substances. Hundreds of thousands of lambs from these and other areas could not be sold as they contained levels of caesium above the safety limit for human consumption set by the government. The ban on lamb was partially lifted ten months later, but meanwhile tests on vegetation in Cumbria, north Wales and Scotland showed that levels of caesium were still high. The monitoring of vegetation has continued since, and at the beginning of 1989 some farms in these regions had still not been declared safe. The environmental, human, economic and political costs of the Chernobyl disaster are still being assessed and it has made many think again about the pros and cons of nuclear power.

The alternatives to nuclear energy, other than those based on fossil fuels, are apparently much less hazardous to the environment. Present nuclear power is generated by the process of 'fission' in which energy is released when atoms are split. There is some hope that nuclear energy can be produced by joining atoms together in a process called 'fusion'. The fuel used in fusion is much cheaper than uranium, the process does not produce radioactive wastes and a fusion power plant would be much safer than a fission plant. However, despite intensive research, the problems of harnessing energy from fusion are still a very long way from being solved, and commercial energy will certainly not be available from fusion reactors for at least 30 years.

Alternative power generation Many opponents of the present environmentally problematic methods of power generation suggest that much more effort should be put into developing so-called 'alternative' energy generation. Not only are fossil-fuel-burning and nuclear industries damaging to the environment, but they also use fuels that will not last forever. Alternative energy sources are less damaging environmentally and are based on renewable resources. They include solar radiation, the wind, energy from moving water, heat from beneath the ground and biological materials such as wood.

Such alternative methods of energy production are not entirely without influence on the countryside, however. At present, the machines used to harness wind energy are large for the amount of electricity they can generate, and although old-style windmills are often considered quaint examples of traditional countryside use, so-called 'wind farms' of modern windmills are thought by many to spoil the landscape. Windmills are also noisy and can disturb bird and insect life and air traffic. Nevertheless, large parts of the British Isles are suitably windy for such machines, and wind is high on the British government's list of alternative energy possibilities.

The building of dams on rivers in upland country to harness hydro power is a well established form of renewable energy production. The building of dams and the ponding back of reservoirs, however, destroys natural habitats which become inundated. The amount of water and the nature of the flow in the river downstream is also changed as flows are regulated, possibly causing a change in the ecology of the river.

Energy from the movement of the ocean's tides as they rise and fall can be harnessed simply by damming a coastal bay or estuary. At present there are no commercial tidal power stations in the UK, but plans have been proposed for a barrage across the Severn Estuary. This project, if built, would inevitably alter the delicate ecological balance that charactises estuaries. In the case of the Severn, this might have serious consequences for a habitat recognised as internationally important for knot and redshank, and protected by the European Community's Birds Directive.

Other threats

Transport provides a widespread threat to the countryside through the construction of new highways and the pollution caused by vehicle exhausts. Major roads and motorways frequently destroy ancient habitats and although roadside verges are often quoted by the Department of Transport as providing new wildlife refuges, these rough grasslands and secondary woodlands are usually inhabited by the most adaptable species which are under no threat from human activities.

In 1984, a Friends of the Earth report listed 28 Sites of Special Scientific Interest (SSSI) that were threatened by recent road schemes in the Midlands and south of England alone. Oxleas Wood in Greenwich, southeast London, is a case in point, threatened by a motorway development plan. Oxleas Wood is notable for its rich variety of fungi, and trees such as the wild service, a rare member of the maple family.

Less obvious effects are those on local animal populations, where roads and railways act as barriers to movement and divide populations, as well as introducing hazards when crossing. Conversely, transport routes can also act to aid dispersal of plants. The Oxford ragwort which is native to Sicily was established in the Botanical Gardens in Oxford before 1690 and colonised the walls of the town. Dispersal to the rest of Britain was largely achieved by the Great Western Railway, the plumed fruits of the plant hitching rides on the carriages and wagons, so that its distribution was closely associated with railway lines.

Urban sprawl continues to nibble at the countryside and farmland surrounding towns and cities. Farmers have complained that the accelerated loss of cropland to bricks and mortar has not only taken land but also fragmented agricultural holdings, making management less efficient. Indeed, these factors have been put forward by some as justification for expansion of farmland onto wildlife habitats. Most conservationists, however, reject this argument since the UK's intensive farming output is not threatened by loss of land to urban growth.

There is little doubt that the spread of commuter settlements and retirement homes, particularly in southern England, has swallowed up large parts of habitats such as heathland. In south Hampshire and Dorset the consequences have been serious for species such as the adder, nightjar, smooth snake and a number of rare dragonflies. Legislation is such that conservationists have little power to stop speculative developers, and compromises have to be reached by appealing to the developers' good nature. The Blackwater Valley Meadows SSSI, for example, will be partially destroyed by a superstore development outside Bracknell in Berkshire. The remaining part of the site will be managed as a conservation area by the Borough Council with developers' money. Similar stories can be told about many important sites. In some cases, however, local authorities have been slow to realise and act to do deals with developers. Five acres of the water meadows round Salisbury Cathedral were destroyed in November 1988 by developers before the local council had woken up to what was going on.

Mining activities have left their mark on the landscape over hundreds of years. Marl has been dug for fertilizer, stone has been quarried for building, limestone quarries have produced fertilizer, and salt, lead, iron, and silver mines have been dug. Sand has been extracted for construction, clay for pottery, and peat and coal for fuel. Holes and waste heaps from all these activities scar our countryside, although in places where the scars have been for some years, new habitats have been created and the modifications accepted. Indeed, the Norfolk Broads are entirely the work of peat cutters digging over 600 years ago. Mechanised peat cutting in Northern Ireland is one of the main threats to habitats in the province.

Waste tips from mining operations are increasingly landscaped but ojectionable and harmful dumping still continues as the waste heaps on North Sea beaches from the Durham collieries testify. Chemical pollution of waterways may also be produced from mines and waste heaps.

Future workings are more likely to use strip or opencast techniques rather than subterranean shafts, and these are even more damaging to the countryside. The extraction of gravel, an essential building material in modern society, is almost all opencast. An application to Buckinghamshire County Council for gravel extraction near Burnham Beeches is currently under consideration. Burnham Beeches is one of the UK's last ancient woodlands, boasting 400-year-old trees that shelter muntjac deer and sparrowhawks among other species. The gravel pit would eventually be twice the size of the Houses of Parliament and lower the local ground-water table, endangering the survival of the trees.

Waste from industrial and urban sources enters and pollutes the environment in a number of ways. Much is buried in holes in the ground, so-called 'landfill' sites. There are thousands of these sites in the UK and they are not well regulated. The laws governing disposal are weak and the bodies that oversee dumps are under-financed and under-staffed. The definition of 'hazardous waste' is hazy and relates only to human health without concern for environmental effects. Whilst the USA and several European countries consider that landfill is an unsatisfactory and dangerous method for disposal of waste, here in the UK it is accepted. Whilst every major industrial country in the European Community has carried out surveys of old dumps and found many to be unacceptably dangerous, in the UK no one knows how many problem sites there are because no one has looked for them.

Polluting gases from industrial processes have been referred to above (see Acid Rain), but many other industrial waste products enter the country's rivers and other waterways. Industries such as power stations often release quantities of warm water into rivers that can adversely affect the aquatic ecosystem, whilst more serious forms of pollution from mining and industrial plants include heavy metals. These pollutants such as lead, cadmium, copper and zinc, can be dangerous to animal and human life in very small quantities if allowed to persist in the environment and to build up in the tissues of living organisms.

Our rivers are also polluted by sewage, which is broken down in water by bacteria using oxygen. Excessive amounts of sewage can severely affect fish and other river animals by depriving them of essential oxygen. At present, water authorities who operate sewage plants are allowed to agree 'discharge consents'. These levels are widely regarded as inadequate to protect the rivers into which the sewage discharges flow.

The UK's sewage plants are badly in need of modernisation, but this will not be carried out until the water authorities have been sold off to private companies. What consequences the proposed privatisation of the water authorities will have for the quality of the UK's waterways remains to be seen, but the prospect for our rivers is not good.

Oil spills from ocean-going tankers create severe threats to coastal wildlife, and the detergents used to diperse oil can be equally damaging. Seabirds are worst affected. Many home in on calm oily seas in rough weather, and on meeting oil slicks, dive, only to surface within the slick and become covered with oil. Oil clogs birds' feathers, making them cold and waterlogged, and often they eventually starve to death. Since seabirds live and move in flocks, whole colonies can be wiped out by a single slick.

Oil spills on coastal habitats can be particularly damaging to sensitive ecosystems, such as on saltmarshes, where plants need to ventilate their root systems through pores or openings that can become clogged by oil.

The development of oil resources on land at Wytch Farm in Dorset has caused recent environmental disturbances. Access roads in an acid heathland environment have been surfaced with limestone chippings which, when pounded by heavy vehicles, release calcareous dust into the surrounding countryside. The most serious disturbances are due to the pipelines laid to the oil refinery at Fawley on the Solent. They have damaged part of the heathland of Foxbury Hill in the Avon Valley SSSI, including a smooth snake habitat.

Recreation in itself can endanger the countryside. The problem of footpath erosion has been mentioned above, but visitors to the countryside should be aware of the other threats they may unknowingly be causing.

Picking wild flowers has resulted in the disappearance of some previously common species, such as the primrose which has declined in many parts of England. Serious naturalists and plant collectors looking for rare local species can also cause the loss of plants in some areas. Several mountain species, such as the blue heath and the Snowdon lily, are only found in one or two places in the UK, and are being trampled out of existence by unaware walkers.

Other forms of recreation that potentially damage the environment include the latest ski-lift developments in the Cairngorms. It is feared that the influx of people will both disturb mountain birds and start serious erosion of the fragile mountain soils.

There has also been widespread concern about the effects of lead poisoning on wildlife, particularly on wildfowl. Swans and mallards, for example, are poisoned by eating spent shotgun pellets and discarded anglers' lead weights when feeding and scavenging amongst grit. These pellets are eroded away in the bird's gizzard and the absorbed lead causes damage to the central nervous system, muscles, liver and kidneys. The number of pairs of breeding swans on the River Thames gradually declined over 20 years from about 60 to less than a dozen in 1984. Since then, public awareness has grown, culminating in an Act of Parliament banning the sale of lead weights in 1987. Thirty-two breeding pairs were recorded in that year.

The Greenhouse Effect is a problem of the global environment. The term refers to the way in which carbon dioxide and other gases, such as methane and water vapour, affect the temperature of our atmosphere. Most of these 'greenhouse gases' are normal parts of the air we breath, and are produced by living things on the planet in the natural course of events. In the atmosphere, they allow light from the sun to reach the earth but prevent longer-waved heat radiation from leaving the atmosphere in the same way as a greenhouse.

Since the beginning of the industrial revolution, the amount of carbon dioxide in the world's atmosphere has been increasing. Today's carbon dioxide levels are 30 per cent higher than they were in the early 19th century. Much of this increase has been created by the burning of fossil fuels such as coal, oil and natural gas which releases carbon dioxide into the atmosphere. The chopping down of trees, which is happening at an accelerating rate in the tropical rainforests, for example, also adds carbon dioxide to the atmosphere as trees are burnt or allowed to decay.

Concentrations in the atmosphere of other greenhouse gases have also been increasing in recent years.

The greenhouse theory suggests that as more of these gases are put into the atmosphere, so more heat is trapped and the global temperature is raised. The theory fits well with the facts as the average world temperature has already risen by ½°C since 1900.

The concentrations of greenhouse gases continue to rise. In the case of carbon dioxide, it is probable that a doubling of pre-industrial levels will happen some time during the next century. The consequent rise in air temperature may be 3°C with the effects becoming more exaggerated towards the poles.

Scientists find it hard to predict what consequences this would have for islands such as ours which are small on the world scale. Our climate may become warmer or it could become cooler, seasons may be less marked or more extreme – it is very difficult to say. Soil moisture, soil fertility, growing seasons, plants and animals would all be affected by the changes. If the temperature rises, for example, conifers may not be as well suited to the new environment as species such as the sweet chestnut, red alder and field maple.

One effect that most people agree upon is that sea levels would rise, perhaps by 1.5 metres (5 feet) or more. The estuaries of the Thames, Severn and Humber, The Wash, the Firth of Forth and Lough Foyle would all be vulnerable to frequent and severe flooding. Inland rivers and wetland areas may also be prone to more frequent flooding as ground water levels would also rise.

What's all the fuss about?

The countryside is a living thing that represents the present stage of the complex interactions between climate, soil, wildlife and human beings. It has always been changing and will continue to change: the flowers bloom and seed with the seasons, rivers carve valleys and deposit floodplains, and occasionally dramatic events, such as the hurricane winds of October 1987, make major transformations to landscapes.

The force of human beings has left its mark on the countryside through the ages. For thousands of years people have chopped down trees and ploughed fields, killed animals and cleared vegetation to survive. Since the human impact on our natural environment is by no means a new phenomenon, the threats to our countryside catalogued above should be seen in this light. If this is the case, it is tempting to turn to conservationists and environmentalists and ask the question: what's all the fuss about?

The answer is this: The trend in human influence on our environment in the modern era has been towards an increasing magnitude and frequency of disturbance. Further, although some of the threats above, such as ploughing and deforestation, are as old as organised human society itself, many of the other threats are new. Pollution from industries has only had significant impact in the last one hundred years or so, while other threats, such as those from nuclear power and the powerful pesticides used by farmers, have only come onto the scene since World War II. The scale of threats has also increased this century from local to nationwide, even global, such as the sea level rise induced by the Greenhouse Effect.

As population has grown and society has become more complex and mechanised, so the threats to our countryside have increased, in number, scale, and intensity of impact. While many other aspects of our society have developed alongside this rise to a well-fed, technological society, the realisation of the environmental price of this advancement has been late in coming.

Protecting the Countryside

As our society has grown and developed, so it has had to be better organised, but while there are many laws governing the way we treat land and change it in towns and cities there are precious few regulations governing the ways in which our countryside is used and abused. For example, there is nothing to stop a farmer uprooting the hedgerows on his land or draining it, thus changing or destroying valuable elements of the countryside. Until recently farmers were even encouraged and financially helped to do so by governments. Although there are some regulations governing the amounts of pollutants put into the environment by industries, these are all too often weak and inadequately upheld.

The attempts that have been made to conserve parts of the countryside are also poorly thought out, difficult to enforce and all too often disregarded in the face of 'more important' activities, such as building new roads. Areas designated as Sites of Special Scientific Interest (SSSIs) are sadly a very apt reflection of these failings.

SSSIs have been recognised by the Nature Conservancy Council (NCC) since 1949, the original idea being not to protect the countryside and its wildlife but to earmark a representative sample of the habitats of plants and animals. By the early 1970s, however, it was becoming clear that the SSSIs were the only parts of the countryside that were going to survive. Since 1982 the Nature Conservancy Council has been involved in cataloguing the threats and values of each SSSI. This process is nearing completion, but as it was being carried out a number of sites were destroyed. There are nearly 5,000 such sites in Britain covering 1.6 million hectares (4 million acres). The final total is estimated to be 6,257 sites.

When an SSSI is fully recognised, however, the story is not over. Any person who owns SSSI land can apply to the NCC for payment to stop them disturbing their land by development. A payment of £287,000 is being paid for a 99 year lease on Lord Thurso's land in Caithness, for example, to protect a peat bog and flow from forestry development. An owner who protects a site voluntarily, on the other hand, will probably receive nothing.

Even these incentives do not always work and SSSIs are still ruined. In 1987, 161 were damaged. The penalties are insufficient and the protection given to SSSIs can still be overridden by planning permission.

The example of Duich Moss, a peat bog on Islay, offers some hope for countryside protection in the future, however. The Scottish Development Office had approved a plan for a drinks company to dig peat on this internationally important habitat for Greenland white-fronted geese, but their decision was overturned by the European Community whose Birds Directive, agreed to by the UK in 1979, called for safeguards to protect certain bird species and their habitats.

In 1989 European environment ministers are meeting in Brussels to debate a new directive on protection of wild plants and animals and their natural habitats. Since in the past we have been so lax in protecting our countryside, perhaps only international agreements can do it for us.

Rights of Way

Various pieces of our countryside are protected to some extent from development that would change the character of the landscape. One of the most important reasons for this protection is to safeguard the rights of the public to visit and enjoy the rich variety of countryside in the UK.

The notion of the public having certain 'common rights' to the countryside dates back over a thousand years in England and Wales. At that time, much land was 'commonly' owned, in other words it was owned by everyone and each person had the right to move across it and to use it. Even much of the land 'owned' by lords of the manor recorded in the Domesday Survey of 1086 was far from secure. Commoners' rights included access to and use of virtually all the things a family needed, particularly important amongst which was the right to graze animals.

Gradually, these common lands were restricted, 'enclosed' or privatised by the more powerful lords of the manor who cordoned off land and effectively denied many of the long-held rights of the people. Over a period of about 400 years to the 19th century, the commoners' system died, the countryside was carved up by a small number of individuals, and many people became workers on landlords' land.

During the Industrial Revolution of the 19th century, there was a large movement of people from the country into the towns as growing industries started to employ greater numbers of workers. It is since these times, as the UK has become more and more organised and pressures on space both in city and country have increased, that people have become more interested in natural history and in the uncultivated countryside as a place for recreation. Some memorable confrontations have taken place over the last century between landowners and people wanting to exercise their 'common rights' of access. These struggles have resulted in the setting up of the various categories of protected countryside that are outlined below, all of which date from the National Parks and Access to the Countryside Act passed by Parliament in 1949.

Although these areas are protected to some degree, all land is still owned by private individuals or organisations. Today there remain just a few remnants of truly common land which are still known as 'commons', even though these too are privately owned. Thus, to all intents and purposes, the entire countryside of the UK is privately owned.

National Parks There are ten areas of wild, attractive landscape in England and Wales which are designated as National Parks. They are the Brecon Beacons, Dartmoor, Exmoor, the Lake District, the Northumberland National Park, the North Yorkshire Moors, the Peak District, the Pembrokeshire Coast, the Yorkshire Dales and Snowdonia.

The public has no special rights of access in these areas and most of the land is still privately owned. The landscape of the National Parks is strictly protected, but not always successfully in the face of political and economic considerations. The conservation of a landscape's characteristic beauty is not promoted by the construction of nuclear power stations, radar early-warning stations, potash mines or dual carriageways, all of which have been built in National Parks.

Areas of Outstanding Natural Beauty A number of Areas of Outstanding Natural Beauty (AONBs) have been designated in England, Wales and Northern Ireland. These are regions that have less protection than National Parks but where obtrusive industrial development is supposed to be discouraged by local and central government, though there is little real power to do so. The public has no special rights of access to AONBs.

Heritage Coasts These are certain coastlines in England, Wales and Northern Ireland which have been recognised as worthy of conservation.

National Scenic Areas Scotland does not have any National Parks, AONBs or Heritage Coasts. Their National Scenic Areas are similar to National Parks and AONBs in that there are restrictions on development above a certain size.

Country Parks Country Parks are areas established by county authorities for recreation. Most are close to large towns and cities and are intended to take some of the pressure off National Parks and Nature Reserves.

Forest Parks Forest Parks are managed by the Forestry Commission, a govenment body which is primarily a commercial timber concern. Its Forest Parks have generally good facilities for the visitor and include some important conservation sites, such as the New Forest. Forest Parks can be visited throughout the UK.

National Trust Land Over half a million acres of land are owned by the National Trust and the National Trust for Scotland. These bodies are independent and rely on voluntary contributions. Most of their land is open to the public, though some is leased to farmers and access is limited to paths and bridleways.

Nature Reserves, Sites of Special Scientific Interest and Environmentally Sensitive Areas These categories have a more or less common purpose which is to conserve certain sites that are important and interesting for their wildlife and landscape. There are over 1,000 Nature Reserves and more than 4,000 Sites of Special Scientific Interest (SSSIs) in Britain. Many of these areas allow open access to the public, but in some cases it is necessary to restrict access. In Northern Ireland, the equivalent of SSSIs are Areas of Special Scientific Interest (ASSIs), of which there were 17 by the beginning of 1988. There are 19 Environmentally Sensitive Areas in the UK.

Although SSSIs and Environmentally Sensitive Areas (ESAs) have little protection in law, most are protected from significant disturbance by public payment to landowners. There are also many cases, however, of SSSIs being damaged and destroyed, mostly by agricultural activity and tree-felling.

An area may be classified as a Reserve by the Nature Conservancy Council (NCC) or by the local authority. NCC-classified reserves are known as National Nature Reserves (NNRs) and local authority-classified reserves are known as Local Nature Reserves (LNRs). There are 234 NNRs and 1,300 LNRs in England, Scotland and Wales. Many are owned or leased and maintained by voluntary Wildlife Trusts, operating under the auspices of the Royal Society for Nature Conservation (RSNC). See page 239.

THE COUNTRY CODE

By following the Country Code, walkers can ensure their visit to an area poses no threat to the conservation of its wildlife. The Code provides a brief set of rules to bear in mind while walking in the countryside and will help you get the most out of your walk, while safeguarding the wildlife for others to enjoy.

You have a right of way on the walks described in this book, but remember that in all cases paths are on land that is privately owned and that if you stray from the path you are trespassing. In this case, the landowner has the right to ask you to return to the path or to leave the land. The things that most upset farmers and landowners are dogs disturbing farm animals and killing game and people damaging crops and property. Be sensible: share the countryside; we all have a right to be there and to enjoy it.

Guard against all risks of fire Fires carelessly started can disturb the natural life of large areas and cause damage worth hundreds of thousands of pounds.

Fasten all gates Farm animals allowed to wander from fields could cause accidents or gorge themselves to death in the wrong field.

Keep dogs under proper control Dogs can worry farm animals to death, spread disease and disturb the countryside's wildlife.

Keep to paths across farmland Walk round the edges of fields and avoid damaging crops or grass. When walking on a narrow track keep in single file.

Avoid damaging fences, hedges and walls Fencing and stone walls are expensive to repair.

Do not leave litter Take any litter home with you – it spoils the countryside and can be dangerous to animals.

Safeguard water supplies Do not pollute rivers and streams. Many of them provide the water we use in our homes as well as water for animals.

Protect wildlife All plants and animals are reliant on each other. Do not be tempted to pick pretty flowers or break branches from trees.

Do not make unnecessary noise Most animals are very timid and can be frightened by sudden or loud noises.

Go carefully on country roads When walking on a road with no footpath, keep to the right to face oncoming traffic. When driving along country roads, beware of slow tractors around bends or flocks of sheep that can block the whole road.

Respect the life of the countryside Country people are often suspicious of town and city dwellers. Help overcome this distrust by keeping to the Country Code.

1 Brandon Hill Nature Park
2 Brown's Folly
3 Limebreach Wood
4 Stockwood Open Space
5 Tucking Mill Trail
6 Weston Moor
7 Willsbridge Valley
8 Breney Common
9 Devichoys Wood
10 Fal-Ruan Estuary
11 Hawkes Wood
12 Kennall Vale Woods
13 Luckett
14 Nansmellyn Marsh
15 North Predannack Downs
16 Park Hoskyn Wood
17 Pelyn Woods
18 Pendarves Wood
19 Red Moor
20 Ropehaven Cliffs
21 Tamar Estuary
22 Ventongimps Moor
23 Arlington Court
24 Braunton Burrows
25 Central Park Nature Park
26 Dunsford Wood
27 Exe Reedbeds
28 Halsdon

29 Northam Burrows Country Park
30 The Old Sludge Beds
31 Otter Estuary
32 Warleigh Point Wood
33 Brownsea Island
34 Powerstock Common
35 Townsend
36 Black Rock
37 Ebbor Gorge
38 Fyne Court
39 Hurscombe
40 Long Wood
41 Velvet Bottom

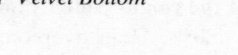

SOUTH-WEST ENGLAND

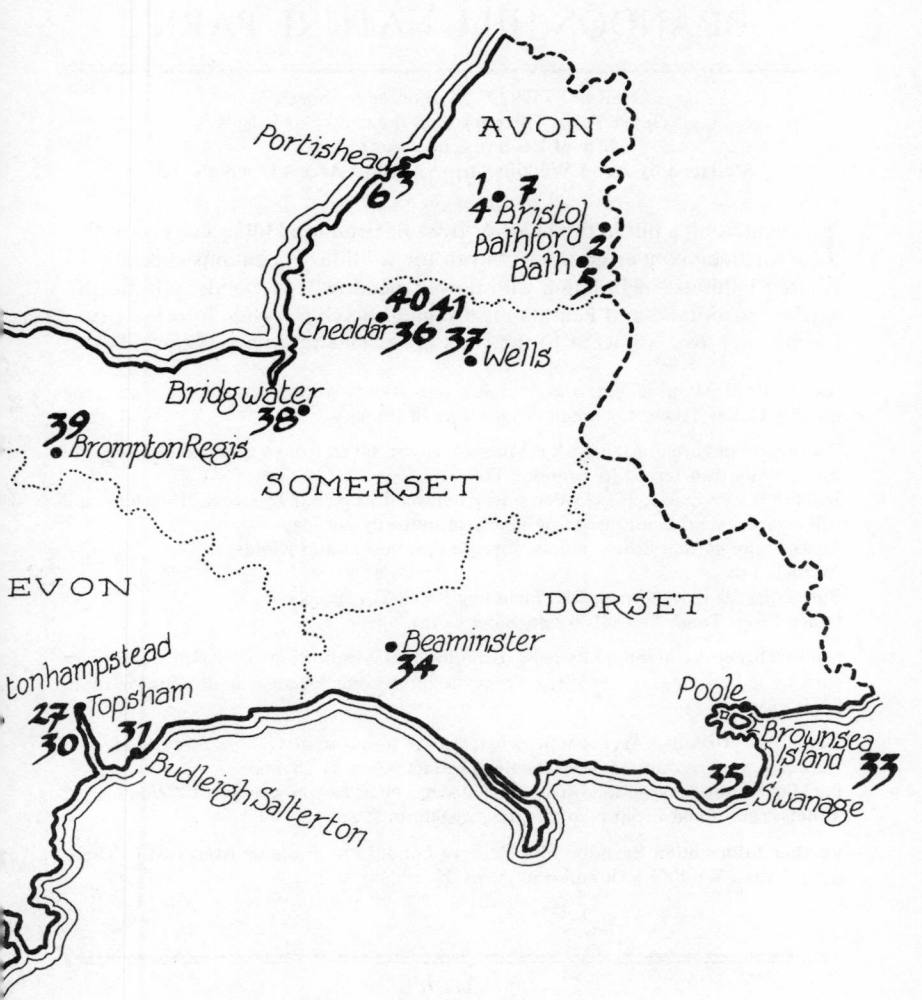

Avon

BRANDON HILL NATURE PARK

OS Ref ST579727   Landranger Sheet 172
Nearest Town The park is in the centre of Bristol
Size of Reserve 2 hectares (5 acres)
Managed by Avon Wildlife Trust (AWT)   **Access** Open all year

L ocated on a hill in the heart of Bristol, Brandon Hill is a city park that has been converted into a haven for wildlife. It contains specially-created habitats, including a wild flower meadow, two ponds, a butterfly garden, woodland and heathland, bringing the countryside into the city for all to enjoy. Adjacent to the park is the Headquarters of the AWT.

Nature Trail About 800 metres (½ mile), unmarked. Walk can include a visit to the historic Cabot Tower for magnificent views of the city.

The heathland area of the park is unusual. It was saved from a Somerset quarry and successfully transferred to Brandon Hill.
Plants Ox-eye Daisy, Hawkweed and Knapweed in meadow; Gorse, Heathers and Bilberry on heathland; flowering plants in butterfly garden.
Birds Many garden birds, mainly during migration and in winter.
Animals Fox.
Butterflies 20 species recorded, including Small Tortoiseshell.
Other Frog, Toad, Smooth Newt, Slow-worm.

Under Threat As an inner city park, Brandon Hill is important as a wildlife sanctuary surrounded by areas under threat from the hustle, bustle, noise and pollution of an inner city.

Guide No   **Disabled Access** Wheelchair access from Great George Street and Berkeley Square only   **School Parties** Contact AWT in advance
Parking Meter parking in surrounding streets. NCP car park in Jacobs Wells Road
Toilets Yes   **Food** From nearby cafés, restaurants, etc.

Further Information Brandon Hill Reserve Guides are available from AWT. There is an Urban Wildlife Exhibition in AWT Headquarters.

Avon

BROWN'S FOLLY

OS Ref ST794665   Landranger Sheet 172
Nearest Town Bathford   **Size of Reserve** 38.5 hectares (95 acres)
Managed by Avon Wildlife Trust (AWT)   **Access** Open all year

B rown's Folly is an area of rich limestone grasslands, ancient woodlands and scrub on the site of the old Bath stone quarries. The famous mid-nineteenth century 'pepper-pot' tower, Brown's Folly, is on the reserve but not open to the public.

Nature Trail There are two waymarked trails (3.2 and 5 km/2 and 3 miles). Paths can be muddy in winter so suitable footwear is essential. Stick to the marked paths and take extreme caution when approaching rock faces. Mines should not be entered. Trails offer commanding views towards Bath. Trail Guides are available from AWT.

With quarries and cliffs of oolitic limestone, the area is designated a geological SSSI and provides valuable insight into Avon's industrial past.
Plants 9 species of orchid (including Fly Orchid), Bath Asparagus, Broad and White Helleborines.
Birds A variety of woodland birds.
Animals Greater Horseshoe Bat.

Guide No   **Disabled Access** No   **School Parties** Contact AWT in advance. Teachers' Information Sheets are available from AWT   **Parking** Car park on Prospect Place
Toilets No   **Food** No

Further Information Contact AWT.

Avon
LIMEBREACH WOOD

OS Ref ST465728   Landranger Sheet 172
Nearest Town Portishead   **Size of Reserve** 6 hectares (15 acres)
Managed by Avon Wildlife Trust (AWT)   **Access** Open all year

L imebreach Wood is part of a large area of ancient woodland. The reserve is notable for its Small-leaved Limes, now declining in Britain.

Nature Trail 3.2 km (2 miles), waymarked. There is a walk of about 1.5 km (1 mile) from the car park to the reserve area in the heart of the woodland. The surrounding wood is privately owned, so please keep to the paths. Paths can be muddy so suitable footwear is essential. Trail Guides are available from AWT.

Coppicing extends the lifespan of the Limes, improves the variety of wildlife in the wood, and gives a hint of how the wood might have looked in Mediaeval times.
Plants Woodspurge, Slender St. John's Wort, Early Purple Orchid.
Trees Small-leaved Lime.
Birds Treecreeper, Goldcrest, Nuthatch, Buzzard.
Animals Small mammals, Badger.
Butterflies Brimstone, Tortoiseshell.

Guide No   **Disabled Access** No   **School Parties** Contact AWT in advance
Parking At the end of Cadbury Camp Lane (private road)   **Toilets** No   **Food** No

Further Information Contact AWT.

Avon

STOCKWOOD OPEN SPACE

OS Ref ST625693 Landranger Sheet 172
Nearest Town Bristol **Size of Reserve** 10 hectares (24½ acres)
Managed by Avon Wildlife Trust (AWT) **Access** Open all year

The reserve is sited on the slopes of a hill offering a panoramic view of south Bristol. Once traditional farmland, Stockwood Open Space is now an area of old grasslands and unploughed meadows enclosed by the suburbs of Bristol. It also boasts very thick hedges alive with birds, and an old woodland known as Ilsyngrove. Two old farm ponds also remain. An old rubbish tip has been left to become overgrown and is developing into a haven for wildlife.

Nature Trail There is a trail of 2.4 km (1½ miles) which can be extended to 3.2 km (2 miles). It is waymarked with white arrows and starts at the north end of Stockwood Road. There are several good viewpoints on the trail. Trail Guides are available from AWT.

In the old grasslands, especially on the valley sides, there are many anthills looking like large tufts of grass. These are a very interesting feature of the Open Space and show that the fields in which they occur have never been ploughed.
Plants Bath Asparagus, Yellow Archangel, Bluebell, Wood Anemone, Yellow Iris, Water Figwort, Cuckoo Flower, Cowslip, Dyer's Greenweed, Birdsfoot Trefoil, Meadowsweet, Field Scabious, Grass Vetchling.
Trees Oak, Field Maple, Hawthorn, Hazel, Lime, Ash, Wild Cherry, Blackthorn, Elder, Willow, Elm, Rose.
Birds Warblers, Finches, Cuckoo, Wheatear, Stonechat, Kestrel, Sparrowhawk, Woodpeckers, Tawny and Little Owls, Wren, Dunnock, Winter Thrush.
Animals Field Mouse.
Insects Bees, Common Field Grasshopper, Dragonfly.
Butterflies Orange Tip, Meadow Brown, Small Heath, Marbled White, Common Blue, Large Skipper.
Other Frog, Newt. At dusk during June and July, female Glow-worms display their 'lights'.

Under Threat During this century, the growth of Bristol has led to the loss of more and more farmland. In the area of the reserve, much of the old farmland has been taken over by houses, a golf course, a school and a public tip. This makes the remaining open space a vital refuge for a rich variety of wild plants and animals. Surrounding areas of farmland continue to be under threat of future development.

Guide No **Disabled Access** Tarmac paths provide some access for wheelchair users
School Parties Contact AWT in advance **Parking** At north end of Stockwood Road
Toilets No **Food** No

Further Information Contact AWT.

Avon

TUCKING MILL TRAIL

OS Ref ST766616   Landranger Sheet 172
Nearest Town Bath   **Size of Reserve** 2.7 km (1¾ miles) long
Managed by Avon Wildlife Trust (AWT)   **Access** Open all year

Tucking Mill valley offers good scenery and interesting geology with outcrops of oolitic limestone. It contains areas of woodland and hillside pastures which exhibit a dramatic change of vegetation in spring over the site of a landslip. The area is best seen in spring.

Nature Trail 2.7 km (1¾ miles), unmarked. Paths on sloping valley sides can be muddy and slippery so suitable footwear is essential. The trail follows public footpaths starting from Combe Down. Trail Guides are available from AWT.

The site is of geological and historical interest with evidence of the valley's industrial past visible in the form of old Bath stone quarries, mills and the Somerset Coal Canal.
Plants Yellow Archangel, Toothwort, Salad Burnet, Rough Hawkbit, Bath Asparagus.
Trees Ash, Hazel, Beech.
Birds Green Woodpecker, Sparrowhawk.
Animals Daubenton's Bat, Rabbit, Badger.
Butterflies Comma, Gatekeeper, Brimstone.

Guide No   **Disabled Access** No   **School Parties** Contact AWT in advance
Parking In Combe Down   **Toilets** No   **Food** No

Further Information Contact AWT.

Avon

WESTON MOOR

OS Ref ST445735   Landranger Sheet 172
Nearest Town Portishead   **Size of Reserve** 10 hectares (25 acres)
Managed by Avon Wildlife Trust (AWT)   **Access** Open all year

Weston Moor contains one of the last remaining reedbeds in Avon, with good views of the Gordano Valley. There is also an area of wet woodland, and a former rubbish tip, providing habitats for different wildlife communities. The reserve is within an area designated an NNR.

Nature Trail 800 metres (½ mile), unmarked apart from a reserve sign at the entrance. The reedbed area of the reserve must not be entered during April to August when birds are nesting. Trail Guides are available from AWT.

The reedbed is a nationally important breeding site for the Reed Warbler. There is a birdwatching hide from which to view the reedbed.

Plants Marsh Orchid, Purple Moor Grass.
Birds Reed and Sedge Warblers, Kestrel, Buzzard, Tawny Owl.
Animals Small mammals, Rabbit.
Butterflies Brimstone, Small Copper, Peacock.

Under Threat The Gordano Valley is threatened by enormous pressure for development for housing, industry, etc.

Guide No   **Disabled Access** No   **School Parties** Contact AWT in advance
Parking Immediately inside reserve entrance or, in bad weather, in Weston-in-Gordano   **Toilets** No   **Food** No

Further Information Contact AWT.

Avon

WILLSBRIDGE VALLEY and MILL

OS Ref ST665706   Landranger Sheet 172
Nearest Town Bristol   **Size of Reserve** 8 hectares (22 acres)
Managed by Avon Wildlife Trust (AWT)   **Access** The reserve is open all year but the Visitor Centre and café are only open from 1st April to 31st October (and closed on Mondays, except Bank Holidays). A charge is made for admission to the Visitor Centre

The reserve is situated in a valley surrounded by housing estates on the edge of Bristol. It includes woodland areas, a meadow, scrub, a stream and a wildlife garden. Three ponds have been built to replace the old mill pond. The impressive 18th-century mill has been converted by the Trust into a wildlife Visitor Centre with an exhibition and café. The wildlife garden was designed by a group of 11–13-year-old WATCH members to encourage wildlife throughout the year.

Nature Trail 1.5 km (1 mile), waymarked. The trail extends beyond the area of the reserve and it is important, while walking, to respect the land and privacy of those living in and around the valley. Strong footwear is recommended for all visitors, particularly in wet weather.

The Centre organises a series of events during the summer that the public is encouraged to attend. Contact the Mill (address below) for details.

Plants Lesser Celandine, Marsh Marigold, Yellow Flag, Hemp Agrimony, Meadowsweet, Pignut, Lousewort, Selfheal, Bretony, Bugle, Quaking Grass, Hemp Agrimony, Angelica.
Trees Sycamore, Laurel, Oak, Wild Cherry, Lime, Willow, Ash, Scots Pine.
Birds Grey Wagtail, Dipper, Blackcap, Chiffchaff, Willow Warbler, Woodpecker, Blackbird, Dunnock, Thrush, Nightingale.
Animals Badger, Rabbit.
Insects Caddisfly, Mayfly, Pond Skater, Whirligig Beetle, Dragonfly.
Butterflies Speckled Wood, Gatekeeper, Comma.

Other Fish such as Bullhead and Stone Loach in the brook.

Under Threat Siston Brook is the fast-flowing stream that runs through the valley. It once drove the mill's wheel and later its turbine. Unfortunately it is very susceptible to pollution as it flows past light industry between housing estates on its course through the district of Kingswood.

Guide By prior arrangement with AWT at Willsbridge Mill Wildlife Visitor Centre, Willsbridge Hill, Bristol BS15 6EX (tel. 0272 326885) **Disabled Access** Available to both floors of the exhibition, the café, toilets, wildlife garden and pond. For further information, contact the Visitor Centre (as above) **School Parties** A variety of activities is available for school groups. Contact the Visitor Centre (as above) for booking details **Parking** The car park is on Long Beach Road, not in the valley itself **Toilets** Next to the café **Food** The café is open 1st April to 31st October, from midday until late afternoon **Shop** The Trust shop sells gifts, souvenirs, wildlife literature and reserve leaflets

Further Information From AWT Headquarters or the Visitor Centre (as above). Leaflets and Trail Guides are available from the shop at the Centre or from AWT Headquarters.

Cornwall

BRENEY COMMON

OS Ref SX057610   Landranger Sheet 200
Nearest Town Bodmin   **Size of Reserve** 55 hectares (135 acres)
Managed by Cornwall Trust for Nature Conservation (CTNC)   **Access** Open all year

T he reserve covers a fairly flat area, sloping gently to the south. It is an important example of a threatened habitat, consisting of a mosaic of dry and wet heath, unimproved acid grassland, Juncus marsh, bog, ponds, streams, willow carr, scrub and semi-natural broadleaved woodland. An area of the reserve is a hummock-hollow complex resulting from past mineral working activity.

Nature Trail 1.2 km (¾ mile), unmarked. Parts of the trail can be wet so suitable footwear is essential.

One pond has a pond-dipping platform.
Plants Plantlife on the reserve is rich and varied, including Royal Fern, Cotton-grass, Marsh Cinquefoil, Ivy-leaved Bellflower, Bog Asphodel, with Pillwort and Western Bladderwort in the acid bog pools.
Birds Breeding birds include Lesser Whitethroat, Tree Pipit, Curlew, Willow Tit and Nightjar.
Insects Abundant butterfly and moth species, including Pearl-bordered and Marsh Fritillaries – 103 species recorded.

Guide Contact CTNC in advance   **Disabled Access** Part of the nature trail and pond-dipping platform are accessible to wheelchair users   **School Parties** Contact CTNC in advance   **Parking** Yes   **Toilets** No   **Food** No

Further Information Reserve maps are available from CTNC.

Cornwall

DEVICHOYS WOOD and PERRAN MEADOWS

OS Ref SW774380   Landranger Sheet 204
Nearest Town Perranarworthal   **Size of Reserve** 15.8 hectares (39 acres)
Managed by Cornwall Trust for Nature Conservation (CTNC)   **Access** Open all year

D evichoys Wood is typical neglected estuarine oak coppice woodland with some areas planted with other species, and partly invaded by rhododendron. The wood occupies a steep valley side overlooking Perran Meadows, a flat area of unimproved wet grassland and scrub with a small ox-bow lake and a river running through.

Nature Trail 1.2 km (¾ mile), unmarked. Paths can be very wet and muddy so suitable footwear is essential.

Plants Devichoys Wood contains typical woodland flora – groves of holly are present within the predominant oak coppice. The Meadows support flora typical of neglected wet grassland.
Birds Dipper and typical woodland birds.
Animals Badger.

Guide Contact CTNC in advance   **Disabled Access** No   **School Parties** Contact CTNC in advance   **Parking** No   **Toilets** No   **Food** No

Further Information Reserve maps are available from CTNC.

Cornwall

FAL-RUAN ESTUARY

OS Ref SW875405 (Ardevora)   SW886415 (Trelonk)   Landranger Sheet 204
Nearest Town Truro   **Size of Reserve** 101 hectares (250 acres)
Managed by Cornwall Trust for Nature Conservation (CTNC)   **Access** Open all year

T he reserve is in two parts, at Ardevora and Trelonk. Both are on the southern shore and in the tidal creeks of the River Fal – part of the drowned valley, or via, of the Fal and Truro rivers. The reserve is all tidal mudflats and saltmarsh.

Nature Trail There is a public footpath to the shore at Ardevora.

Birds The main interest of the reserve is for birdwatching – it is a nationally important site with winter populations of waders and wildfowl of up to 10,000. There is a birdwatching hide (access on foot only) at Trelonk.

Guide Contact CTNC in advance   **Disabled Access** No   **School Parties** Contact CTNC in advance   **Parking** On roadside   **Toilets** No   **Food** No

Further Information Reserve maps are available from CTNC.

Cornwall

HAWKES WOOD

OS Ref SW986709   Landranger Sheet 200
Nearest Town Wadebridge   **Size of Reserve** 3.2 hectares (8 acres)
Managed by Cornwall Trust for Nature Conservation (CTNC)   **Access** Open all year

T he reserve occupies the valley sides and bottom at the confluence of two streams. It consists of a mixed broadleaved semi-natural wood with some introduced species, and partly old oak coppice – the remnant of a much larger wooded area in the valley now replanted with conifers.

Nature Trail 400 metres (¼ mile), unmarked. Paths can be muddy so suitable footwear is essential.

Plants Good for ferns. Contains plants typical of semi-natural woodland.
Birds About 50 species recorded.
Animals Badger and other common mammals.

Guide Contact CTNC in advance   **Disabled Access** No   **School Parties** Contact CTNC in advance   **Parking** On roadside at Treneague   **Toilets** No   **Food** No

Further Information Reserve maps are available from CTNC.

Cornwall

KENNALL VALE WOODS

OS Ref SW754375   Landranger Sheet 204
Nearest Town Penryn   **Size of Reserve** 8.5 hectares (21 acres)
Managed by Cornwall Trust for Nature Conservation (CTNC)   **Access** Open all year

T he reserve consists of woodland occupying steep valley sides, a water-filled quarry and a fast-flowing river. The mixed broadleaved plantation is on an ancient woodland site with a small remnant of semi-natural oakwood on the northern slope.

Nature Trail 1.2 km (¾ mile), unmarked. Tracks can be very muddy in parts so suitable footwear is essential.

The reserve is of considerable industrial archaeological interest since it contains the remains of the water-powered Kennall Gunpowder Works. The leats system and water mills can still be seen.

Plants The Tunbridge Filmy Fern can be found amongst other typical woodland flora. Abundant bryophyte flora and fungi.

Birds Most typical woodland birds are present and Dippers breed.

Animals Badger and other typical woodland mammals.

Guide Contact CTNC in advance **Disabled Access** No **School Parties** Contact CTNC in advance **Parking** On roadside **Toilets** No **Food** No

Further Information Reserve maps are available from CTNC.

Cornwall

LUCKETT

OS Ref SX392728 Landranger Sheet 201
Nearest Town Luckett, near Callington **Size of Reserve** 3.6 hectares (9 acres)
Managed by Cornwall Trust for Nature Conservation (CTNC) **Access** Open all year

T he reserve is on a steep east-facing valley side and consists of seminatural broadleaved woodland with clearings of scrub and heath. It is within a scheduled SSSI.

Nature Trail 1.2 km (¾ mile), unmarked.

The reserve is good for spotting plants and butterflies.

Plants Bladderseed, Flax-leaved St. John's Wort, Bastard Balm, Yellow Bartsia and several orchids.

Insects Over 80 species of Lepidoptera recorded and 8 species of Odonata (dragonflies).

Guide Contact CTNC in advance **Disabled Access** No **School Parties** Contact CTNC in advance **Parking** Beside track at SX393730 **Toilets** No **Food** No

Further Information Reserve maps are available from CTNC.

Cornwall

NANSMELLYN MARSH

OS Ref SW762543 Landranger Sheet 200/204
Nearest Town Perranporth **Size of Reserve** 3.4 hectares (8½ acres)
Managed by Cornwall Trust for Nature Conservation (CTNC) **Access** Open all year

T he reserve is an area of low-lying reedbed and willow carr with smaller adjacent drier areas and a length of river.

Nature Trail A roadside path runs down the western side of the reserve, or there is a short path to the birdwatching hide from the adjacent Social Club. The path to the hide is fairly wet.

Chiefly a birdwatching area.

Plants Reedmace, Water Horsetail, Flag Iris, Greater Tussock Sedge, Water Mint, Southern Marsh Orchid – typical reedbed flora.

Birds Sedge Warbler, Chiffchaff, Willow Warbler, Grasshopper Warbler (breeding), Cetti's Warbler, Water Rail, Cirl Bunting, as well as many other commoner species.

Butterflies 90 species recorded.

Guide Contact CTNC in advance   **Disabled Access** No   **School Parties** Contact CTNC in advance   **Parking** On roadside or in Social Club car park   **Toilets** No **Food** No

Further Information Reserve maps are available from CTNC. There is an information display in the adjacent Social Club.

Cornwall
NORTH PREDANNACK DOWNS

OS Ref SW688174   Landranger Sheet 203
Nearest Town Lizard   **Size of Reserve** 40 hectares (99 acres)
Managed by Cornwall Trust for Nature Conservation (CTNC)   **Access** Open all year

A mosaic of flat wet and dry Lizard heathland, partly an SSSI, with some seasonal pools.

Nature Trail 2.4 km (1½ miles), unmarked. Tracks can be very muddy so suitable footwear is essential.

Plants Typical of Lizard heathland – Cornish Heath (*Erica vagans*), several orchids, Pale Butterwort, Petty Whin.

Insects 14 species of Odonata (dragonflies) recorded from Hayle Kimbro Pool which extends on to the reserve.

Other Adders commonly sighted.

Guide Contact CTNC in advance   **Disabled Access** No   **School Parties** Contact CTNC in advance   **Parking** At entrance to Predannack Airfield (SW696164) **Toilets** No   **Food** No

Further Information Reserve maps are available from CTNC.

Cornwall
PARK HOSKYN WOOD

OS Ref SW749495   Landranger Sheet 204
Nearest Town Truro   **Size of Reserve** 2 hectares (4½ acres)
Managed by Cornwall Trust for Nature Conservation (CTNC)   **Access** Open all year

The reserve occupies a steep valley side and wet valley bottom and consists of mixed broadleaved woodland, part of which may be semi-natural oakwood, together with a planted area, some willow carr and old hazel coppice.

Nature Trail 500 metres (⅓ mile), unmarked. Paths can be very muddy so suitable footwear is essential.

Flora and fauna typical of small woods.

Guide Contact CTNC in advance   **Disabled Access** No   **School Parties** Contact CTNC in advance   **Parking** At SW753497   **Toilets** No   **Food** No

Further Information Reserve maps are available from CTNC.

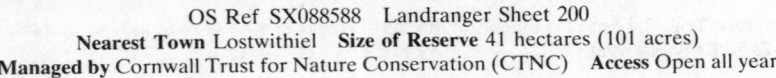

Cornwall
PELYN WOODS

OS Ref SX088588   Landranger Sheet 200
Nearest Town Lostwithiel   **Size of Reserve** 41 hectares (101 acres)
Managed by Cornwall Trust for Nature Conservation (CTNC)   **Access** Open all year

A mixed broadleaved plantation on an ancient woodland site, mostly on steep valley sides. Includes streams and an old quarry. Small remnant areas of semi-natural woodland are present – mostly an oak/ash mixture – but the planted beech is now dominant.

Nature Trail 2.4 km (1½ miles), unmarked. Tracks can be very wet and muddy so suitable footwear is essential.

Plants Typical woodland flora with abundant ferns and some areas dominated by Bluebells or Snowdrops. Abundant bryophytes (80 species recorded) and fungi. 52 species of lichen recorded.

Guide Contact CTNC in advance   **Disabled Access** No   **School Parties** Contact CTNC in advance   **Parking** Beside reserve entrance   **Toilets** No   **Food** No

Further Information Reserve maps are available from CTNC.

Cornwall
PENDARVES WOOD

OS Ref SW645375   Landranger Sheet 203
Nearest Town Camborne   **Size of Reserve** 16.5 hectares (40½ acres)
Managed by Cornwall Trust for Nature Conservation (CTNC)   **Access** Open all year

T he wood occupies a flat area and is a 19th-century plantation with a lake. A large part of the wood is overgrown by rhododendron and cherry-laurel which is gradually being cleared.

Nature Trail 1.2 km (¾ mile), unmarked. Tracks can be wet and muddy so suitable footwear is essential.

Trees Many exotic species of trees and shrubs are present. Willow and Alder are found in wetter areas, while other areas are dominated by Beech or Sycamore. Part is a conifer plantation.
Birds 74 species recorded, with 40 species known to breed on the reserve.
Insects Excellent site for Odonata (dragonflies) with 15 species present.

Guide Contact CTNC in advance   **Disabled Access** No   **School Parties** Contact CTNC in advance. The reserve is used extensively by local schools. Teachers' Educational Notes and booklets for schoolchildren are available from CTNC
Parking Beside reserve entrance   **Toilets** No   **Food** No

Further Information Reserve maps are available from CTNC.

Cornwall
RED MOOR and SOUTHERN RED MOOR

OS Ref SX070622   Landranger Sheet 200
Nearest Town Bodmin   **Size of Reserve** 96 hectares (238 acres)
Managed by Cornwall Trust for Nature Conservation (CTNC)   **Access** Open all year

D esignated an SSSI, the reserve covers a fairly flat area of mixed wet and dry heathland, bog, ponds, scrub, willow carr and broadleaved woodland. The value of the reserve is that a great diversity of habitats, from permanent standing water to dry open heathland, are to be found close together. It is an important example of a threatened habitat being improved and maintained by a conservation trust. The southern part of the reserve is inaccessible.

Nature Trail 1.5 km (1 mile), waymarked and numbered to correspond with map on back of information booklet. Parts of the trail can be wet and there are snakes on the reserve, so suitable footwear is essential.

Plants Plant life is rich and varied, including Royal Fern, Bog Asphodel, Cotton-grass, Marsh Cinquefoil, Round-leaved Sundew, and 31 noteworthy species of higher plants present. Rich lichen flora in the woodland area, a good site for bryophytes.
Birds Breeding birds include Tree Pipit, Willow Tit, Sparrowhawk. 97 species have been recorded in all. 60 species known to breed.
Animals Most common mammals have been recorded.
Insects 13 species of Odonata (dragonflies); particularly important for aquatic beetles; 64 species of Lepidoptera recorded.
Other Grass Snakes and Adders are often seen. Pond-dipping is possible with good chances of seeing frogs, toads, newts, tadpoles, etc.

Guide Contact CTNC in advance   **Disabled Access** The trail is suitable for wheelchair users   **School Parties** Contact CTNC in advance   **Parking** About 100 metres (110 yards) from the reserve main entrance   **Toilets** No   **Food** No

Further Information Information booklets, with maps, are available from CTNC.

Cornwall
ROPEHAVEN CLIFFS

OS Ref SX034490   Landranger Sheet 204
Nearest Town St. Austell   **Size of Reserve** 20 hectares (50 acres)
Managed by Cornwall Trust for Nature Conservation (CTNC)   **Access** Open all year

T he reserve occupies a 2-km (1¼-mile) stretch of east-facing cliffs on the western side of St. Austell Bay. The central area of the reserve is mixed broadleaved woodland and the rest consists of scrub, maritime grassland and steep cliffs.

Nature Trail The shore line is mostly inaccessible, but the Cornwall South Coast Footpath runs alongside the whole length of the reserve and there is a short footpath within the reserve down to the shore.

Plants Rich bryophyte flora.
Birds 90 species recorded as breeding, on passage or wintering. About 30 other species can be seen, mainly in winter, from the reserve, on the water or flying further out to sea.

Guide Contact CTNC in advance   **Disabled Access** No   **School Parties** Contact CTNC in advance   **Parking** Car park at reserve entrance   **Toilets** No   **Food** No

Further Information Reserve maps are available from CTNC.

Cornwall
TAMAR ESTUARY

OS Ref SX432630   Landranger Sheet 201
Nearest Town Plymouth   **Size of Reserve** 405 hectares (1,000) acres
Managed by Cornwall Trust for Nature Conservation (CTNC)   **Access** Open all year

T he reserve covers an area of the western coastline of the Tamar Estuary, including Kingsmill Lake. Visitors have access only to the edge of the reserve as it consists entirely of tidal mudflats and saltmarsh. It is accessible at Kingsmill (SX414623), Cargreen (SX436626), Landulph Marsh (SX433613) and Lower Moditonham (SX419613).

An excellent site for birdwatching.
Birds Avocet, Kingfisher, Shelduck, Redshank, Widgeon, Gadwall, Black-tailed Godwit, Water Rail, Greenshank, Grey Heron, Red-breasted Merganser, Pochard.

Guide Contact CTNC in advance   **Disabled Access** No   **School Parties** Contact CTNC in advance   **Parking** At Kingsmill, Cargreen, Landulph Church and Lower Moditonham   **Toilets** No   **Food** No

Further Information Reserve maps are available from CTNC.

Cornwall
VENTONGIMPS MOOR

OS Ref SW781512   Landranger Sheet 204
Nearest Town Perranporth   **Size of Reserve** 8 hectares (20 acres)
Managed by Cornwall Trust for Nature Conservation (CTNC)   **Access** Open all year

S cheduled an SSSI, the reserve occupies a valley bottom site comprising a mosaic of wet and dry heath and scrubland, with semi-natural broad-leaved woodland, a stream and several pools.

Nature Trail Although there is no formal trail, a public footpath crosses one end of the reserve and a short path runs on to the heathland from the road. The whole area is very wet so suitable footwear is essential.

The reserve is of particular importance for its rich flora.
Plants 125 species of flowering plants and ferns recorded, including Dorset Heath, Eyebright, Cornish Moneywort, Yellow Bartsia, Yellow Centaury, Sundew, Orchids and Bog Myrtle.
Birds 49 species recorded.
Insects 13 species of Odonata (dragonflies); 99 species of Lepidoptera, including Marsh Fritillary.

Other Abundant bryophytes and fungi.

Guide Contact CTNC in advance   **Disabled Access** No   **School Parties** Contact CTNC in advance   **Parking** Beside road   **Toilets** No   **Food** No

Further Information Reserve maps are available from CTNC.

Devon

ARLINGTON COURT

OS Ref SS611405   Landranger Sheet 180
Nearest Town Barnstaple   **Size of Reserve** 1,125 hectares (2,780 acres)
Managed by The National Trust (NT)   **Access** Park and gardens open daily (except Saturday) November to end of March, dawn to sunset; April to end of October, 11.00–18.00 (11.00–17.00 in October). Open Saturdays of Bank Holiday weekends. A charge is made for admission but there are concessions for groups. NT members admitted free.

The Arlington Court Estate is situated in the River Yeo Valley and has been an NT property since 1949. Only part of the Estate is open to the public, including the park, lake and woods. The house itself was built in 1822 and the grounds include a formal Victorian garden and a 'wilderness' area.

Nature Trail There is a circular 2.4-km (1½-mile) walk through the woods and beside the lake. Nature Trail leaflets are available from the shop at Arlington Court.

Birds The Park includes a lakeside Heronry and wildfowl sanctuary. A birdwatching hide overlooks the lake.
Animals Red Deer

Guide Contact the Administrator, James Stout, at Arlington Court, Arlington, Near Barnstaple, Devon EX31 4LP (tel. 027 182 296).
Disabled Access Yes; wheelchairs are available   **School Parties** By prior arrangement with the Administrator (as above)   **Parking** Yes   **Toilets** Yes, including for the disabled   **Food** Licensed restaurant serving home-made light lunches and teas as well as morning coffee; snack room in peak season; picnic area.

Further Information Contact the Administrator (as above) or The National Trust.

Devon

BRAUNTON BURROWS

OS Ref SS463351 (start of trail)   Landranger Sheet 180
Nearest Town Braunton   **Size of Reserve** 1,000 hectares (2,470 acres)
Managed by Nature Conservancy Council (NCC)   **Access** Open all year

B raunton Burrows is a National Nature Reserve (NNR) and consists of one of the largest dune systems in the country. The sand dunes reach a height of 30 metres (100 feet) in places. Vegetation and wildlife is typical of mobile and stable sand dunes, blow-outs and damp slacks. Artificial ponds have been dug to encourage the breeding of some of the country's endangered species.

Nature Trail Braunton Burrows Ecology Trail – the basic trail takes a circuit of about 3 km (2 miles) through the heart of the dunes. An optional loop crosses the complete width of the dune system and adds 1.5 km (1 mile) to the walk. The trail is unmarked. This trail has been established by Thematic Trails, an educational publishing unit based at Oxford Polytechnic. *Braunton Burrows Ecology Trail* by Janet Keene (1987/40 pages) is available from Thematic Trails, Faculty of Environment, Oxford Polytechnic, Oxford OX3 0BP.

Plants Hartstongue Fern, Comfrey, Hemp Agrimony, Marram Grass, Hawthorn, Blackthorn, Creeping Willow, Sand Sedge, Reed Mace, Soft Rush, Mosses, Sea Holly, Buck's-horn Plantain, Red Fescue, Orchids, Evening Primrose, Lichens, Viper's Bugloss.
Trees Sallow, Alder.
Animals Common Lizard.
Other Common Frog, Palmate Newt, Pond Snail, Dragonflies, Damselflies, Brown-lipped Snail.

Information Centre Opening in Braunton in 1989.

Guide By prior arrangement with Reserve Warden, Broadeford Farm, Heddon Mill, near Braunton, North Devon EX33 2NQ.
Disabled Access No   **School Parties** By prior arrangement with the Warden (as above). A workbook version of *Braunton Burrows Ecology Trail* is available for educational groups. A teaching pack of 24 slides can also be supplied. Contact Thematic Trails at Oxford Polytechnic (address above) for details
Parking Yes   **Toilets** No   **Food** No

Further Information Braunton Burrows Ecology Trail is part of a series of trails with accompanying educational literature produced by Thematic Trails.

Devon

CENTRAL PARK NATURE PARK

OS Ref SX475560   Landranger Sheet 201
Nearest Town The reserve is in the centre of Plymouth
Size of Reserve 10 hectares (25 acres)   **Managed by** Plymouth Urban Wildlife Group (PUWG) in conjunction with the Plymouth City Council Parks Section
Access Open all year

T he Nature Park is part of a large urban park in the centre of the city of Plymouth. The reserve lies within a valley on the eastern side of Central Park and comprises a variety of habitats, including mixed woodland, formal tree plantation, butterfly garden, pond and grassland.

Nature Trail 800 metres (½ mile), with information panels at either end of the trail showing the route.

Wildlife on the reserve is typical of an urban park.

Under Threat The reserve aims to protect Plymouth's wildlife and semi-natural habitats. As such, it is under threat from the intensive management practices carried out within Central Park, eg. manicured grass and planting of ornamental standard trees.

Guide No   **Disabled Access** All rides in the park have tarmac surfaces and are suitable for wheelchair users   **School Parties** Yes   **Parking** There are 2 large car parks in Central Park   **Toilets** Yes, within Central Park   **Food** No

Further Information Information leaflets are available from PUWG.

Devon

DUNSFORD WOOD

OS Ref SX802884   Landranger Sheet 191
Nearest Town Moretonhampstead   **Size of Reserve** 56 hectares (140 acres)
Managed by Devon Wildlife Trust (DWT)   **Access** Open all year

D unsford Wood lies within the Dartmoor National Park and is part of the Teign Valley SSSI. It consists of river valley woodland, heath-covered rocky slopes and fertile floodplain scrub and grassland.

Nature Trail There is no formal trail, but level footpaths run through the reserve.

Plants Dunsford is one of the principal sites in south-west England for the Wild Daffodil which grows in profusion.
Birds Pied Flycatcher, Green and Great Spotted Woodpeckers, Dipper, Buzzard and several varieties of Tit and Warbler are notable breeding species.
Animals Fallow Deer, Dormouse, Otter and Mink occur on the reserve.
Insects Butterflies and Dragonflies are common, and the large conspicuous mounds of the Wood Ant can be seen all over the reserve.

Guide By prior arrangement with DWT   **Disabled Access** No   **School Parties** By prior arrangement with DWT   **Parking** In Dartmoor National Park car park at Steps Bridge   **Toilets** Yes   **Food** There is a pub adjacent to the entrance/car park

Further Information Information booklets are available from DWT. There is a Dartmoor National Park Information Caravan parked in the car park during the summer season.

Devon

EXE REEDBEDS

OS Ref SX957885   Landranger Sheet 192
Nearest Town Topsham   **Size of Reserve** 25 hectares (62 acres)
Managed by Devon Wildlife Trust (DWT)   **Access** Open all year

A n area of the Exe estuary, covering an extensive reedbed and a narrow fringe of saltmarsh. The whole area is designated an SSSI and is of very high wildlife value, offering much to be seen in all seasons.

Nature Trail The reserve is adjacent to The Old Sludge Beds Reserve (page 55) and both reserves may be enjoyed by walking from the car park along the tow path on the east side of the canal via both reserves, continuing as far as The Turf Hotel, and returning along the west side of the canal.

Birds The Exe estuary is important for its populations of wintering wildfowl and waders. In spring and autumn large numbers of passage migrants gather in the reedbeds.

Guide By prior arrangement with DWT   **Disabled Access** No   **School Parties** By prior arrangement with DWT   **Parking** At the University Boathouse off the Countess Wear Road (OS Ref SX941895)   **Toilets** No   **Food** There is a hotel 2 km (1¼ miles) south of the reedbeds.

Further Information Contact DWT.

Devon

HALSDON

OS Ref SS554131   Landranger Sheet 191/180
Nearest Town Dolton   **Size of Reserve** 57 hectares (142 acres)
Managed by Devon Wildlife Trust (DWT)   **Access** Open all year

D esignated an SSSI, Halsdon is one of DWT's newest reserves, containing mixed deciduous river valley woodland, riverside meadows, marsh and a 2.4-km (1½-mile) length of the River Torridge.

Nature Trail There are 3 waymarked trails of varying lengths and degrees of difficulty through the reserve. The shortest takes only 30 minutes to walk, the longest about 2 hours.

Plants In the marsh can be found the rare Marsh Cinquefoil, Devil's Bit Scabious, Marsh Ragwort, Skullcap and 9 species of sedge.
Trees Amongst others, 2 uncommon trees, the Devon Whitebeam and the Wild Service Tree, both regarded as indicators of ancient woodland, occur on the reserve.

Birds There is a typical and varied community of oakwood birds, including Buzzard and Lesser Spotted Woodpecker. Heron, Dipper and Grey Wagtail are regularly seen on the river.
Animals The commoner mammals are present and Otter and Mink frequent the river.

Guide By prior arrangement with DWT **Disabled Access** No **School Parties** Yes
Parking Yes **Toilets** No **Food** Available from pubs in Dolton

Further Information Leaflet, with map, available from DWT.

Devon
NORTHAM BURROWS COUNTRY PARK

OS Ref SS433294 (start of trail) Landranger Sheet 180
Nearest Town Bideford **Size of Reserve** 259 hectares (640 acres)
Managed by Devon County Council **Access** Open all year

Northam Burrows is a protected country park coastal region consisting of areas of sand dunes, saltmarsh, rushes, tall grasses and low grass flat burrows.

Nature Trail Westward Ho! Ecology Trail – The walk follows a circular route of about 6.5 km (4 miles). The trail is unmarked. This trail has been established by Thematic Trails, an educational publishing unit based at Oxford Polytechnic. *Westward Ho! Ecology Trail* by Janet Keene (1985/32 pages) is available from Thematic Trails, Faculty of Environment, Oxford Polytechnic, Oxford OX3 0BP.

The wide range of habitats included in the reserve supports a variety of wildlife.

Under Threat The reserve aspects of Northam Burrows Country Park are under pressure from the number of people entering the area for general holiday purposes.

Information Centre As well as permanent displays, the Visitors' Centre lists the birds seen during the current week and the plants in flower that day. It is open daily from Easter to autumn, 9.00–13.00 and 14.00–17.00, although these times may vary depending on the season. Country Park Visitors' Centre, Northam Burrows, Northam, Bideford, North Devon (tel: 0272 479708).
Guide By prior arrangement with the Warden at the Visitors' Centre (as above).
Disabled Access There is an easy walkway from the car park to the Visitors' Centre but general accessibility is limited by nature of the landscape.
School Parties By prior arrangement with the Warden at the Visitors' Centre (as above). A workbook version of *Westward Ho! Ecology Trail* is available for educational groups, and a teaching pack of 24 slides can also be supplied. Contact Thematic Trails at Oxford Polytechnic (address above) for details.
Parking Near Visitors' Centre and also at start of trail **Toilets** At Visitors' Centre
Food Available at Westward Ho! (start of trail)

Further Information Westward Ho! Ecology Trail is part of a series of trails with accompanying educational literature produced by Thematic Trails.

Devon

THE OLD SLUDGE BEDS

OS Ref SX952888   Landranger Sheet 192
Nearest Town Topsham   **Size of Reserve** 5 hectares (12 acres)
Managed by Devon Wildlife Trust (DWT)   **Access** Open all year

S andwiched between the River Exe and the Exeter Canal, this reserve
has developed on the site of abandoned sewage settling lagoons, and
offers a particularly good example of aquatic plant succession.

Nature Trail Although there is no nature trail as such, paths run through the
reserve or along the canal, linking it with the neighbouring reserve of Exe
Reedbeds (page 53).

Birds The reserve has become a major stopping-off point and feeding area for
migrating birds. Over 140 species of ducks, waders and passerines have been
recorded, including Cetti's Warbler, an uncommon breeding bird in Britain.
Insects Dragonflies are abundant and 3 nationally scarce species are found on the
ponds.
Other The reserve provides an ideal habitat for aquatic invertebrates.

Guide By prior arrangement with DWT   **Disabled Access** No   **School Parties** By
prior arrangement with DWT   **Parking** At the University Boathouse off the
Countess Wear Road (SX941895)   **Toilets** No   **Food** Available from nearby pubs.

Further Information Contact DWT.

Devon

OTTER ESTUARY

OS Ref SY076822   Landranger Sheet 192
Nearest Town Budleigh Salterton   **Size of Reserve** 20 hectares (50 acres)
Managed by Devon Wildlife Trust (DWT)   **Access** Open all year

D esignated an SSSI, the reserve embraces the whole estuary of the
River Otter, from White Bridge to the foot of the shingle spit at its
mouth.

Nature Trail A good waymarked footpath runs right round the reserve.

There is an observation hide on the east side of the estuary.
Plants Typical saltmarsh species.
Birds The rich invertebrate life in the mudflats supports a good wintering
population of wildfowl and waders. It is a regular and popular stopping-off point
for migrant birds.

Insects Amongst a variety of interesting insects to be spotted on the reserve is the uncommon Long-horned Cricket.

Guide By prior arrangement with DWT   **Disabled Access** Footpath on western side of estuary is level and even   **School Parties** By prior arrangement with DWT **Parking** Large paying car park overlooking estuary   **Toilets** No   **Food** Available in Budleigh Salterton

Further Information Leaflet, with map, available from DWT.

Devon
WARLEIGH POINT WOOD

OS Ref SX447610   Landranger Sheet 201
Nearest Town Tamerton Foliot, near Plymouth
Size of Reserve 30 hectares (75 acres)
Managed by Devon Wildlife Trust (DWT)   **Access** Open all year

O ne of the finest examples of coastal oak woodland in Devon, with magnificent views of the Tamar/Tavey estuary.

Nature Trail Although there is no formal waymarked trail, there are good-surfaced paths round the reserve.

Plants Masses of Bluebells, Primroses and Ramsons (Wild Garlic). The rare Wavy-leaved St. John's Wort grows in small acid flushes.
Trees Wild Service Tree, an uncommon species associated with ancient woodlands, is present along with Oak, Sweet Chestnut, Silver Birch, Hazel, Alder and Spindle.
Birds A good number of woodland birds breed at Warleigh, while on the estuary Redshank and Shelduck are common. Great Crested Grebe and occasionally Pochard and Goldeneye can be seen in winter.
Insects Speckled Wood Butterflies are numerous and an uncommon cricket, the Short-winged Conehead can be found.

Under Threat Nearby Tamerton Lake Estuary is threatened by the proposed development of a marina.

Information Centre A disused railway station adjacent to the reserve has been developed as a nature centre for Warleigh Point Wood by Plymouth City Council.
Guide No   **Disabled Access** Yes   **School Parties** By prior arrangement with DWT **Parking** In lane leading to reserve   **Toilets** No   **Food** No

Further Information Information leaflet, with map, available from DWT.

Dorset
BROWNSEA ISLAND

OS Ref SZ028878   Landranger Sheet 195
Nearest Town Poole   **Size of Reserve** 202.3 hectares (500 acres)
Managed by The National Trust (NT) and the Dorset Trust for Nature
Conservation (DTNC)
Access The island is open from Easter to end of September, daily from 10.00–19.30,
or dusk if earlier. Only part of the island is freely accessible to the public; access to
the DTNC Nature Reserve is restricted. Contact the DTNC Warden at The Villa,
Brownsea Island, Poole Harbour, Dorset BH15 1EE (tel. 0202 709445) for details of
access to the Reserve. Public boats to the island leave from Poole Quay or
Sandbanks. A landing fee is charged to all non-NT members. No dogs.

B rownsea Island lies in Poole Harbour. The public area consists
mainly of heath and woodland, while the DTNC Reserve also
contains a marsh, reedbed, salt-water lagoon and two lakes. The island
provides fine views of Purbeck, Corfe Castle and the Dorset coast.

Nature Trail A waymarked trail of about 2.4 km (1½ miles) explores the southern
part of the island, excluding the DTNC Reserve, although a public observation
hide at the start of the walk provides views over the lagoon. Nature Trail leaflets
are available from the NT shop on the island.
Trees Scots Pine, Sycamore, Ash, Oak, Beech, Alder, Willow, Birch.
Birds Seabirds, Waders, Wildfowl, Tern, Cormorant, Peacock, Pheasant.
Animals Sika Deer, Red Squirrel, Rabbit.

Guide Contact the NT Warden at Brownsea Island, Poole Harbour, Dorset BH15
1EE (tel. 0202 707744)   **Disabled Access** Yes. Contact the NT Warden (as above)
for details   **School Parties** By prior arrangement with the NT Warden (as above)
Parking On the mainland   **Toilets** On the island   **Food** Cafeteria and tuck shop near
the quay. No barbecues   **Shop** National Trust shop near the quay.

Further Information Leaflets, with maps, are available from the Warden (as above)
or from The National Trust, Wessex Regional Office, Stourton, Near Warminster,
Wiltshire (tel. 0747 840224).

Dorset
POWERSTOCK COMMON

OS Ref SY540973   Landranger Sheet 194
Nearest Town Beaminster   **Size of Reserve** 115 hectares (285 acres)
Managed by Dorset Trust for Nature Conservation (DTNC)   **Access** Open all year

P owerstock Common is an ancient woodland site now partly planted
with conifers. It includes old oak woodland, ancient hedgebanks,

coppiced areas, heathy grassland, ponds and a disused railway line with grassy embankments. Much of the reserve is designated an SSSI.

Nature Trail There is a 2.8-km (1¾-mile) circular walk waymarked with red arrows. There is an Information Panel close to the entrance of the reserve, showing the beginning and end of the nature trail.

Plants Orchids, Lady's Mantle, Devil's Bit Scabious, Twayblade, Purple Moor Grass, Fleabane, Bog Pimpernel, Cross-leaved Heath, Dog's Mercury, Lesser Valerian, Fairy Flax, Pendulous Sedge, Stinking Iris, Wayfaring Tree, Figwort, Yellow Wort, Salad Burnet, Coltsfoot, Mouse-eared Hawkweed, Horseshoe Vetch, Toadflax, Sheep's Fescue, Great Horsetail, Carline Thistle, Guelder Rose.
Trees Dominating conifers include Norway and Sitka Spruce, Douglas Fir and Scots Pine, but there is some Ash, Hazel, Oak and Alder.
Birds Siskin, Reedpoll, Blackcap, Nightingale.
Animals Roe, Fallow and Sika Deer, Badger.
Butterflies 37 species have been recorded, including Silver-washed and Marsh Fritillaries and Purple Hairstreak.
Other Adders are common in grassy areas.

Under Threat This reserve provides a good example of the way in which areas of natural growth can be overcome and destroyed by the relentless growth of conifer plantations. They cover much of the original woodland area and about half the ancient field systems. DTNC aims to change these areas back to deciduous woodland.

Guide For groups only, by prior arrangement with DTNC   **Disabled Access** By prior arrangement with DTNC   **School Parties** By prior arrangement with DTNC **Parking** Small car park at entrance to reserve   **Toilets** No   **Food** No

Further Information Leaflets, with maps, are available at the reserve or from DTNC, or from local Tourist Information Centres.

Dorset

TOWNSEND

OS Ref SZ024782   Landranger Sheet 195
Nearest Town Swanage   **Size of Reserve** 13 hectares (32 acres)
Managed by Dorset Trust for Nature Conservation (DTNC)   **Access** Open all year

Townsend reserve occupies an area of limestone grassland rising to a height of 99 metres (325 feet), providing superb views of Swanage and its bay, the chalk ridge of the Purbeck Hills and the Isle of Wight. It is connected to Durlston Country Park by public footpaths.

Nature Trail Although there is no formal trail, there are many clear paths to follow.

The area was once quarried for Purbeck Stone. There is a quarry entrance, with the broken remains of its crab-stones, on the reserve. The hummocky nature of the ground is another legacy of byegone quarrying, as are the Scar Banks (steep-sided mounds of quarry waste). These now provide a habitat for plants which attract a number of butterfly species, some of which are becoming quite rare because of the widespread destruction of their downland habitat and the disappearance of their food plants.

Plants Grasses (including some typical of old pasture), Bastard Toadflax, Kidney Vetch, Horseshoe Vetch, Ox-eye Daisy, Pepper Saxifrage, Greater Knapweed, Common Vetch, Cuckoo Pint, Lesser Celandine, Hartstongue Fern and the rare Early Spider Orchid.
Birds Lesser Whitethroat and other common species.
Insects Meadow Grasshopper, Great Green Bush-cricket, Bloody-nosed Beetle.
Butterflies Small Blue, Chalkhill Blue, Lulworth Skipper (a rare butterfly, practically confined to Dorset), Marbled White, Speckled Wood.

Guide For groups only, by prior arrangement with DTNC   **Disabled Access** No   **School Parties** By prior arangement with DTNC   **Parking** In road beside reserve   **Toilets** In Swanage (nearby)   **Food** In Swanage

Further Information Reserve leaflets are available as part of a pack called *Nature Reserves on the Dorset Coast* available from DTNC (price £1.20).

Somerset

BLACK ROCK

OS Ref ST483546   Landranger Sheet 182
Nearest Town Cheddar   **Size of Reserve** 73 hectares (180 acres)
Managed by The Somerset Trust for Nature Conservation (STNC)
Access Open all year

The reserve consists of rough grassland, plantation, natural woodland and scree. The reserve is divided in two by a dry valley, Black Rock Drove.

Nature Trail There is a 1.5-km (1-mile) trail which can be extended to a slightly longer one of 2.4 km (1½ miles). The trail is waymarked with green arrows and there are numbered stop signs along the route. The trail climbs above Black Rock Drove to give views down Cheddar Gorge towards Exmoor and to the highest point to Mendip at Blackdown. Nature Trail leaflets are available at the entrance to the reserve.

The site is part of the Cheddar Gorge SSSI on account of its plant communities.
Plants Lesser Meadow Rue, Rock Stonecrop, Spring Cinquefoil, Ragwort, Small Scabious, Salad Burnet, Early Purple Orchid, lichens, ferns (including the uncommon Limestone Polypody and Brittle Bladder Ferns), Wall Pepper.
Trees Ash, Hazel, Sycamore, Larch, Scots Pine.
Birds Willow Warbler, Redstart, Whitethroat, Finches.
Animals Wood Mouse, Yellow Necked Mouse, Dormouse, Rabbit, Grey Squirrel, Fox, Badger.
Butterflies Small Blue, Common Blue, Brown Argus, Dark Green Fritillary, Small Essex and Grizzled Skipper, Yellow Brimstone.

Guide No   **Disabled Access** No   **School Parties** Welcomed
Parking Roadside only   **Toilets** No   **Food** No

Further Information Contact STNC.

Somerset
EBBOR GORGE

OS Ref ST525485   Landranger Sheet 182
Nearest Town Wells   **Size of Reserve** 46 hectares (114 acres)
Managed by The Nature Conservancy Council (NCC)
Access Open all year

E bbor Gorge is a fine example of a Mendip valley, carved out of the carboniferous limestone by an ancient river. Designated a National Nature Reserve (NNR), the reserve contains both high canopy and coppiced woodland as well as valley meadows, scrub and open grassland.

Nature Trail There are 2 trails. The shorter walk (marked with black posts) takes just 30 minutes, while the longer 1½-hour walk (red posts) is more strenuous, climbing to 244 metres (800 feet) and giving superb views. Strong walking shoes are recommended. Walkers should keep off the screes and rockfalls and should not attempt to enter the caves – they are treacherous. Both walks start and finish at the stone stile in the car park. Trail leaflets are available from the Nature Conservancy Information Centre in the car park.

Plants Dog's Mercury, Enchanter's Nightshade, Hartstongue Fern.
Trees Ash, Wych Elm, Beech, Pedunculate Oak, Hornbeam.
Birds Buzzard, Sparrowhawk, Kestrel.
Animals Badger.
Other Greater and Lesser Horseshoe Bats sometimes hibernate in the caves and rock fissures of the Gorge.

Information Centre The Nature Conservancy Information and Display Centre in the car park illustrates the geology and some of the wildlife to be seen on the reserve.

Guide Contact the Reserve Warden, Peter Mountford, 6 Priory Place, Wells (tel. 0749 79546)   **Disabled Access** The shorter walk is recommended to wheelchair users. There are also facilities for the visually handicapped. Please contact the Warden (as above) for further details   **School Parties** Contact the Warden (as above)
Parking Yes   **Toilets** No   **Food** No

Further Information Contact the Warden (as above) or the NCC, South West Region, Roughmoor, Bishops Hull, Taunton, Somerset TA1 5AA (tel. 0823 283211).

Somerset

FYNE COURT

OS Ref ST223321   Landranger Sheet 182
Nearest Town Bridgwater   **Size of Reserve** 9 hectares (22 acres)
Managed by The Somerset Trust for Nature Conservation (STNC)
Access Open all year. No dogs.

F yne Court is the headquarters of the STNC. Situated on the lower slopes of the Quantock Hills, it is a Victorian estate of artificial lakes, unimproved grassland and artificial woodland being converted to something more natural. The buildings within the estate include the following: an Information Centre, a shop, administrative offices, a lecture hall and a schoolroom for use by visiting parties.

Nature Trail There are numerous paths through the woodland of the estate, plus a laid out **Tree Trail** with marked posts to follow. Two trails start from Fyne Court and take in the surrounding countryside. The **Fyne Court Circular Walk** is 8.8 km (5½ miles) long and starts from the car park at Fyne Court. The **Five Pond Wood Nature Trail** lies about 400 metres (¼ mile) north of Fyne Court and is just over 1.5 km (1 mile) long. Access is on foot from the grounds of Fyne Court. The paths can be muddy in wet weather so suitable footwear is essential. Leaflets for all the trails (including a schools' activity trail leaflet) are available from the shop.

Fyne Court is noted for its fine old trees and large variety of tree species. Within the estate is an Arboretum, planted as part of the 1973 'Tree Planting Year' campaign, where many unusual species can be seen growing. There is also a Tree Nursery producing young native British trees and shrubs.
Plants Typical woodland plants grow on the reserve. *Five Pond Wood* has a particularly delightful carpet of wild flowers in spring and early summer. The 'Deadwood' area of the estate contains many species of fungus.
Trees *Five Pond Wood* contains naturally occurring Ash, Hawthorn, Hazel, Holly and Sallow, along with planted species such as Beech, Laurel, Snowberry, Poplar, Sycamore and Sweet Chestnut. *The Arboretum* has many interesting species such as Canoe Birch, Japanese Red Cedar, Tulip Tree, Deodar, Cedar of Lebanon, Snake-bark Maple, Paper-bark Maple, Wellingtonia, Spanish Chestnut and Quince. On the *Circular Walk*, Japanese Larch, Western Hemlock, Douglas Fir, European Larch, Sweet Chestnut, Oak, Beech and Sitka Spruce can also be seen.
Birds Most common birds inhabit the woods and hedgerows, including several species of Tit and Finch, Woodpecker, Jackdaw and Jay.
Animals Badger, Fox, Rabbit, Vole, Mole, Wood Mouse.

Guide Can sometimes be arranged for groups by prior arrangement with STNC
Disabled Access Yes, within the estate itself   **School Parties** Welcomed. No special arrangements necessary but prior notification appreciated. One pond is reserved for school groups   **Parking** In car park   **Toilets** At STNC headquarters
Food Available Sunday afternoons in summer only; picnic area   **Shop** Open every afternoon, 14.00–17.00, except in January and February, selling leaflets and nature goods of all descriptions.

Further Information Contact STNC at Fyne Court.

Somerset

HURSCOMBE

OS Ref SS974317   Landranger Sheet 181
Nearest Town Brompton Regis   **Size of Reserve** 19 hectares (46 acres)
Managed by The Somerset Trust for Nature Conservation (STNC)
Access Open all year

T he reserve lies within the Exmoor National Park and occupies the northern end of Wimbleball Lake. It is an area of scrub, marsh, rough grass, old and new woodland, and open water. The surrounding land is intensively farmed, so the contrasting shelter and variety of habitats on the reserve are of value to wildlife.

Nature Trail On the west side of the lake, above Bessom Bridge, starting along the bridleway that runs through the reserve. The trail is 3.2 km (2 miles) long and is marked by numbered posts. Trail leaflets are available at the reserve or from STNC (price 20p).

The reserve is noted for its butterfly population.
Plants Meadowsweet, Jointed Rush, Ragged Robin, Marsh St. John's Wort, Sheep's Bit, Lousewort, Birdsfoot Trefoil.
Trees Ash, Alder, Larch, Oak, Beech, Wild Service.
Birds Kestrel, Buzzard, Raven, Tawny Owl, Whinchat, Redstart, Pied Flycatcher, Woodpeckers, Willow Warbler, Blackcap, Great Crested Grebe, Wigeon, Teal, Pochard, Tufted Duck, Mallard, Coot, Goldeneye.
Animals Pipistrelle Bat, Badger, Rabbit, Fox, Roe Deer, Shrew, Mouse, Vole.
Butterflies Over 30 species recorded, including Pearl-bordered, Silver-washed and Marsh Fritillaries.

Guide No   **Disabled Access** No   **School Parties** Welcomed   **Parking** In car park
Toilets At car park   **Food** Picnic area

Further Information Contact STNC.

Somerset

LONG WOOD

OS Ref ST488551   Landranger Sheet 182
Nearest Town Cheddar   **Size of Reserve** 17 hectares (42 acres)
Managed by The Somerset Trust for Nature Conservation (STNC)
Access Open all year

T he reserve consists of ancient, mainly broadleaved, woodland in a dry river valley near the head of Cheddar Gorge. The wood is at its best in spring when the woodland plants are flowering.

Nature Trail 2.4 km (1½ miles), marked with white arrows and numbered posts. Trail leaflets are available at the Black Rock Gate entrance to the reserve.

The site is classified as a geological SSSI on account of its underground cave systems.
Plants Candle Snuff and Heart Rot Fungi, Wild Garlic, Meadowsweet, Herb Paris, Usnea (a species of lichen that will only grow in very clean, unpolluted air), Wood Anemone, Toothwort, Garlic Mustard, Cuckoo Flower.
Trees Hazel, Beech, Oak, Sycamore, Field Maple, Ash, Poplar.
Birds Green Woodpecker.
Animals Grey Squirrel, Roe Deer, Fox, Badger.
Butterflies Orange-tip, Green-veined White.

Guide No   **Disabled Access** No   **School Parties** Welcomed   **Parking** Roadside only
Toilets No   **Food** No

Further Information Contact STNC.

Somerset
VELVET BOTTOM

OS Ref ST503555   Landranger Sheet 182
Nearest Town Cheddar   **Size of Reserve** 17 hectares (42 acres)
Managed by The Somerset Trust for Nature Conservation (STNC)
Access Open all year

V elvet Bottom Nature Reserve lies on the floor of a dry river valley bounded by carboniferous limestone. The valley floor has a high lead content and there are lead industry slag heaps lining the sides of the valley. It is an area of rough grassland with small areas of woodland and scrub. The reserve is within the Charterhouse-on-Mendip SSSI.

Nature Trail The reserve is about 2 km (1¼ miles) long and very narrow in shape. Although there is no formal trail, a footpath runs the length of the reserve.

The area has been used extensively for lead working since pre-Roman times. Although this halted in the 1880s, its effects can be seen in the series of 'levels' formed by the lead workers, and in the numerous slag heaps, as well as in the flora and fauna to be seen on the site.
Plants Unusual plants particularly associated with lead, eg. Alpine Penny-cress and Spring Sandwort.
Birds Redstart, Grasshopper Warbler, Buzzard, Kestrel.
Animals Fox, Badger, Rabbit, Hare, Stoat, Weasel, Roe Deer.
Butterflies The reserve is noted for its butterfly population – 26 species have been recorded, with Marbled White and Dark Green Fritillary particularly numerous.
Other The dry grassland is also an ideal habitat for Adder and Common Lizard.

Guide No   **Disabled Access** No   **School Parties** No   **Parking** Roadside only
Toilets No   **Food** No

Further Information Reserve leaflets are available from dispensers at either end of the reserve, or from STNC (price 10p).

1 East Blean Wood	10 Russia Dock Woodland	21 Wallis Wood
2 Hothfield Common	11 Stave Hill Nature Park	22 Arundel Wildfowl Pa
3 Bramley Bank	12 Sydenham Hill Wood	23 Woodsmill Countrysi
4 Camley Street Natural Park	13 Tump 53	Centre
5 The Chase	14 The Warren	24 Blackmoor Copse
6 Dulwich Upper Wood	15 Bagmoor Common	25 Clouts Wood
7 Gunnersbury Triangle	16 Dollyper's Hill	26 Jones's Mill
8 Hutchinsons and Chapel Banks	17 Nower Wood	27 Rack Hill
9 Lavender Pond Nature Park	18 Thorpe Hay Meadow	28 Vincients Wood
	19 Thundry Meadows	29 Whitesheet Hill
	20 Vann Lake	

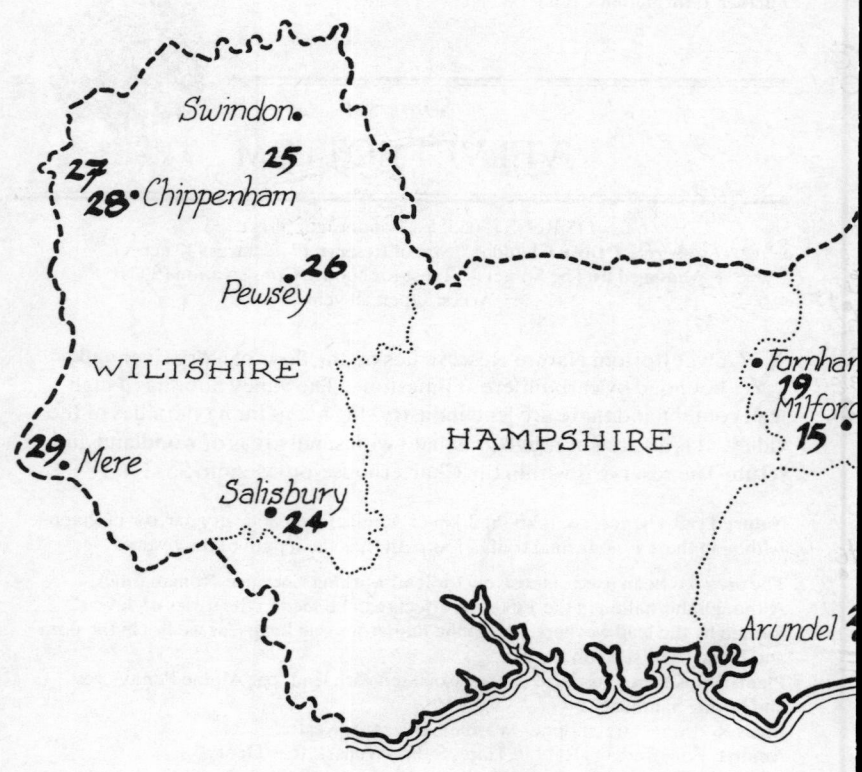

SOUTH-EAST ENGLAND

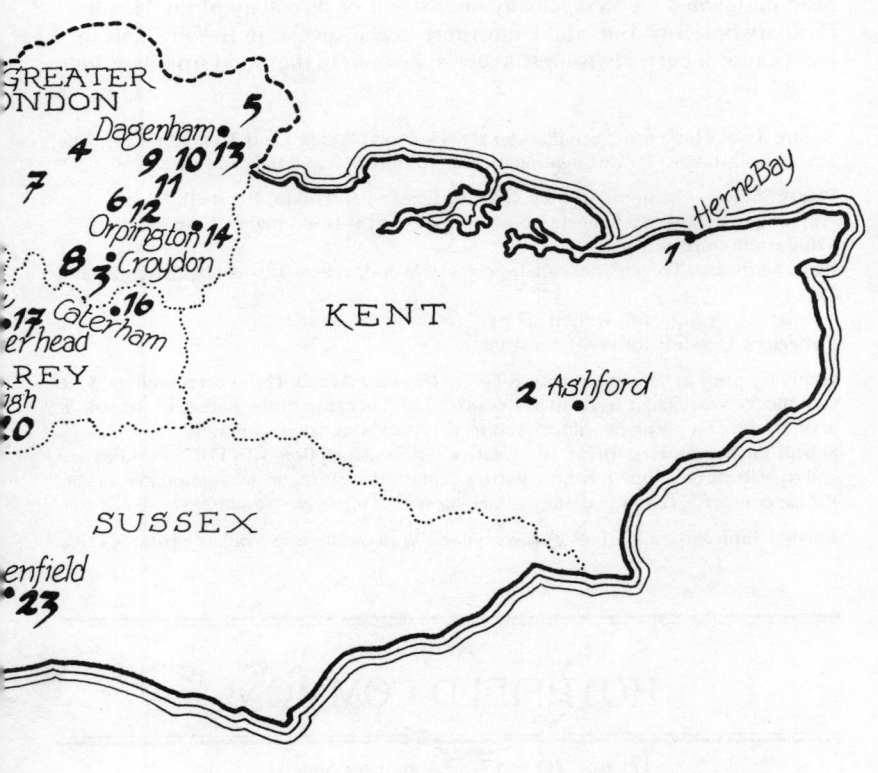

Kent

EAST BLEAN WOOD

OS Ref TR188643 Landranger Sheet 179
Nearest Town Herne Bay **Size of Reserve** 112 hectares (277 acres)
Managed by Kent Trust for Nature Conservation (KTNC) **Access** Open all year

E ast Blean Wood is a remnant of the ancient forest of Blean. It is an area of mixed coppice, oak high forest and conifer plantation that has been designated an SSSI, chiefly on account of its colony of the Heath Fritillary butterfly, one of the most threatened species in Britain. This rare and beautiful butterfly is most likely to be seen in the wood from late June to late July.

Nature Trail There are 2 waymarked trails – 1 km (⅔ mile) and 3 km (2 miles). The longer walk takes you through most of the different habitats in the wood.

Plants Sanicle, Common Spotted Orchid, Lesser Periwinkle, Bluebell, Wood Anemone, Yellow Archangel, Common Cow-wheat (food plant of the Heath Fritillary butterfly).
Birds Nuthatch, Treecreeper, all 3 species of Woodpecker, Tawny Owl, Nightingale, Jackdaw.
Animals Grey Squirrel, Rabbit, Hare.
Butterflies Heath Fritillary, Brimstone.

Guide By prior arrangement with KTNC **Disabled Access** The shorter walk may be suitable for wheelchair users in dry weather, but, because of the nature of the soil, it is often difficult going in winter, and in very wet weather in summer.
School Parties As East Blean is a relatively new acquisition of KTNC, facilities are still to be fully developed. School parties cannot, therefore, be accommodated as yet. Please contact KTNC for details **Parking** No **Toilets** No **Food** No

Further Information Leaflets and Woodland Walk guides are available from KTNC.

Kent

HOTHFIELD COMMON

OS Ref TQ969459 Landranger Sheet 189
Nearest Town Ashford **Size of Reserve** 58 hectares (143 acres)
Managed by Kent Trust for Nature Conservation (KTNC) **Access** Open all year

H othfield Common is one of the last remaining areas of heathland in Kent and is designated an SSSI and an LNR. The reserve also includes a number of acid bogs (rare in Kent) and some woodland.

Nature Trail 1.5 km (1 mile), waymarked. Parts of the trail can become wet under foot so suitable footwear is essential. The route is not strenuous, taking about 1 hour to walk and offering some lovely views over the open heathland.

Plants Botanical interest is centred on the acid bogs which support several species of Sphagnum Moss, Round-leaved Sundew, Bog Asphodel and Heath Spotted-orchid.
Birds Over 60 bird species have been recorded on the Common, and breeding birds include Green Woodpecker, Treecreeper, Nuthatch, Tree Pipit and Yellow Hammer.
Animals Fox, Badger, Weasel, Stoat, Vole, Shrew.
Insects The insects of the Common are unusual for Kent and include several species of Dragonfly and tiny solitary Sand Wasps.
Other Grass Snakes have occasionally been recorded.

Guide By prior arrangement with KTNC   **Disabled Access** A shortened nature trail route is suitable for wheelchair users   **School Parties** Facilities for educational groups can be arranged and an educational information pack is available for primary schools. Please contact KTNC several weeks in advance   **Parking** Yes
Toilets Yes, including for the disabled   **Food** No

Further Information Educational information packs, nature trail guides and reserve leaflets are available from KTNC.

London

BRAMLEY BANK

OS Ref TQ2636   Landranger Sheet 176
Nearest Town Croydon   **Size of Reserve** 10.5 hectares (26 acres)
Managed by London Wildlife Trust (LWT)   **Access** Open all year

B ramley Bank Reserve lies on west and south-west facing slopes of underlying chalk and pebbly sands topped with clay. The area consists mainly of broadleaved woodland (some ancient and some secondary), an Austrian Pine plantation, an area of acid grassland, a large pond and an old gravel pit.

Nature Trail 800–1200 metres (½–¾ mile), waymarked. There are benches along the path which runs from one end of the reserve to the other.

Plants Wild flower meadow and Hawthorn coppice.
Birds A range of common woodland species.
Animals Bats, Grey Squirrel, Vole, Field Mouse.

Guide By prior arrangement with LWT   **Disabled Access** No
School Parties Contact LWT in advance   **Parking** Heathfield Estate car park adjoins the northern end of the reserve. At the southern end there is roadside parking only
Toilets No   **Food** No

Further Information Contact LWT.

London
CAMLEY STREET NATURAL PARK

OS Ref TQ299834   Landranger Sheet 176
Nearest Town Camden Town, London NW1   **Size of Reserve** 1 hectare (2¼ acres)
Managed by London Wildlife Trust (LWT) with help from a volunteer 'Support
Group'   **Access** Open every day of the year from 9.30–17.30 (later in summer)

C amley Street Natural Park is a man-made urban nature reserve now
maturing well. A large pond is surrounded by a marshy area, young
woodland and scrub, and wild flower meadows. The park provides city-
dwellers with a unique and valuable opportunity to come into contact with
the natural world.

Nature Trail There is a waymarked circular path system around the Park (about
500 metres/550 yards), allowing visitors access to many areas.

Nets are provided for pond-dipping (deposit payable) and there is a birdwatching
hide overlooking the pond.
Plants Over 200 plant species have been recorded. Meadow areas are spectacular in
summer.
Birds 55 species recorded, including Heron, Kestrel and Black Redstart. Moorhens,
Coots, Mallards and Tufted Duck have all nested on and around the pond.
Animals Squirrel, Hedgehog.
Insects 12 species of butterfly, 16 moth and 5 dragonfly.
Other First recording of spider *Osteavius Gelanopygius* for the London area. Frogs,
newts and toads all breed and are regularly sighted.

Under Threat The Park and entire surrounding area are under threat from the King's
Cross Development. A campaign to fight the threat has been launched.

Visitor Centre The Centre hosts frequent 'community events', wildlife workshops,
etc., as well as a continuous push-button slide show, changing exhibitions, the 'Food
Web Game' and goods for sale.

Guide There are staff on site every day. Groups (other than school parties) wishing to
visit the Park should contact the Park Manager on 01-833 2311 in advance.
Disabled Access The buildings and main paths are accessible to wheelchair users.
School Parties Welcomed, but bookings *must* be made well in advance. A classroom
is available for school use and a teacher is based permanently on site. To make a
booking, contact the teacher at the Park on 01-833 2311.
Parking In surrounding streets   **Toilets** Yes, including for the disabled   **Food** No

Further Information Information leaflets are available from the Park (12 Camley
Street, London NW1 0NX) or from LWT.

London
THE CHASE

OS Ref TQ515855 Landranger Sheet 177
Nearest Town Dagenham **Size of Reserve** 46.9 hectares (116 acres)
Managed by London Wildlife Trust (LWT) **Access** Open all year

T he Chase is a large area of land on either side of the River Beam which runs the length of the reserve. The area contains wetlands, grasslands, scrub and woodland and supports a wealth of interesting plant and animal life. This reserve is new to the LWT and facilities are not yet developed.

Nature Trail A 1–2-km (½–1¼-mile) waymarked trail is planned for the future.

Plants The very rich plantlife includes Spiny Restharrow, Lesser Spearwort and Purple-loosestrife.
Birds Waterfowl and waders on the wetland; Warblers, etc., in the scrub. Notable species include Snipe, Teal, Long-eared Owl, Lapwing, Redshank, Reed Warbler, Water Rail.
Insects Butterflies, dragonflies and the rare Roesel's Bush-cricket.
Other Grass Snake, Frog, Toad and Common Newt all breed on the site.

Under Threat Wetland sites are rapidly disappearing in London, the former Thames grazing marshes being probably the most threatened. Rainham Marshes (SSSI), in the neighbouring borough of Havering, is a good example of such an area which is imminently threatened by a proposed new road.

Information Centre Planned for the future

Guide By prior arrangement with LWT **Disabled Access** Planned for the future
School Parties Contact LWT **Parking** Yes **Toilets** Yes **Food** No

Further Information Contact LWT headquarters or local team on 01-593 8096.

London
DULWICH UPPER WOOD NATURE PARK

OS Ref TQ338712 Landranger Sheet 177
Nearest Town Norwood, London SE19 **Size of Reserve** 2.2 hectares (5½ acres)
Managed by Trust for Urban Ecology (TRUE) **Access** Open all year

T he reserve consists of sycamore-dominated urban woodland which has developed from a patch of ancient woodland and the neglected gardens of now-demolished Victorian houses. The wood is at its best in spring and summer.

Nature Trail 800 metres (½ mile), waymarked. There is a viewing area on the Upper Terrace. Trail Guides are available.

The wood contains over 200 species of trees and vascular plants, and more than 200 species of fungi, as well as a great variety of invertebrates. There is evidence of the ancient woodland boundary, eg. pollarded oak and ditch.

Plants Solomon's Seal, Cuckoo-pint.

Trees A tree nursery has been started on the reserve to preserve local strains.

Birds Great and Lesser Spotted Woodpeckers, Green Woodpecker, Kestrel, Sparrowhawk, Redstart.

Animals Fox, Hedgehog, Grey Squirrel.

Butterflies Speckled Wood, Peacock, Small White, Common Blue.

Information Centre There is a Portacabin in the wood and the Warden is present during normal weekday working hours.

Guide By prior arrangement with the Warden on 01-761 6230 **Disabled Access** Not at present, but a suitable entrance and paths, and additional handrails, are planned for the near future **School Parties** Visits by school parties must be booked in advance by telephoning the Warden (as above) **Parking** There is limited parking space inside the entrance gate and along Farquhar Road **Toilets** Yes, adjacent to the Portacabin **Food** No

Further Information Contact the Warden (as above) or TRUE.

London

GUNNERSBURY TRIANGLE

OS Ref TQ201786 Landranger Sheet 176
Nearest Town Chiswick, London W4 **Size of Reserve** 2.5 hectares (6 acres)
Managed by London Wildlife Trust (LWT) **Access** Open 9.30–17.00 Monday to Friday, 14.00–16.00 Sundays (but only the second and fourth Sundays of the winter months). Closed Saturdays. Members of the public are welcome to visit, either just to look round or to participate in community work days, when volunteers help to maintain paths, dig ponds, clear brambles, etc. To find the date of the next open day or work day, please telephone the reserve (01-747 3881), check the signboard at the entrance, or look in the local press

The Triangle is an area of secondary semi-natural woodland situated about 9.6 km (6 miles) from the centre of London, the entrance being only about 46 metres (50 yards) from Chiswick Park Underground Station. It contains a number of habitats, including birch woodland, willow woodland, grasslands and a pond. The site was surrounded by 3 railway lines, giving the reserve its triangular shape. One of these is now disused and forms one of the footpaths on the reserve. During the early 1900s, gravel was extracted from the site with the result that parts of the reserve are low-lying and swampy. The site has LNR status and is therefore relatively safe from development, despite its location.

Nature Trail About 800 metres (½ mile), waymarked with numbered posts corresponding to information in leaflet. Paths can be muddy in wet weather. It takes about 45 minutes to walk round the site.

The Triangle is one of the few remaining areas of semi-natural woodland in West London.

Plants Celery-leaved Buttercup, Water-Plantain, Hemlock Water Dropwort, Pendulous Sedge, Prickly Buckler Fern.

Trees Birch, Willow, Sycamore, Yew, Mountain Ash, Holly.

Birds 44 species recorded, including Tawny Owl, Great Spotted Woodpecker and a number of different Warblers. Of these, 39 species are thought to breed on the site.

Animals The reserve is noted for its Foxes which are often seen by visitors, especially towards dusk. Other mammals present include Field Vole, Hedgehog, etc.

Other Common Frog, Common Toad, Smooth Newt.

Information Centre There is an information hut on the reserve.

Guide By prior arrangement with Warden at reserve on 01-747 3881 (answer-phone when no-one in office)   **Disabled Access** A tarmac entrance ramp allows wheelchair access. A toilet for the disabled is planned for the near future

School Parties Groups of all ages, including GCSE and A-level students, visit the reserve. The information hut can be used as a classroom. There is a teacher/warden on site to lead groups. Further details from the reserve on 01-747 3881   **Parking** For up to 6 cars or 2 mini-buses   **Toilets** Yes   **Food** Tea/coffee can be arranged for organized groups, if notice is given

Further Information A number of handouts, including nature trail leaflets, is available from the reserve. Information packs are available for schools and community groups.

London

HUTCHINSONS and CHAPEL BANKS

OS Ref TQ2636   Landranger Sheet 176
Nearest Town Croydon   **Size of Reserve** 30 hectares (74 acres)
Managed by London Wildlife Trust (LWT)   **Access** Open all year

The reserve lies on south-west and west facing banks, the land dropping steeply to the valley bottom. Hutchinsons Bank consists of chalk grassland and scrub and a small area of woodland. Chapel Bank is mainly woodland.

Nature Trail Although there is no formal trail, the reserve is covered by an extensive network of footpaths.

Plants The reserve is rich with calcareous grassland species.
Animals Rabbit, Fox.
Butterflies Large and varied butterfly populations.
Other Lizards.

Guide No   **Disabled Access** No   **School Parties** No   **Parking** Restricted to roadside verges   **Toilets** No   **Food** No

Further Information Contact LWT.

London
LAVENDER POND NATURE PARK

OS Ref TQ365807   Landranger Sheet 177
Nearest Town Rotherhithe, London SE16   **Size of Reserve** 0.8 hectares (2 acres)
Managed by Trust for Urban Ecology (TRUE)   **Access** Open weekdays and some
weekends when Warden is on duty

T he Park consists of a large man-made freshwater pond fringed by
reedbeds, alder carr and mixed woodland. It is within the Surrey
Docks redevelopment area.

Nature Trail Although there is no formal trail within this reserve, the Park is included
in a 2-hour walk which runs through the entire Surrey Docks area. For details,
telephone 01-252 0294.

Plants Alder carr, marshland vegetation including Purple Loosestrife and Marsh
Marigold.
Birds Nesting Waterfowl, occasional exotic migrants.

Information Centre The now disused Pump House is to be converted for community
and environmental education use.

Guide By prior arrangement with TRUE   **School Parties** By prior arrangement with
Site Teacher on 01-232 0498. The site is used extensively for education purposes,
especially primary   **Parking** Yes   **Toilets** Yes, including for the disabled from
Autumn 1989   **Food** In Pump House when open. Currently available from Surrey
Quays Shopping Centre (15 minutes' walk away)

Further Information Available from the Warden at the reserve or on 01-232 0498.

London
RUSSIA DOCK WOODLAND

OS Ref TQ360800   Landranger Sheet 177
Nearest Town Rotherhithe, London SE16   **Size of Site** 14 hectares (34½ acres)
Managed by London Borough of Southwark   **Access** Open all year

T he area that was once Russia Dock has been transformed into a linear
park, creating a landscape of woodland, ponds and streams
surrounding the remains of the old dock. It is within the Surrey Docks
redevelopment area but is not a formal reserve.

Nature Trail There is no formal trail within Russia Dock Woodland, but the area is
covered by a maze of footpaths, providing a walk of no more than 4 km (2½ miles).
The Woodland is included in a 2-hour walk which runs through the entire Surrey
Docks area. For details, telephone 01-252 0294.

Trees Willow, Poplar.

Birds Common urban and woodland species, including Blackcap, Chiffchaff, Spotted Flycatcher and Lesser Spotted Woodpecker. Also exotic migrants and Waterfowl.

Guide The Trust for Urban Ecology (TRUE) runs occasional guided walks through Russia Dock Woodland, Lavender Pond Nature Park (left) and Stave Hill Nature Park (below) each summer. Contact TRUE for details.

Disabled Access The Woodland is fully accessible to disabled people

School Parties No   **Parking** On adjacent roads   **Toilets** No   **Food** No, but good pubs in Old Rotherhithe and a food hall in Surrey Quays Shopping Centre (15 minutes' walk away)

Further Information Contact TRUE or London Borough of Southwark.

London
STAVE HILL NATURE PARK

OS Ref TQ361800   Landranger Sheet 177
Nearest Town Rotherhithe, London SE16   **Size of Reserve** 2.3 hectares (6 acres)
Managed by Trust for Urban Ecology (TRUE)   **Access** Open all year

This Park is an experiment in creating natural habitats on wasteland. The area, formerly a disused dock basin and quayside, has been gently landscaped and will develop into a mosaic of scrub, woodland and wild flower meadows, with two ponds. The area is well used by birds throughout the year, has a large population of frogs and attracts numerous insects. The meadow areas are managed to maintain a show of wild flowers from April through to late autumn. The Park is within the Surrey Docks redevelopment area. Although not within the Park, Stave Hill itself (a public viewing point) provides marvellous views.

Nature Trail There is a Herb and Wild flower Trail of about 400 metres (¼ mile). Contact TRUE for details. The Park is also included in a longer 2-hour walk through the entire Surrey Docks area. For details, telephone 01-252 0294.

Plants Impressive show of wild flowers throughout growing season. The site is of interest as an experiment in habitat creation, with demonstrations of different wild flower seed mixes, methods of planting trees and shrubs, etc.

Birds Summer: Skylark, Kestrel, other common urban birds, some exotic visitors. Winter: large mixed flocks of Finches.

Information Centre Warden's accommodation/TRUE headquarters is nearby (but not accessible to disabled visitors).

Guide By prior arrangement with TRUE   **Disabled Access** The surfaced paths can be used by people with walking difficulties and by wheelchair users if helpers are present. There are no very steep slopes and only a few shallow steps   **School Parties** By prior arrangement with TRUE   **Parking** Limited at edge of Park, more on nearby roads   **Toilets** In Warden's accommodation nearby   **Food** No, but good pubs in Old Rotherhithe and food hall in Surrey Quays Shopping Centre (15 minutes' walk away)

Further Information Site Guides are available from TRUE.

London
SYDENHAM HILL WOOD

OS Ref TQ344726   Landranger Sheet 177
Nearest Town Dulwich, London SE26   **Size of Reserve** 8 hectares (20 acres)
Managed by London Wildlife Trust (LWT)   **Access** Open all year

Sydenham Hill Wood is one of the last surviving fragments of the Great North Wood which once covered much of south London. It consists mainly of ancient sessile oak and hornbeam woodland with some patches of secondary woodland along an old railway track or in areas that were once Victorian gardens.

Nature Trail The trail route is marked by white posts and takes just under 1 hour to complete. The old railway line bed is flat but other areas of the wood are quite steep. Nature Trail Guides are available from LWT.

Despite centuries of human activity, the wood supports by far the widest range of wildlife in Southwark – 56 types of bird, 138 species of plant, more than 40 sorts of butterfly and moth, and an abundance of insects and mammals.

Plants In the ancient part of the wood, Solomon's Seal, Wood Anemone, Ramson and Wood Sorrel can be found. The wood is also the only London site for the moss *Mnium Punctatum*.

Trees Oak, Hornbeam, Ash, Birch, Beech, Sycamore, Cedar of Lebanon, Monkey-puzzle.

Birds All 3 species of Woodpecker, Goldcrest, Long-tailed Tit, Pied Wagtail, Tawny Owl.

Animals Squirrel, Noctule and Pipistrelle Bats, Fox, Hedgehog, Bank Vole, Common Shrew.

Insects 12 species of butterfly, including Brimstone, Comma, Small Tortoiseshell and Peacock, breed in the wood. A pond attracts Dragonflies.

Other The bridge on Cox's Walk, designed by Charles Barrie, is of historical interest as Pisarro painted a picture of Lordship Lane from it. The Victorian Gothic folly is also of interest.

Under Threat Beechgrove is an adjacent site threatened with development. A recent planning application was turned down, but an appeal or another application may follow. Owned by Dulwich Estates, it is the site of an old house, half wooded and half covered in scrub/grassland. Lapsewood, adjoining Beechgrove, is an area of secondary woodland currently zoned for housing by London Borough of Southwark. It would seem, however, that the Borough is in the process of re-zoning it as open space, so the threat may soon be removed.

Information Centre A small Information Centre is open irregularly when staff are on the site.

Guide By prior arrangement with LWT.   **Disabled Access** Part of the site is to be made accessible to wheelchair users in the near future. Contact LWT for further information.   **School Parties** By prior arrangement with LWT   **Parking** Freely available, including coach parking, in Crescent Wood Road   **Toilets** No   **Food** No

Further Information Contact LWT.

London

TUMP 53

OS Ref TQ467804   Landranger Sheet 177
Nearest Town Thamesmead, London SE28   **Size of Reserve** 1.5 hectares (3½ acres)
Managed by London Wildlife Trust (LWT)   **Access** Open all year

Tump 53 is a nature park within the urban environment of Thamesmead New Town. The site was previously an ammunition dump, and was part of the extensive Woolwich Arsenal which covered the area. It consists of a water-filled moat and a central 'island' – the 'Tump' itself. In the central area of the Tump there is a wild flower meadow surrounded by hawthorn copse. The moat and surrounding reedbeds provide freshwater habitats.

Nature Trail A short trail leads into the reserve.

Plants Bristly Ox-tongue, Horn-wort, Water Crowfoot, Lesser Spearwort and other freshwater species.
Birds 58 species recorded up to November 1988, including 5 pairs of Reed Warbler and common garden birds.
Insects Dragon and damselflies, including Emperor and Common Darter Dragonflies.
Other Freshwater invertebrates include Water Scorpion. Vertebrates include newts, toads and frogs.

Under Threat The whole of the surrounding area of Thamesmead is still being developed and the Tump may become one of very few wildlife refuges in years to come. In terms of education, it is of paramount importance.

Nature Centre Planned for the future to provide an educational centre and a base for staff.

Guide By prior arrangement with the Thamesmead Field Officer on 01-310 1500 ext. 354   **Disabled Access** Some access is possible for wheelchair users. Contact Field Officer for details   **School Parties** Welcomed. 900 children visited during the summer of 1988. Pond-dipping is available for visiting parties   **Parking** Nearby   **Toilets** No   **Food** No

Further Information Reserve leaflets, with maps, are available. Contact LWT or Thamesmead Field Officer for information.

London

THE WARREN

OS Ref TQ484680   Landranger Sheet 177
Nearest Town Orpington   **Size of Reserve** 12 hectares (30 acres)
Managed by London Wildlife Trust (LWT)   **Access** Open all year

T he Warren is a predominantly woodland site on higher ground above the River Cray. The mixed broadleaved woodland includes two areas of coppice. A large pond within the wood is rich in aquatic fauna.

Nature Trail There is no formal trail but a good footpath network provides easy access.

Plants Woodland flora includes Butcher's Broom, Wood Spurge, Wood Anemone, Bluebell, Foxglove. Meadow (by railway) contains Centaury, Birdsfoot Trefoil.
Trees Hornbeam, Oak, Beech, Silver Birch.
Birds All common woodland birds, including 3 species of Woodpecker, Tawny Owl, Yellowhammer, Lesser Whitethroat.
Animals Bats, Fox, Rabbit, Weasel, Grass Snake.
Insects Up to 8 species of dragonfly use ponds, including Large Hawker. Butterflies include Common Blue, Skipper, Speckled Wood.
Other The pond is home to 3 species of newt, frogs and numerous invertebrates.

Guide Contact LWT in advance   **Disabled Access** No   **School Parties** No
Parking Some parking available for cars in adjacent Sweeps Lane and Sheepcote Lane, but no space for coaches   **Toilets** No   **Food** No

Further Information Reserve leaflets are available from LWT.

Surrey
BAGMOOR COMMON

OS Ref SU926423   Landranger Sheet 186
Nearest Town Milford   **Size of Reserve** 14 hectares (34 acres)
Managed by Surrey Wildlife Trust (SWT)   **Access** Open all year

T he reserve was at one time open heath but has now reverted to birch woodland. There are a number of open spaces with rough grass and other plants.

Nature Trail There is no waymarked trail but footpaths run through the reserve.

Plants Purple Moor Grass, Opposite-leaved Golden Saxifrage, Hemp Agrimony, Lady Fern.
Trees Birch, Scots Pine, Oak, Aspen.
Birds Woodpecker, Willow Tit, Kingfisher.
Animals Roe Deer.
Insects Agrion Damselfly, Broad-bordered Bee Hawk-moth.
Butterflies Woodland butterflies, notably White Admiral and Purple Emperor, are a feature of the reserve.

Guide By prior arrangement with SWT   **Disabled Access** No   **School Parties** No
Parking No   **Toilets** No   **Food** No

Further Information A pack of 25 reserve cards, with maps, is available from SWT headquarters, price £2.50 (inc. p & p). Copies of up to 6 individual reserve cards are available free of charge, on receipt of an s.a.e.

Surrey

DOLLYPER'S HILL

OS Ref TQ315584   Landranger Sheet 187
Nearest Town Caterham   **Size of Reserve** 11 hectares (27 acres)
Managed by Surrey Wildlife Trust (SWT)   **Access** Open all year

D ollyper's Hill is a mixture of woodland, scrub and grassland. The wooded section at the northern end of the reserve consists of old ash and hazel coppice with some maple. This is at its best in spring when it is a mass of bluebells and wood anemones.

Nature Trail Not at present, but planned for the future. However, there are footpaths running through the reserve.

Plants Bluebell, Wood Anemone, Primrose, Forget-me-not.
Trees Ash, Hazel, Maple.
Animals Fox.

Guide By prior arrangement with SWT   **Disabled Access** No   **School Parties** By prior arrangement with SWT   **Parking** No   **Toilets** No   **Food** No

Further Information A pack of 25 reserve cards, with maps, is available from SWT headquarters, price £2.50 (inc. p & p). Copies of up to 6 individual reserve cards are available free of charge on receipt of an s.a.e.

Surrey

NOWER WOOD

OS Ref TQ193546   Landranger Sheet 187
Nearest Town Leatherhead   **Size of Reserve** 33 hectares (81½ acres)
Managed by Surrey Wildlife Trust (SWT)   **Access** Access is limited. For details, please contact the Trust's Education Officer on Leatherhead (0372) 379509. No dogs

T he reserve is a mixed deciduous wood with a few scattered Scots pine. It is ancient in origin and has been managed over the centuries for timber and game. This past use and recent conservation management have resulted in a mosaic of habitats for wildlife. There are three main ponds and a swamp with some sphagnum moss; all are artificial.

Nature Trail There are 2 general waymarked trails (800 metres/½ mile and 2.5 km/ 1½ miles), plus other more specialised walks. Contact SWT for more details.

There is a birdwatching hide and a deerwatching platform on the reserve.
Trees Oak, Sweet Chestnut, Birch, Hazel, Beech.
Birds Sparrowhawk, Stock Dove, Woodcock, Woodpeckers, Wood Warbler, Tree-creeper, Nuthatch.

Animals Roe Deer, Fox, Badger.

Guide By prior arrangement with SWT. Contact Trust headquarters or the Reserve Warden on Leatherhead (0372) 379509   **Disabled Access** Not at present, but planned for the future   **School Parties** By prior arrangement with SWT. Contact the Reserve Warden (as above)   **Parking** Large car park at reserve entrance open most days during the school term from about March to November.
Toilets No   **Food** No

Further Information A pack of 25 reserve cards, with maps, is available from SWT headquarters, price £2.50 (inc. p & p). Copies of up to 6 individual reserve cards are available free of charge, on receipt of an s.a.e.

Surrey
THORPE HAY MEADOW

OS Ref TQ030701   Landranger Sheet 176
Nearest Town Chertsey   **Size of Reserve** 6.5 hectares (16 acres)
Managed by Surrey Wildlife Trust (SWT) The purchase of this reserve by SWT was made possible with financial assistance from Cadbury's Wildlife Bar via WWF-UK, and from the Nature Conservancy Council.   **Access** Open all year

T he reserve is a small, five-sided meadow lying on the alluvial gravels of the Thames Flood Plain. The meadow is surrounded by ditches and old hedgerows.

Nature Trail Although there is no waymarked trail, there are well-used paths crossing the reserve.

The reserve is thought to be the last remaining example of a Thames Valley hay meadow in Surrey. It contains a range of lime-loving plants which are characteristic of this type of unimproved meadow.
Plants The grassland is dominated by Rough-stalked Meadow Grass, Crested Dog's Tail Grass and Lesser Knapweed. Other species include Yellow Rattle, Ox-eye Daisy, Smooth Hawk's-beard, Meadow Barley, Meadow-fescue Grass, Common Reed, Meadow Brome (a grass only recorded from one other Surrey location in recent years), Meadow Foxtail Grass, Yorkshire-fog Grass, Pepper Saxifrage, Meadowsweet, Meadow Cranesbill, Clustered Bellflower, Hoary Plantain, Salad Burnet, Lady's Bedstraw.
Trees Old hedgerows include Ash, Hawthorn, Field Maple, Spindle, Dogwood and Buckthorn. There are 5 species of willow, including Purple and Almond, on the reserve.
Butterflies Orange-tip, Common Blue, Ringlet.

Guide By prior arrangement with SWT.   **Disabled Access** No   **School Parties** No
Parking No   **Toilets** No   **Food** No

Further Information A pack of 25 reserve cards, with maps, is available from SWT headquarters, price £2.50 (inc. p & p). Copies of up to 6 individual reserve cards are available free of charge, on receipt of an s.a.e.

Surrey
THUNDRY MEADOWS

OS Ref SU898440   Landranger Sheet 186
Nearest Town Farnham   **Size of Reserve** 15 hectares (37 acres)
Managed by Surrey Wildlife Trust (SWT) This reserve was purchased by SWT
with financial assistance from the Nature Conservancy Council and the World Wide
Fund for Nature.   **Access** Open all year

The reserve consists of unimproved wet and dry meadows in the River Wey Valley. The variety of alluvial soils supports a rich vegetation enhanced by moisture from the river and spring waters. In 1987 a new pond was created in the eastern end of the reserve to provide a still-water habitat. This has already started to attract a variety of wildlife.

Nature Trail 1.5 km (1 mile), waymarked. Care should be taken as there are areas of deep water on the reserve.

Plants Bog Bean, Climbing Corydalis, Dyer's Greenweed, Golden Saxifrage (both British species), Heath Spotted Orchid, Lady's Smock, Marsh Cinquefoil, 14 species of sedge, Southern Marsh Orchid. The riverside vegetation includes Amphibious Bistort, Dame's Violet, and Musk (Monkey Flower).
Birds Common Snipe, Sandpipers, Redshank, Woodcock, Heron, Mandarin Duck, Kingfisher.
Butterflies Pearl-bordered Fritillary, Purple Emperor.
Other Dragonflies, including Banded and Demoiselle Agrions, Brown and Southern Hawkers.

Guide By prior arrangement with SWT   **Disabled Access** No   **School Parties** By prior arrangement with SWT   **Parking** Limited parking across road from reserve entrance   **Toilets** No   **Food** No

Further Information Reserve leaflets giving general information and nature trail details are available from SWT. A pack of 25 reserve cards, with maps, is also available, price £2.50 (inc. p & p). Copies of up to 6 individual reserve cards are available free of charge, on receipt of an s.a.e.

Surrey
VANN LAKE

OS Ref TQ157394   Landranger Sheet 187
Nearest Town Cranleigh   **Size of Reserve** 12 hectares (30 acres)
Managed by Surrey Wildlife Trust (SWT) The reserve was purchased in 1987 with financial assistance from the Nature Conservancy Council, the World Wide Fund for Nature and Mole Valley District Council.   **Access** Open all year

T he wooded area of Vann Lake is a particularly fine example of ancient woodland on Weald Clay. The lake was made in the 18th century to provide power. There is a good marginal flora.

Nature Trail There is a waymarked trail and there are plans to improve it.

Plants Bluebell, Greater Butterfly Orchid, Pendulous Sedge, Cowslip, Spurge Laurel, Broad and Violet Helleborines.
Trees Alder, Chequer, Wild Service.
Birds About 110 species have been recorded.
Insects The lake attracts a number of dragonflies. Flies are abundant and one new species to Britain has been recorded.
Butterflies Purple Emperor, White Admiral, Silver-washed Fritillary, Purple Hairstreak.
Other About 575 species of fungi have been recorded on the reserve, including 7 new to Britain and one new to science. The lake is rich in plankton with diatoms, protozoans, rotifers, and many cladocerans in evidence. Ten species of fish are known to live in the lake.

Guide By prior arrangement with SWT **Disabled Access** No **School Parties** No
Parking Contact SWT to arrange parking before visiting the reserve **Toilets** No
Food No

Further Information A pack of 25 reserve cards, with maps, is available from SWT headquarters, price £2.50 (inc. p & p). Copies of up to 6 individual reserve cards are available free of charge, on receipt of an s.a.e.

Surrey

WALLIS WOOD

OS Ref TQ121388   Landranger Sheet 187
Nearest Town Cranleigh   **Size of Reserve** 13.4 hectares (33 acres)
Managed by Surrey Wildlife Trust (SWT)   **Access** Open all year. The reserve is not generally suitable for visits by large parties

W allis Wood is a typical example of Weald Clay oak-hazel coppice woodland with a stream, small pond and surrounding pasture.

Nature Trail There is no formal trail but there are a number of obvious footpaths around the wood, providing a walk of about 800 metres (½ mile).

Spring migrant birds are a feature of this reserve.
Plants Bluebell, Broadleaved and Violet Helleborines, Primrose, Wild Daffodil, Wood Anemone, Wood Sorrel.
Trees Oak, Hazel, Ash, Hornbeam, Midlands Hawthorn, Wild Apple, Wild Cherry, Wild Service.
Birds Typical woodland birds, including 5 species of Tit, as well as spring migrants.
Butterflies Purple Emperor, Purple Hairstreak, Silver-washed Fritillary, Speckled Wood.

Guide By prior arrangement with SWT **Disabled Access** No **School Parties** By

prior arrangement with SWT **Parking** Small car park at entrance to wood
Toilets No **Food** No

Further Information A pack of 25 reserve cards, with maps, is available from SWT headquarters, price £2.50 (inc. p & p). Copies of up to 6 individual reserve cards are available free of charge, on receipt of an s.a.e.

Sussex

ARUNDEL WILDFOWL PARK

OS Ref TV015085   Landranger Sheet 197
Nearest Town Arundel   **Size of Reserve** 22.2 hectares (55 acres)
Managed by The Wildfowl Trust (WT)   **Access** Open daily 9.30–17.30 in summer or 9.30–16.00 in winter. Closed 25th December. There is an admission charge for all visitors over 4 years old but there are reductions for children, senior citizens and groups

This wetland reserve lies in a picturesque setting between the River Arum and Swanbourne Lake. Half the area consists of landscaped ponds with easy access, while the other area is wild and includes scrapes, ponds, reedbeds, meadow and woodland. The Entrance Building includes an Education Wing, Cinema/Lecture Hall, Exhibition Area and Viewing Gallery.

Nature Trail There are 2.4 km (1½ miles) of paths round the reserve. Maps are displayed at various points. WT Walkabout Guides are available.

The reserve is home to some 1,200 wildfowl, with Swan Lake as the attractive central feature. There are 7 observation hides overlooking ponds, reedbeds, and wader scrapes. A range of activities takes place throughout the year for children and adults.
Plants Wetland species, eg. Hemp Agrimony, Greater Willowherb, Meadowsweet, Purple Loosestrife, Yellow and Blue vetches, reeds and sedges.
Birds Water Rail, Teal, Snipe, Greenshank, Redshank, Green Sandpiper, many types of Duck, Goose and Swan.

Guide Yes   **Disabled Access** Yes, paths are level and there are low windows in hides
School Parties Welcomed. Much educational material is available   **Parking** Yes
Toilets Yes, including for the disabled   **Food** Yes   **Shop** Selling books and gifts

Further Information Contact The Wildfowl Trust, Mill Road, Arundel, Sussex BN18 9PB (tel. 0903 883355).

Sussex
WOODS MILL COUNTRYSIDE CENTRE

OS Ref TQ218138   Landranger Sheet 198
Nearest Town Henfield   **Size of Reserve** 6 hectares (15 acres)
Managed by Sussex Wildlife Trust (SWT)   **Access** Open April to end of September
(Tues, Wed, Thurs and Sat 2.00–18.00; Sundays and Bank Holidays 11.00–18.00).
Closed Mondays and Fridays (except Bank Holidays). There is an admission fee.
Dogs are not permitted

T he Centre is a reserve of mixed habitat, including marsh, meadow, reedbed, lake, streams and woodland. Woods Mill is the headquarters of the Sussex Wildlife Trust.

Nature Trail 1.2 km (¾ mile), waymarked. Adult and Junior Trail Guides are available from the shop.

The 18th-century water mill houses a natural history exhibition, which includes a vivarium for Harvest Mice and, weather permitting, an observation beehive. A number of special events, including workshops, day courses and exhibitions (all on a 'countryside' theme), are held at the Centre. Details and booking information from SWT. Along the nature trail is a pond where dipping can take place (nets are provided), and a woodland birdwatching hide.
Plants Bluebell, Wood Anemone, Common Spotted Orchid.
Birds Great and Lesser Spotted Woodpeckers, Kingfisher, Sparrowhawk, Warblers, Water Rail.
Animals Roe Deer, Fox, Stoat, Weasel, Badger.
Butterflies A good range, including White Admiral.

Guide Guided walks by prior arrangement with SWT   **Disabled Access** No
School Parties By prior arrangement with SWT. There is a custom-built classroom in the Centre available for school parties   **Parking** For 75 cars   **Toilets** Yes
Food Available only for special events   **Shop** Offering a range of gifts.

Further Information Details of special events are available from SWT.

Wiltshire
BLACKMOOR COPSE

OS Ref SU233288   Landranger Sheet 184
Nearest Town Salisbury   **Size of Reserve** 31 hectares (77 acres)
Managed by Wiltshire Trust for Nature Conservation (WTNC)
Access Open all year

B lackmoor Copse is an area of semi-natural woodland, mainly oak with hazel coppice. The wood is divided by rides and there is a pond.

Nature Trail 2.4 km (1½ miles), unmarked. There is an alternative shorter route of 1.2 km (¾ mile). Although level, paths can be wet and muddy, so suitable footwear is essential. Nature Trail leaflets are available from WTNC.

The Copse is particularly famous for its butterflies. It also supports a very interesting diversity of flora since the area slopes gently from north to south and the lower part is quite damp. King Charles' Pond is an important drinking and bathing place for birds and animals.

Plants Water Avens, Meadowsweet, Primrose, Common Spotted Orchid, Aromatic Water Mint, Dog Violet, Honeysuckle, Wood Anemone.
Trees Oak, Ash, Hazel, Alder, Silver Birch, Sallow, Yew, Larch.
Birds Great Spotted Woodpecker, Wren, Warblers, Nuthatch, Nightingale.
Animals Badger, Roe Deer, Bats, Dormouse.
Butterflies Purple Emperor, Purple Hairstreak, Silver-washed Fritillary.

Guide By prior arrangement with WTNC **Disabled Access** No **School Parties** By prior arrangement with WTNC. A Blackmoor Copse Resource Pack for teachers is available from WTNC **Parking** On wide roadside verges **Toilets** No **Food** No

Further Information Contact WTNC.

Wiltshire

CLOUTS WOOD

OS Ref SU137794 Landranger Sheet 173
Nearest Town Swindon **Size of Reserve** 6 hectares (15 acres)
Managed by Wiltshire Trust for Nature Conservation (WTNC)
Access Open all year

C louts Wood is an outstanding area of ancient woodland, thought to have been continuously wooded since the last Ice Age. It lies on a steep chalk hillside.

Nature Trail 2.4 km (1½ miles), waymarked. The path is steep in places. Nature Trail leaflets are available from WTNC.

Plants Bath Asparagus, Green Hellebore, Yellow Archangel, Red Campion, Bluebell, Greater Stitchwort, Herb Paris.
Trees Oak, Ash, Lime, Wild Cherry, Sycamore, Field Maple.
Birds Sparrowhawk, numerous Wrens, Blackbirds, Blue Tits and Great Tits.
Animals Badger, Roe Deer, Fox, Rabbit, Squirrel, Wood Mouse, Bats, Bank Vole.

Under Threat Forty-five percent of ancient woodlands has been lost nationally through changes in land use, ie. commercial forestry, development for factories and houses, waste disposal dumps, etc. As an SSSI, the future of Clouts Wood and its wildlife is protected by law.

Guide By prior arrangement with WTNC **Disabled Access** No **School Parties** The Reserve is used by a number of local schools, and groups of children are taken there on a regular basis. Contact WTNC in advance **Parking** In a layby off the A361 Swindon to Avebury road (SU136800) **Toilets** No **Food** No

Further Information There are information boards on the reserve.

Wiltshire

JONES'S MILL

OS Ref SU169611   Landranger Sheet 173
Nearest Town Pewsey   **Size of Reserve** 12 hectares (29 acres)
Managed by Wiltshire Trust for Nature Conservation (WTNC) **Access** Open all year

J ones's Mill is unique among the Wiltshire Trust reserves because of its
fenland qualities. The water meadows were once part of a farming
system and, since falling into disuse, have evolved into a fen-like habitat.

Nature Trail 3 km (2 miles), unmarked. This reserve is particularly wet so suitable
footwear is essential.

Fenlands are rare in Wiltshire and are exciting because of their varied wildlife. The
reserve illustrates all the stages of succession from open water through to fen and,
ultimately, to woodlands.
Plants Marsh and Common Valerian, Southern Marsh Orchid, Bogbean, Water
Avens, Yellow Flag, Devil's Bit Scabious, Water Figwort, Brooklime.
Birds Kingfisher, Sparrowhawk, Tawny Owl, Heron, Mallard, Moorhen, Tufted
Duck, Reed and Sedge Warblers, Wren.
Animals Water Shrew, Water Vole.
Insects Dragonflies and damselflies.
Other Grass Snake.

Under Threat Many areas of old hay meadows have been drained, ploughed, resown,
fertilised and sprayed. There are very few unimproved meadows left in Wiltshire.

Guide By prior arrangement with WTNC   **Disabled Access** No
School Parties Arrangements can be made to conduct *small* parties if plenty of notice
is given. Contact WTNC   **Parking** Limited parking on roadside verge   **Toilets** No
Food There are a number of good hotels and inns in Pewsey

Further Information Reserve Guides are available from WTNC.

Wiltshire

RACK HILL

OS Ref ST841768   Landranger Sheet 183
Nearest Town Chippenham   **Size of Reserve** 8 hectares (19¾ acres)
Managed by Wiltshire Trust for Nature Conservation (WTNC)
Access Open all year

R ack Hill is situated in the Wiltshire Cotswolds and is a perfect
example of limestone downland on a steep south-west facing slope.
Overlooking Castle Combe and the beautiful valley of the By Brook,
Rack Hill is a popular walking area.

Nature Trail 2.7 km (1¾ miles), including return along same route. The waymarked path can be muddy in winter. Nature Trail leaflets are available from WTNC and from the local post office.

Plants Grasses, eg. Quaking, Sheep's Fescue; Fairy Flax, Harebell, Fragrant and Pyramidal Orchids, Green-winged Orchis; lichens, mosses and Bracket Fungi on ancient gnarled trees.
Birds Green Woodpecker, Dipper, Chiffchaff, Long-tailed Tit.
Animals Wood Mouse, Bank Vole, Weasel, Fox.
Butterflies Comma, Brimstone, Chalkhill Blue, Skipper, Speckled Wood.

Under Threat Limestone downland is a rare and decreasing habitat in Wiltshire.

Guide By prior arrangement with WTNC **Disabled Access** No **School Parties** By prior arrangement with WTNC **Parking** Large public car park nearby **Toilets** In the village of Castle Combe **Food** There are several excellent hotels and inns in Castle Combe

Further Information Contact WTNC.

Wiltshire

VINCIENTS WOOD

OS Ref SU899733 Landranger Sheet 173
Nearest Town Chippenham **Size of Reserve** 3 hectares (7½ acres)
Managed by Wiltshire Trust for Nature Conservation (WTNC)
Access Open all year

Vincients Wood is on the western edge of Chippenham and is almost completely surrounded by a new housing development. It is therefore an important haven for wildlife and an excellent facility for local residents, especially schoolchildren.

Nature Trail 1.5 km (1 mile), waymarked. Paths are fairly easy walking but can be muddy in winter. Nature Trail leaflets are available from WTNC.

Plants Bluebell, Sweet Woodruff, Meadowsweet, Red Campion, Violet, Primrose.
Trees Ash, Hazel, Aspen, Oak, Field Maple.
Birds Great Spotted Woodpecker, Blackbird, wintering Fieldfare and Redwing, Blue Tit, Chiffchaff.
Animals Grey Squirrel.
Butterflies Orange-tip, Small Tortoiseshell.
Other Many kinds of fungi thrive amongst the damp rotting logs and leaves, including Wood Blewits, Jew's Ear and Trooping Crumble Cap.

Guide By prior arrangement with WTNC **Disabled Access** No **School Parties** By prior arrangement with WTNC **Parking** Limited roadside parking in Derriads Lane (ST900732) **Toilets** No **Food** No

Further Information Contact WTNC.

Wiltshire
WHITESHEET HILL

OS Ref ST798350   Landranger Sheet 183
Nearest Town Mere   **Size of Reserve** 2.8 hectares (7 acres)
Managed by Wiltshire Trust for Nature Conservation (WTNC)
(leased from the National Trust)   **Access** Open all year

Whitesheet Hill is within the Stourhead Estate which forms part of the impressive chalk downland landscape of South Wiltshire. Traditionally maintained by sheep grazing, the reserve contains a rich chalk grassland flora, attracting a diversity of downland butterflies. The tussocky grass makes an ideal habitat for the Short-tailed Vole.

Nature Trail 2.1 km (1⅓ miles), waymarked. The site is exposed and can be very windy; walking shoes necessary. The trail can be extended to about 3 km (2 miles). Nature Trail leaflets are available from WTNC or Stourhead National Trust Information Centre.

Plants Pyramidal Orchid, Horseshoe Vetch, Cowslip, Kidney Vetch, Birdsfoot Trefoil, Chalk Milkwort, Wild Thyme, Squinancy Wort, Devil's Bit Scabious, Autumn Gentian, Clustered Bellflower.
Birds Yellowhammer, Kestrel, Meadow Pipit, Skylark.
Animals Short-tailed Vole.
Butterflies Green Hairstreak, Adonis Blue, Meadow Brown, Skipper, Marbled White.
Other Brown-Lipped Snail.

Under Threat Intensive agriculture and the use of fertilisers and chemical sprays have reduced Wiltshire's chalk downlands by 75%, making sites such as Whitesheet Hill both rare and vulnerable, which is why it is legally protected as an SSSI.

Guide By prior arrangement with WTNC   **Disabled Access** No   **School Parties** Arrangements with WTNC should be made well in advance   **Parking** Small car park at ST798350, or on wide road verges   **Toilets** No   **Food** No

Further Information Contact WTNC.

1 Coed Cilygnoeslwyd
2 Ddôl Uchaf
3 Y Graig
4 Castle Woods
5 Cemaes Head
6 Coed Simdde Lwyd
7 Goodwick Moor
8 Pengelli Forest
9 Skokholm Island
10 Skomer Island
11 Teifi Marshes
12 Coed-y-Bedw
13 Coed-y-Bwl
14 Gelli-hir Wood
15 Hambury Wood
16 Melincourt Falls
17 Ogmore Down
18 Park Pond
19 Prior's Wood
20 South Gower Coast
21 Taf Fechan
22 Cleddon Shoots
23 Croes Robert
24 Cwm Merdog
25 Magor Marsh
26 Priory Wood
27 Prisk Wood
28 Strawberry Cottage Wood
29 Cors Goch
30 The Spinnies
31 Bayley Einon Woodland Trail
32 Glaslyn
33 Priory Groves
34 Roundton Hill
35 Severn Farm Pond

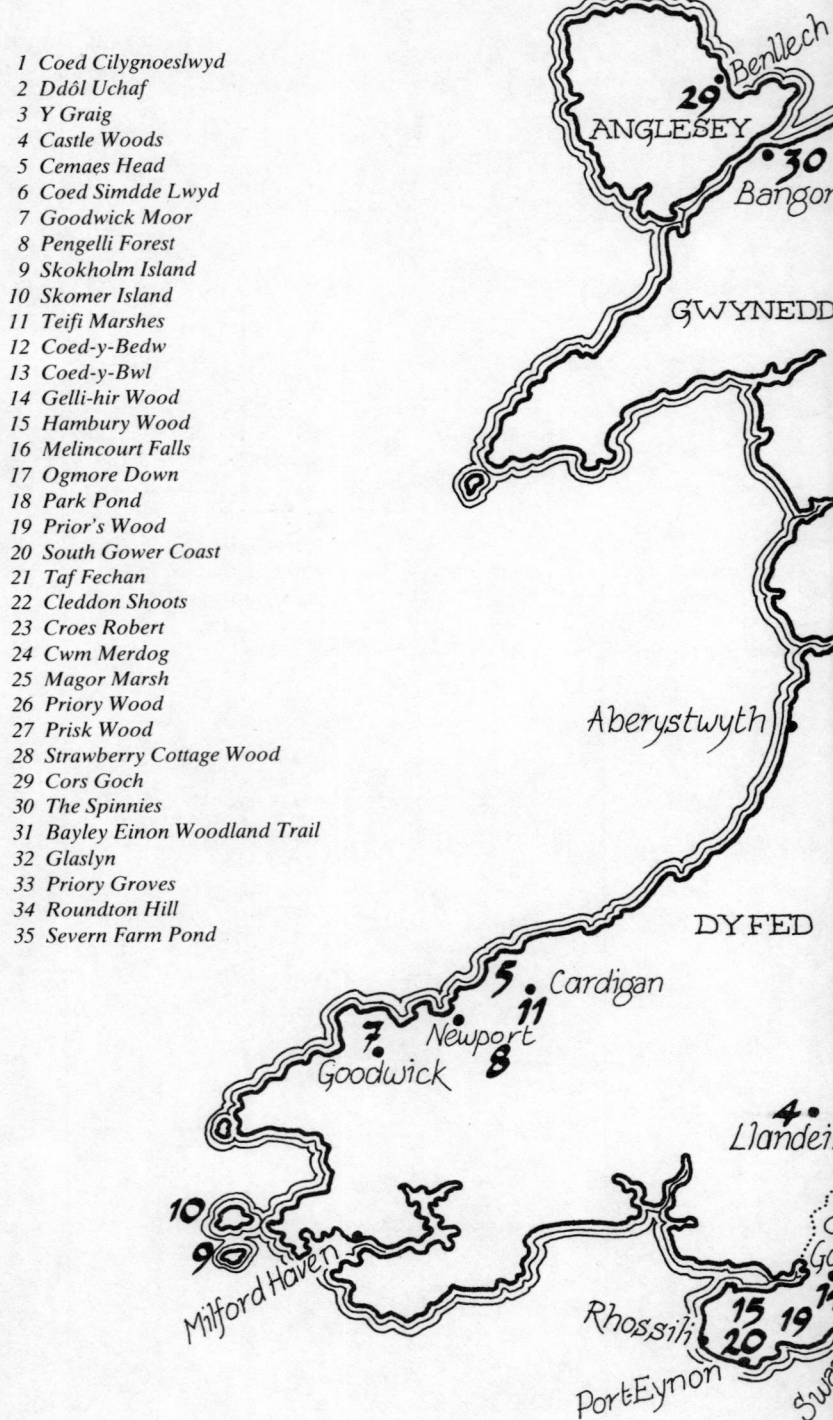

WALES

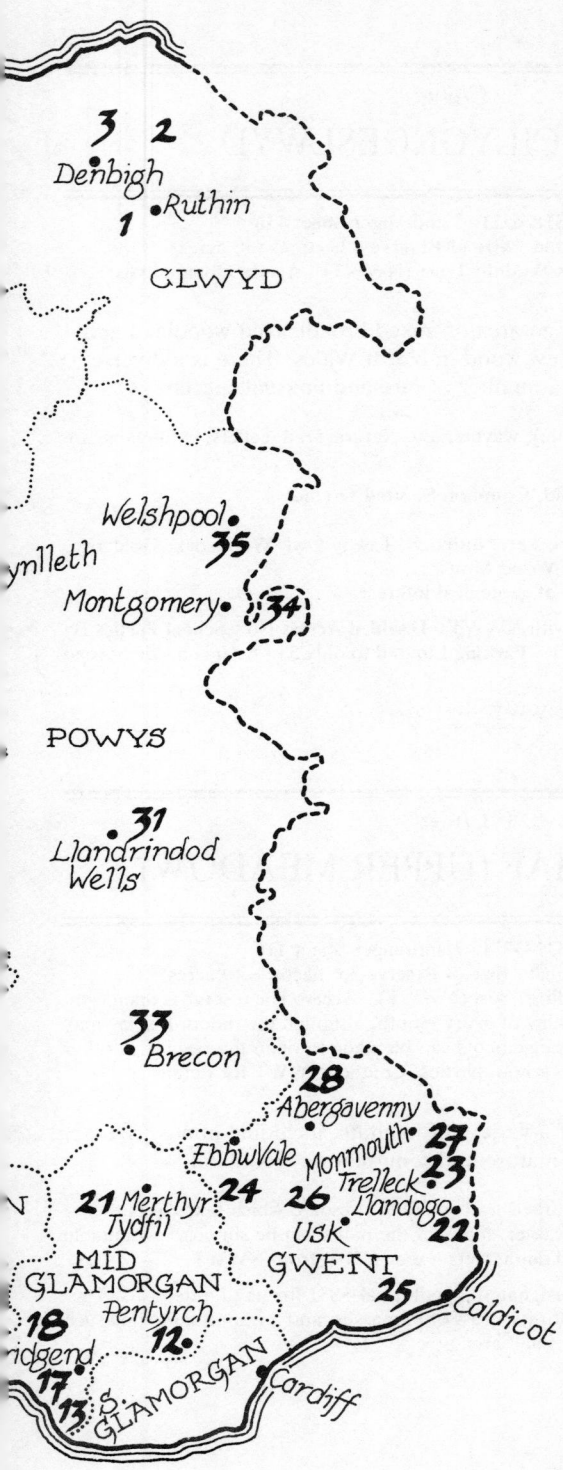

3 2
Denbigh
1 •Ruthin

CLWYD

Welshpool•
35
ynlleth
Montgomery• **34**

POWYS

•**31**
Llandrindod
Wells

33
•Brecon

28
•Abergavenny
Ebbw Vale Monmouth **27**
23
21 Merthyr **24** **26** Trelleck
Tydfil   Usk Llandogo
22
MID
GLAMORGAN   GWENT
18 Pentyrch...   **25**
idgend   **12**•   •Caldicot
17
13 S.•Cardiff
GLAMORGAN

N

Clwyd
COED CILYGNOESLWYD

OS Ref SJ126553   Landranger Sheet 116
Nearest Town Ruthin   **Size of Reserve** 4 hectares (10 acres)
Managed by North Wales Wildlife Trust (NWWT)   **Access** Open all year

T he reserve consists of an area of mixed broadleaved woodland and includes the largest Yew wood in North Wales. There is a diverse limestone flora containing a number of rare and unusual species.

Nature Trail 400 metres (¼ mile), waymarked. Nature Trail leaflets, with maps, are available from NWWT.

Plants Greater Butterfly Orchid, Common Spotted Orchid.
Trees Yew, Spindle.
Birds Greater Spotted Woodpecker, Nuthatch, Tawny Owl, Woodcock, Goldcrest.
Animals Stoat, Weasel, Vole, Wood Mouse.
Other Limestone pavement is of geological interest.

Guide By prior arrangement with NWWT   **Disabled Access** No   **School Parties** By prior arrangement with NWWT   **Parking** Limited to only 5 or 6 cars on side of road
Toilets No   **Food** No

Further Information Contact NWWT.

Clwyd
DDÔL UCHAF (UPPER MEADOW)

OS Ref SJ143714   Landranger Sheet 116
Nearest Town Denbigh   **Size of Reserve** 3.6 hectares (9 acres)
Managed by North Wales Wildlife Trust (NWWT)   **Access** The reserve is open from 10.00–16.00 on the third Saturday of every month, although the indoor display may be curtailed in the winter. Arrangements can be made to open the reserve at other times, particularly to school parties. Contact NWWT for details

T his reserve consists of a variety of habitats, including ponds, rivers, calcareous grassland, mature and semi-mature woodland.

Nature Trail There is a waymarked trail round the reserve which takes about 45 minutes to walk. After wet weather, many of the paths can be slippery, so suitable footwear is essential. Nature Trail leaflets are available from NWWT.

The reserve is shortly to be designated a geological SSSI for its tufa deposits. The reserve is also specially noted for its Grass of Parnassus, and it is unusual to find such a variety of habitats in such a small area.

Plants Grass of Parnassus, Orchids.
Birds The birdlife is rich but mainly of common species.
Other All 3 types of Newt occur and there is a rich and varied fungal flora.

Information Centre There is an Information Centre at the Reserve.

Guide By prior arrangement with NWWT   **Disabled Access** Limited
School Parties By prior arrangement with NWWT   **Parking** Yes   **Toilets** Yes
Food No

Further Information Contact NWWT.

Clwyd

Y GRAIG (THE ROCK)

OS Ref SJ084722   Landranger Sheet 116
Nearest Town Denbigh   **Size of Reserve** 5.7 hectares (14 acres)
Managed by North Wales Wildlife Trust (NWWT)   **Access** Open all year

Y Graig is a limestone hill in the Vale of Clwyd with good views of the surrounding countryside. Part of the reserve is grazed and managed for its limestone grassland flora, while part supports mixed broadleaved woodland. A disused limestone quarry adds to the wildlife interest.

Nature Trail There are 2 waymarked trails. The **Summit Route** leads you uphill through a variety of woodland to the open grassland of the summit. The **Quarry Route** is a shorter and less strenuous walk to the old limestone quarry and lime-kiln. Visitors to the quarry are advised not to climb on the cliff faces and to take care on the roof of the kiln. Nature Trail leaflets, with maps, are available from NWWT.

Plants Common Rock-rose, Early Purple Orchid, Ploughman's-spikenard.
Birds Woodpeckers, Goldcrest, Pied Flycatcher, Stonechat, Wheatear, Dunnock, Yellowhammer, Whinchat.
Animals Bats.
Other Anthills show that Y Graig has never been ploughed or cattle-grazed.

Guide By prior arrangement with NWWT   **Disabled Access** No   **School Parties** By prior arrangement with NWWT   **Parking** Limited to only 3 cars on side of road
Toilets No   **Food** No

Further Information Contact NWWT.

Dyfed
CASTLE WOODS

OS Ref SN610225   Landranger Sheet 159
Nearest Town Llandeilo   **Size of Reserve** 25 hectares (62 acres)
Managed by Dyfed Wildlife Trust (DWT)   **Access** Open all year

C astle Woods comprise two main areas of woodland along a steep south and west facing escarpment above the Tywi floodplain. Towering above the main block of woodland is the long-ruined Dinefwr Castle.

Nature Trail A path runs through the woods from Llandeilo to the Castle ruins. It is waymarked with badger footprint signs. Access to the castle ruins is restricted to advertised open days.

Plants Wood Anemone, Bluebell, Dog's Mercury, Primrose, Toothwort.
Birds Woodpeckers, Nuthatch, Treecreeper, Warblers, Redstart, Flycatchers.
Animals Badger, Fox, Hare, Rabbit, Fallow Deer, Grey Squirrel.
Butterflies Silver-washed Fritillary, Comma, Speckled Wood.
Other The reserve is also rich in lichens, including the large Lungwort.

Information Centre The footpath leads past Llandyfeisant Church, now used as an Information Centre by DWT. It includes a range of woodland displays.

Guide By prior arrangement with DWT   **Disabled Access** No   **School Parties** Yes
Parking In Llandeilo   **Toilets** In Llandeilo   **Food** In Llandeilo

Further Information Reserve leaflets, with maps, are available from DWT.

Dyfed
CEMAES HEAD

OS Ref SN132500   Landranger Sheet 145
Nearest Town Cardigan   **Size of Reserve** 18.2 hectares (45 acres)
Managed by Dyfed Wildlife Trust (DWT)   **Access** Open all year

C emaes Head is the most northerly headland in Pembrokeshire with a range of habitats from more sheltered cliffs to the most exposed. There are extensive areas of sheep- and rabbit-grazed grassland, maritime heath and bracken.

Nature Trail The Pembrokeshire Coast Path provides good access through the reserve. Footpaths are signposted. Cemaes Head Nature Trail booklets are available from DWT.

Plants Maritime species, such as Red Fescue, Spring Squill.

Birds Chough, Raven, Peregrine, Fulmar, Cormorant, Stonechat, Wheatear.
Animals Rabbit, Bank Vole, Badger, Fox.
Other Grey Seals breed on inaccessible beaches, and are sometimes to be seen swimming offshore, as are schools of Dolphins and Porpoises.

Guide By prior arrangement with DWT **Disabled Access** No **School Parties** No
Parking Car park at SN136494 **Toilets** No **Food** No

Further Information Reserve leaflets, with maps, are available from DWT.

Dyfed

COED SIMDDE LWYD

OS Ref SN720786 Landranger Sheet 135
Nearest Town Aberystwyth **Size of Reserve** 40.5 hectares (100 acres)
Managed by Dyfed Wildlife Trust (DWT) **Access** Open all year

S essile oak woodland on a steep, in places precipitous, south-facing slope above the Rheidol Valley. The reserve incorporates, at its western end, the Rheidol Falls.

Nature Trail There is no formal trail, but a series of public footpaths and bridleways provides excellent access to the reserve.

Plants Wood Anemone, Golden Saxifrage, Foxglove, Bluebell, Sheep's-bit, Yellow Pimpernel, Common Cow-wheat, Primrose, Dog Violet. Nine species of fern recorded, including Wilson's Filmy Fern.
Trees Sessile Oak, Birch, Alder, Ash, Cherry, Wych Elm, Small-leaved Lime, Blackthorn, Sycamore.
Birds Buzzard, Jackdaw, Jay, Raven, Long-tailed Tit, Pied Flycatcher, Redstart, Wood Warbler, Red Kite, Tree Pipit.
Other Of special interest are the large and active Wood Ant nests. Wood Ants are local to west Wales.

Guide By prior arrangement with DWT **Disabled Access** No **School Parties** No
Parking There are 2 car parking areas alongside the road below the reserve
Toilets No **Food** No

Further Information Reserve leaflets, with maps, are available from DWT.

Dyfed

GOODWICK MOOR

OS Ref SM945375 Landranger Sheet 157
Nearest Town Goodwick **Size of Reserve** 16.2 hectares (40 acres)
Managed by Dyfed Wildlife Trust (DWT) **Access** Open all year

The main features of this reserve are a reedbed, flood plain mire, carr scrub and a complex network of ditches running between two streams which form the eastern and western boundaries of the reserve. Ponds have been created to form areas of open water.

Nature Trail A public footpath crosses the reserve and links up with a boardwalk to form a circular route taking you into the very heart of the reedbed. Paths can be muddy so suitable footwear is essential. The walk should take about 1½ hours at a leisurely pace.

Plants Royal Fern and Bog Myrtle are 2 specialities.
Birds Sedge and Reed Warblers, Snipe in winter, Buzzard.
Animals Otter.
Butterflies Comma, Painted Lady, Ringlet.

Under Threat Nationally, wetlands of this sort are under considerable threat from drainage and agricultural improvement schemes. Other land to the west of the reserve, which was formerly marsh, was reclaimed by infilling with slate waste and rubbish. Leased by the DWT in 1975, Goodwick Moor has been saved from a similar fate.

Guide By prior arrangement with DWT   **Disabled Access** No   **School Parties** No
Parking In car park on sea-front   **Toilets** On sea-front   **Food** No

Further Information Reserve leaflets, with maps, are available from DWT.

Dyfed
PENGELLI FOREST

OS Ref SN123390   Landranger Sheet 145
Nearest Town Newport   **Size of Reserve** 68 hectares (169 acres)
Managed by Dyfed Wildlife Trust (DWT)   **Access** Open all year

Pengelli Forest is the largest block of ancient woodland in west Wales, a relic of the forest that used to cover most of the country.

Nature Trail A network of footpaths runs through the forest, many of them following the route of an old tramway. The paths are waymarked.

The reserve is designated an SSSI. Tree cover has been continuous despite the area being grazed by animals in the past. As a result, there are plants and animals in the forest that are rare elsewhere and which have survived because the area has always been worked as a woodland. A hide is situated in one corner of the reserve overlooking a field in which there is a very actively used Badger sett.
Plants Early Dog Violet, Adderstongue Fern, Midland Hawthorn, Water Avens.
Trees Main tree species are Oak, Birch, Ash and Alder.
Birds Pied Flycatcher, Redstart, Sparrowhawk, Woodcock (in winter).
Animals Dormouse, Badger.
Insects Dark Bush and Speckled Bush Crickets.
Butterflies White-letter and Purple Hairstreaks.

Guide By prior arrangement with DWT   **Disabled Access** No   **School Parties** No
Parking On roadside   **Toilets** No   **Food** No

Further Information Reserve leaflets, with maps, are available from DWT.

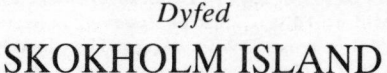

Dyfed
SKOKHOLM ISLAND

OS Ref SM735050   Landranger Sheet 158
Nearest Town Milford Haven   **Size of Reserve** 97 hectares (240 acres)
Managed by Dyfed Wildlife Trust (DWT)   **Access** The island is open from April to
October, Saturday to Sunday on a weekly basis. Day visiting is possible for guided
groups on Mondays only from early June to the end of August. All arrangements
to visit must be made through the DWT office. Access to the island is by boat from
Martin's Haven, a small beach near the village of Marloes

P rimarily a bird sanctuary, Skokholm is an island of outstanding
ornithological importance. It lies about 3 km (2 miles) south west of
the mainland cliffs of the Marloes Peninsula. The island takes the form of
a diamond-shaped plateau with numerous rocky outcrops. Most of the
perimeter is precipitous, but access to the shoreline is possible in a few
places.

Nature Trail The island has a series of paths, making all areas of the reserve
accessible.

Weekly visits may be just for a restful opportunity to watch birds, or may include a
course on such subjects as the birdlife of Skokholm, wildlife art or photography.
These courses are run by the DWT and must be booked and paid for in advance
(accommodation £120–140, plus course fees). There are several birdwatching hides
on the island.
Birds Skokholm is designated a Grade 1 SSSI and is famed for its large populations
of Manx Shearwaters and Storm Petrels, and for its strong colonies of Puffins with
smaller numbers of Razorbills and Guillemots. Oystercatchers breed on the island
and migrant birds include Sand Martins, Pied Flycatchers, Redstarts, Blackcaps and
Yellow Wagtails. Rare species recorded include Osprey, Spotted Crake, Pectoral
Sandpiper and Barred Warbler.
Other The island supports a large population of Rabbits. Grey Seals and occasionally
Porpoises and Dolphins may be seen.

Guide Guided parties by prior arrangement only on Mondays from early June to end
of August   **Disabled Access** No   **School Parties** No   **Parking** In National Trust car
park at Martin's Haven (fee payable)   **Toilets** Yes   **Food** No (except as part of a
week's paid accommodation)

Further Information Colour brochures, reserve leaflets with maps, and details of
courses are available from DWT.

Dyfed

SKOMER ISLAND

OS Ref SM725095   Landranger Sheet 158
Nearest Town Milford Haven   **Size of Reserve** 291 hectares (720 acres)
Managed by Dyfed Wildlife Trust (DWT)   **Access** The island is open from Easter to
the end of September, but is closed on Mondays (except Bank Holidays). Access is
by boat from Martin's Haven, a small beach near the village of Marloes. A landing
fee is payable on arrival at the island. Dogs are prohibited

S komer is the largest of the Pembrokeshire islands. It lies about 800
metres (½ mile) off the mainland. It has a fairly flat plateau with a
series of rock outcrops that form ridges running east to west, between which
run streams. There are also a number of ponds. A striking feature is the
narrow isthmus (only 4 metres/4½ yards wide) which connects the main
part of the island to The Neck.

Nature Trail A waymarked 4-km (2½-mile) trail circuits the island.

Skomer is one of the most important seabird sites in southern Britain. Most numerous
is the Manx Shearwater breeding in burrows all over the island. Two other members
of the Petrel family breed on the island – Fulmar and Storm Petrel. Puffins are
numerous and there are important colonies of Guillemot and Razorbill. Other
seabirds include Kittiwake, Gulls, Shag and Cormorant, while the cliffs are also used
by Buzzard, Peregrine, Kestrel, Raven and Chough.
Plants The island sports a surprising profusion of Bluebell and Red Campion in May
and June, as well as other common flowering plants.
Animals Rabbit, Skomer Vole (rarely seen by visitors); Grey Seals are often seen.

Information Centre On the island.

Guide Not normally available, but there is a guided walk every Wednesday
Disabled Access No   **School Parties** By prior arrangement with DWT   **Parking** In
National Trust car park at Martin's Haven (fee payable)   **Toilets** Yes   **Food** No

Further Information Reserve booklets, with maps, are available from DWT in
advance or on arrival at Skomer Island.

Dyfed

TEIFI MARSHES

OS Ref SN181457   Landranger Sheet 145
Nearest Town Cardigan   **Size of Reserve** 18 hectares (44 acres)
Managed by Dyfed Wildlife Trust (DWT)   **Access** Open all year

This reserve comprises an area of marshland close to the River Teifi estuary with pools, reedbeds and water meadows. The reserve lies on the outskirts of Cardigan.

Nature Trail A 400-metre (¼-mile) path and boardwalk lead from the reserve entrance and car park to a birdwatching hide overlooking the main lagoon. Wellingtons required!

The reserve is particularly noted for winter (August to April) wildfowl, dragonflies and wetland vegetation.
Plants A wide range of wetland plants grows on the Marshes.
Birds Wigeon, Mallard, Teal, Pintail, Goldeneye (on the river); also Hen Harrier.
Animals Otters frequent the Marshes.
Insects Dragonflies.

Guide By prior arrangement with DWT   **Disabled Access** No   **School Parties** No
Parking At the edge of the reserve   **Toilets** In Cardigan town, 450 metres (500 yards) from the reserve   **Food** In Cardigan town

Further Information Reserve maps are available from DWT.

Glamorgan
COED-Y-BEDW

OS Ref ST117829   Landranger Sheet 171
Nearest Town Pentyrch, Near Cardiff   **Size of Reserve** 16.5 hectares (41 acres)
Managed by Glamorgan Wildlife Trust (GWT)   **Access** Open all year

Coed-y-Bedw is an area of ancient deciduous woodland ranging from wet oak/birch in the east to drier beechwood in the west. There are two lime-rich springs and an acidic spring. Much of the site occupies a steep north-facing slope.

Nature Trail 800 metres (½ mile), waymarked. Paths can be muddy in damp weather.

The site is designated an SSSI. The curious mixture of acidic and calcareous waters in the stream supports an interesting assemblage of invertebrates, including a number of rare species.
Plants The field layer is dominated by Bluebells in acid areas and Ramsons in the basic areas; Giant Horsetail; rich herb layer with assemblages of lime-loving and lime-hating plants.
Birds Resident birds include Nuthatch, Great Spotted Woodpecker, Treecreeper; summer visitors include Pied Flycatcher, Willow Warbler and Blackcap.

Guide By prior arrangement with GWT   **Disabled Access** No   **School Parties** By prior arrangement with GWT   **Parking** In Gwaelod-y-garth   **Toilets** No   **Food** No

Further Information Reserve leaflets, with maps, are available from GWT.

Glamorgan
COED-Y-BWL

OS Ref SS909751   Landranger Sheet 170
Nearest Town Bridgend   **Size of Reserve** 2.4 hectares (6 acres)
Managed by Glamorgan Wildlife Trust (GWT)   **Access** Open all year

C oed-y-Bwl is an area of ancient woodland entirely enclosed by a stone
wall. It was originally an elm wood but the elm population was
destroyed by Dutch Elm disease in the mid-seventies. However, a good
deal of well developed woodland remains and much tree planting has taken
place. The GWT received The Prince of Wales Award in 1975 in
recognition of the work carried out by the Trust to promote and preserve
the wood as a nature reserve.

Nature Trail An 800-metre (½-mile) circular path runs through the wood.

Coed-y-Bwl is renowned for its Wild Daffodil display in early spring.
Plants Wild Daffodil, Dog's Mercury, Wood Anemone, Bluebell, Red Campion,
Yellow Archangel.
Trees Ash, Sycamore, Oak, Willow, Rowan, Alder, Wild Cherry, Whitebeam.
Birds Blackcap, Whitethroat, Spotted Flycatcher, Willow Warbler, Chiffchaff,
Nuthatch, Treecreeper, Great Spotted Woodpecker, Kestrel, Buzzard, Tawny Owl.
Butterflies Speckled Wood and Holly Blue, Silver-washed, Dark Green and Pearl-
bordered Fritillaries, Brimstone, Orange-tip.
Other Interesting range of fungi in autumn.

Guide By prior arrangement with GWT   **Disabled Access** No   **School Parties** By
prior arrangement with GWT   **Parking** Layby provides limited parking
Toilets No   **Food** No

Further Information Reserve leaflets, with maps, are available from GWT.

Glamorgan
GELLI-HIR WOOD

OS Ref SS562925   Landranger Sheet 159
Nearest Town Gowerton, Near Swansea
Size of Reserve 28.7 hectares (71 acres)
Managed by Glamorgan Wildlife Trust (GWT)   **Access** Open all year

G elli-Hir Wood lies at the northern edge of Fairwood Common. The
woodland grades from wet oak/birch wood in the south and east to
drier ash/elm wood in the north and west. There is a variety of habitats,
including open rides, streams and a pond.

Nature Trail Various waymarked paths may be taken up to a maximum length of about 1.5 km (1 mile).

There is a birdwatching hide overlooking the pond.
Plants Rich ground flora.
Birds Buzzard, Tawny Owl, Sparrowhawk and many woodland birds. Mallard and Teal breed on the pond.
Insects Moths and butterflies are well represented, including Comma, Silver-washed Fritillary and Holly Blue.

Guide Contact GWT in advance   **Disabled Access** No   **School Parties** Contact GWT in advance   **Parking** Limited parking on road adjacent to reserve   **Toilets** No **Food** No

Further Information Reserve leaflets, with maps, are available from GWT.

Glamorgan
HAMBURY WOOD
(shown on maps as Castle Wood)

OS Ref SS472929   Landranger Sheet 159
Nearest Town Swansea   **Size of Reserve** 4.8 hectares (12 acres)
Managed by Glamorgan Wildlife Trust (GWT)   **Access** Open all year

This ancient oak/hazel wood is on the Gower Peninsula and provides excellent viewing points over the Burry estuary.

Nature Trail There is a 1-km (⅔-mile) waymarked circular walk, with viewing points and seats.

Plants Field layer has improved greatly since enclosure in mid-70s.
Trees Oak, Hazel, Field Maple, Elder, Holly.
Birds Buzzards nest in the wood.

Guide By prior arrangement with GWT   **Disabled Access** No   **School Parties** By prior arrangement with GWT   **Parking** On roadside   **Toilets** No   **Food** No

Further Information Reserve leaflets, with maps, are available from GWT.

Glamorgan
MELINCOURT FALLS

OS Ref SN825017   Landranger Sheet 170
Nearest Town Neath   **Size of Reserve** 5.2 hectares (13 acres)
Managed by Glamorgan Wildlife Trust (GWT)   **Access** Open all year

The main attraction of Melincourt is the spectacular 21-metre (70-foot) waterfall set in an unspoilt wooded valley/gorge, reached by a gently sloping path.

Nature Trail 800 metres (½ mile) to falls and back. Signs at the entrance to the reserve, in the car park and at the falls indicate the way.

The sheer unspoilt beauty of the valley and falls is the main attraction, but there is much for the naturalist, particularly the botanist.
Plants There is a rich bryophyte flora as the air is moist all year round. Filmy Fern grows near the waterfall.
Trees The valley is surrounded by ancient woodland.
Birds Dippers and a variety of woodland birds.

Information Centre In Aberdulais, about 6 km (3¾ miles) south west of Melincourt.

Guide For larger groups, by prior arrangement with GWT   **Disabled Access** Not suitable for wheelchair users   **School Parties** By prior arrangement with GWT
Parking Space for several coaches   **Toilets** No   **Food** No

Further Information Reserve leaflets, with maps, are available and there are interpretative signs at the reserve.

Glamorgan
OGMORE DOWN

OS Ref SS894763   Landranger Sheet 170
Nearest Town Bridgend   **Size of Reserve** 26.5 hectares (65½ acres)
Managed by Glamorgan Wildlife Trust (GWT)   **Access** Open all year

An area of open limestone grassland lying between two limestone quarries, and including a sloping area of limestone heath. There are a great number of flowers to be seen on the reserve, especially in spring.

Nature Trail There is no formal trail, but the whole reserve provides an open area for walking any distance up to at least 800 metres (½ mile).

Limestone heath is both uncommon and unusual, being composed of a characteristic and curious assemblage of lime-loving and lime-hating plants.
Plants Mountain Everlasting (rare in southern Britain).
Birds Nesting Skylarks and various open land birds. Kestrels are frequently seen.

Guide By prior arrangement with GWT   **Disabled Access** No   **School Parties** By prior arrangement with GWT   **Parking** Adequate on level ground by road
Toilets No   **Food** No

Further Information Reserve leaflets, with maps, are available from GWT.

Glamorgan
PARK POND

OS Ref SS881843   Landranger Sheet 170
Nearest Town Bridgend   **Size of Reserve** 2 hectares (5 acres)
Managed by Glamorgan Wildlife Trust (GWT)   **Access** Open all year

P ark Pond Reserve is adjacent to Glamorgan Nature Centre, the headquarters of Glamorgan Wildlife Trust. As well as the pond, the reserve includes surrounding areas of reedbed, willow carr and oak/ash woodland. The reserve is easily accessible with a large car park and boardwalk with bridge over a waterfall.

Nature Trail There is a waymarked trail of about 500 metres (550 yards).

Various amphibians and wildfowl visit the pond. Orchids and a great number of wild flowers can be seen in season. There is also a birdwatching hide and a pond-dipping pier.
Plants Marsh Orchid, Water Plantain, Creeping Willow, Fleabane.
Birds Numerous birds can be seen on or near the reserve, including wildfowl, Green Woodpecker, Buzzard, Sparrowhawk, numerous Passerines, breeding Reed Bunting and Moorhen.
Animals Small mammals.
Insects Butterflies, and a great many dragonflies, including the Emperor Dragonfly.
Other Great Crested Newt.

Information Centre Glamorgan Nature Centre is adjacent to the reserve. It is open weekday mornings and some afternoons.

Guide Groups requiring a guide should contact staff at Glamorgan Nature Centre on arrival or in advance (preferably).   **Disabled Access** Yes, to Nature Centre
School Parties By prior arrangement with GWT   **Parking** Ample for cars, with room for a coach   **Toilets** Yes   **Food** No

Further Information Contact GWT at Glamorgan Nature Centre. Reserve leaflets, with maps, are available.

Glamorgan
PRIOR'S WOOD

OS Ref SS557938   Landranger Sheet 159
Nearest Town Swansea   **Size of Reserve** 17.4 hectares (43 acres)
Managed by Glamorgan Wildlife Trust (GWT)   **Access** Open all year

P rior's Wood is gently sloping woodland with a rich mixture of tree species and some uncommon shrubs. The reserve also includes an area of rich calcareous meadow supporting a variety of meadow species.

Nature Trail About 600 metres (656 yards), waymarked. Paths can be rather wet in autumn/winter so suitable footwear is essential.

Plants Rich ground flora in wood, including the rare Royal Fern. Meadow species include Whorled Caraway.
Birds Very wide variety of resident birds and summer visitors.
Insects Numerous butterflies.

Guide By prior arrangement with GWT   **Disabled Access** No   **School Parties** By prior arrangement with GWT   **Parking** On road, then follow public footpath to wood   **Toilets** No   **Food** No

Further Information Reserve leaflets, with maps, are available from GWT.

Glamorgan
SOUTH GOWER COAST

OS Ref SS434862 to SS470844   Landranger Sheet 159
Nearest Towns Rhossili, Port Eynon and Oxwich
Size of Reserve 96.3 hectares (238 acres) total
Managed by Glamorgan Wildlife Trust (GWT)   **Access** Open all year

The Glamorgan Wildlife Trust manages a number of small reserves along the South Gower Coast. (The whole South Gower coastline is owned/leased by various conservation organizations who manage the area in cooperation.) They contain some of the most magnificent sea cliffs in Britian and are of extraordinary botanical diversity.

Nature Trail The South Gower Coast path runs around the Gower Peninsula. The stretch of path crossing the GWT area is about 2 km (1¼ miles) long. The path is signposted.

The Coast Path crosses a wide variety of habitats amid magnificent scenery, with views of nesting seabirds.
Plants Tremendous variety (over 200 species), including *Draba Aizoides*, the Yellow Whitlow Grass, known only on the Gower Peninsula in the UK.
Birds Seabirds, Merlin, and various others.
Animals Seals regularly seen.

Information Centres Nature Conservation Council (at Oxwich) and National Trust (at Rhossili) Information Centres are within easy driving distance.

Guide Contact GWT in advance   **Disabled Access** No   **School Parties** Contact GWT in advance   **Parking** At Port Eynon   **Toilets** Yes, at Port Eynon   **Food** No

Further Information Reserve leaflets, with maps, are available from GWT.

Glamorgan

TAF FECHAN

OS Ref SO037085 Landranger Sheet 171
Nearest Town Merthyr Tydfil **Size of Reserve** 41 hectares (102 acres)
Managed by Glamorgan Wildlife Trust (GWT) **Access** Open all year

Taf Fechan Reserve is a large area of country park in the Taf Valley. The valley is broad and open in some parts, narrow in others and ends in a large open area, an old quarry floor that has reverted to nature with trees and open grassland. The River Taff cuts a spectacular gorge down the centre of the valley. The bordering slopes comprise large areas of oak woodland and limestone grassland.

Nature Trail The 5-km (3-mile) waymarked trail follows the route of an old tramway.

Of industrial archeological interest are the old tramway to Cyfarthfa ironworks, a ruined fulling mill and a feeder canal to Cyfarthfa Lake.
Plants The ancient broadleaved woodland on the reserve is one of the richest sites for mosses and liverworts in Glamorgan (over 100 species).
Birds Nesting Dippers, Buzzard and a great variety of woodland and open country birds can be seen.

Guide By prior arrangement with GWT **Disabled Access** No **School Parties** By prior arrangement with GWT **Parking** At the Blue Pool (SO037076) and near Cefn Coed Bridge (SO045097) **Toilets** No **Food** No

Further Information Reserve leaflets, with maps, are available from GWT and there are interpretative signs on the reserve.

Gwent

CLEDDON SHOOTS

OS Ref SO520040 Landranger Sheet 162
Nearest Town Llandogo **Size of Reserve** 8 hectares (20 acres)
Managed by Gwent Wildlife Trust (GWT) **Access** Open all year

The reserve consists of an area of ancient and semi-natural deciduous woodland on the steep east-facing slopes of the Wye Valley. Cleddon Brook rushes down these slopes over a series of small waterfalls – the 'Shoots'.

Nature Trail There is no waymarked trail but a network of paths runs through the reserve. Paths are very steep in places.

The reserve is part of an area designated an SSSI.

Plants Many mosses and liverworts, especially along the brook; also ferns, eg. Hartstongue and the rare Narrow Buckler Fern.
Trees This type of acid Sessile Oak wood, with oak standards and beech and oak coppice, is rare in the county of Gwent; also Ash, Cherry, Yew, Alder, Holly, Hazel, Wych Elm.
Birds Pied Flycatcher, Nuthatch, Treecreeper, Woodpeckers, Grey Wagtail.

Guide Contact the Conservation Officer at GWT   **Disabled Access** No
School Parties Contact GWT in advance   **Parking** For about 12 cars, at the top of the reserve   **Toilets** No   **Food** No

Further Information Reserves booklets, including maps, are available from GWT.

Gwent

CROES ROBERT

OS Ref SO475060   Landranger Sheet 161
Nearest Town Trelleck   **Size of Reserve** 15 hectares (37 acres)
Managed by Gwent Wildlife Trust (GWT)   **Access** Open all year

C roes Robert Reserve is an area of recently-coppiced deciduous woodland with several small streams running through it. The wood is on a steep hillside with views of the Black Mountains.

Nature Trail There is no formal waymarked trail, but sheltered rides round the wood form a network of paths. Maximum length of walk about 3 km (2 miles).

Plants Guelder Rose, Blackthorn.
Trees Ash, Wych Elm.
Birds Abundant and various woodland birdlife.
Animals Fallow Deer.

Guide Contact the Conservation Officer at GWT   **Disabled Access** No
School Parties Contact GWT   **Parking** For 10 cars   **Toilets** No   **Food** No

Further Information Reserve booklets, with maps, are available from GWT.

Gwent

CWM MERDOG

OS Ref SO187063   Landranger Sheet 161
Nearest Town Ebbw Vale   **Size of Reserve** 22 hectares (55 acres)
Managed by Gwent Wildlife Trust (GWT)   **Access** Open all year

T he main part of the reserve consists of ancient beech woodland with a typically sparse ground flora. In between areas of beech are wet flushes which tend to be dominated by alder and willow. There is also a revegetated coal tip and an area of old grassland. Evidence of old drift mines can be seen along the mountain side.

Nature Trail About 3 km (2 miles), waymarked. The path is steep in places. The summit of the old coal tip provides a superb view down the valley. No attempt should be made to enter the old mines.

Plants Bluebell, Wood Anemone, Broadleaved Helleborine, Ivy-leaved Bellflower, Bog St. John's Wort, Marsh Violet. Bracken is the commonest fern on the reserve but 3 other species have been recorded, including Mountain Fern and Narrow Buckler Fern.
Birds Redstart, Pied Flycatcher, Buzzard.

Guide Contact the Conservation Officer at GWT   **Disabled Access** No
School Parties Contact GWT   **Parking** For about 20 cars in picnic site car park (Blaenau Gwent Borough Council)   **Toilets** No   **Food** No

Further Information Reserves booklets, including maps, are available from GWT.

Gwent

MAGOR MARSH

OS Ref ST424867   Landranger Sheet 171
Nearest Town Caldicot   **Size of Reserve** 24 hectares (60 acres)
Managed by Gwent Wildlife Trust (GWT)   **Access** Open all year. No dogs

This reserve is the only major remnant of the formerly extensive fenland habitat of the Gwent Levels. It consists of several wet meadows, hay fields, reedbed, willow scrub and woodland. There are several drainage ditches or 'reens' and a large pond.

Nature Trail About 3 km (2 miles), unmarked. Paths can be very wet so waterproof footwear is essential. Please keep to the footpath as parts of the reserve are dangerous due to their marshy nature.

The reserve supports a rich variety of wetland plants, some now local or rare in the county, and is also important for its breeding birds. The reen habitat of the Levels is unique to Wales and is a very rare habitat in the British Isles. The pond and reedbed are overlooked by a birdwatching hide.

Plants Many rare plants in the reens, including Frogbit, Arrowhead and Flowering Rush. Hay meadows support a rich variety of species, including Meadow Thistle and many sedges. In the grazed fields can be seen Ragged Robin, Marsh Marigold, and Yellow Flag.
Birds Warblers, Water Rail, Little Grebe, Snipe, Cuckoo.

Guide Contact the Conservation Officer at GWT   **Disabled Access** No
School Parties Contact GWT in advance   **Parking** For about 12 cars   **Toilets** No
Food No

Further Information Reserve maps are available from GWT.

Gwent
PRIORY WOOD

OS Ref SO353058   Landranger Sheet 161
Nearest Town Usk   **Size of Reserve** 5 hectares (12 acres)
Managed by Gwent Wildlife Trust (GWT)   **Access** Open all year

P riory Wood is an area of varied broadleaved woodland with an abundance of wild cherry.

Nature Trail About 800 metres (½ mile), unmarked. The path is of a fairly easy gradient.

Trees Wild Cherry, Oak, Beech, Silver Birch.
Birds Pied Flycatcher, Hawfinch, Lesser Spotted Woodpecker.
Animals Badger.
Other Hole in tree used by Noctule Bats in summer.

Guide Contact the Conservation Officer at GWT   **Disabled Access** No
School Parties Contact GWT   **Parking** For about 4 cars   **Toilets** No   **Food** No

Further Information Reserve booklets, with maps, are available from GWT.

Gwent
PRISK WOOD

OS Ref SO533087   Landranger Sheet 162
Nearest Town Monmouth   **Size of Reserve** 6.5 hectares (13 acres)
Managed by Gwent Wildlife Trust (GWT)   **Access** Open all year

A n area of mixed broadleaved woodland in the Wye Valley, with streams and flushes. The wood is especially attractive in spring.

Nature Trail About 800 metres (½ mile), unmarked.

Plants Herb Paris, Early Purple Orchid, Hard Shield Fern.
Trees Ash, Wych Elm, Small-leaved Lime, Beech, Alder.
Birds Woodpeckers, Flycatchers, Sparrowhawk, Woodcock.
Animals Fallow Deer, Dormouse.

Guide Contact the Conservation Officer at GWT   **Disabled Access** No
School Parties Contact GWT   **Parking** For 4 cars   **Toilets** No   **Food** No

Further Information Reserve booklets and maps showing the location of the reserve are available from GWT.

Gwent
STRAWBERRY COTTAGE WOOD

OS Ref SO314215 Landranger Sheet 161
Nearest Town Abergavenny **Size of Reserve** 6.2 hectares (15 acres)
Managed by Gwent Wildlife Trust (GWT) **Access** Open all year

T he reserve consists of an area of predominantly sessile oak woodland on a south-west facing slope above the River Honddu.

Nature Trail About 1.2 km (¾ mile), unmarked. The path is steep in parts but mostly of moderate gradient.

Plants Forster's (Southern) Wood-rush, Nettle-leaved Bellflower.
Trees Small-leaved Lime, Oak, Ash, Silver Birch, Aspen, Yew, Beech.
Birds Pied Flycatcher, Wood Warbler, Redstart.
Animals Badger sett in adjacent field, Fox.

Guide Contact the Conservation Officer at GWT **Disabled Access** No
School Parties Contact GWT **Parking** For 5 cars **Toilets** No **Food** No

Further Information Reserve booklets, with maps, are available from GWT.

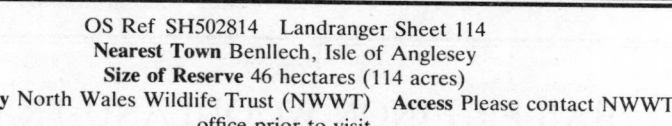

Gwynedd
CORS GOCH

OS Ref SH502814 Landranger Sheet 114
Nearest Town Benllech, Isle of Anglesey
Size of Reserve 46 hectares (114 acres)
Managed by North Wales Wildlife Trust (NWWT) **Access** Please contact NWWT office prior to visit

C ors Goch is a very diverse reserve, the main feature being the valley fen. Also present are limestone grassland, quarry, heathland, unimproved meadows, limestone pavement, hay meadows and a good-sized lake.

Nature Trail The circular 1.2-km (¾-mile) trail is waymarked with numbered posts. Nature Trail Guides, with maps, are available from NWWT.

Plants Grass of Parnassus, Black Bog Rush, Green-veined Orchid, Bog Myrtle.
Birds Reed Bunting, Grasshopper Warbler, Barn Owl, Little Grebe, Great Crested Grebe, Tufted Duck, Ruddy Duck.

Guide By prior arrangement with NWWT **Disabled Access** No **School Parties** By prior arrangement with NWWT **Parking** On roadside only **Toilets** No **Food** No

Further Information Contact NWWT.

Gwynedd
THE SPINNIES

OS Ref SH613722   Landranger Sheet 115
Nearest Town Bangor   **Size of Reserve** 2.8 hectares (7 acres)
Managed by North Wales Wildlife Trust (NWWT)   **Access** Open all year

The Spinnies is a coastal site with a wide range of habitats, including brackish lagoon, woodland, scrub, grassland and reedbeds. The reserve is next to the mudflats at the mouth of the Menai Straits and so is an excellent place for birdwatching.

Nature Trail 230 metres (250 yards) to the birdwatching hide. The path is gravelled so ordinary footwear is adequate.

Over 170 species of bird have been seen on or from the reserve, including several rarities. The area is rich in waders and wildfowl throughout the year, their numbers peaking in autumn.
Birds Species seen on the reserve include Sedge Warbler, Water Rail, Moorhen, Mallard, Little Grebe, overwintering Kingfisher, Teal, Shoveler, Widgeon, Gadwall, Greenshank, Shelduck, Merganser, Mute Swan.

Guide By prior arrangement with NWWT   **Disabled Access** The path and the birdwatching hide are accessible to wheelchair users   **School Parties** By prior arrangement with NWWT   **Parking** Yes   **Toilets** No   **Food** No

Further Information Reserve leaflets, with maps, are available from NWWT, and additional information is given inside the birdwatching hide.

Powys
BAILEY EINON WOODLAND TRAIL

OS Ref SO083614   Landranger Sheet 147
Nearest Town Llandrindod Wells   **Size of Reserve** 4.6 hectares (11½ acres)
Managed by Radnorshire Wildlife Trust (RWT)   **Access** Open all year

Bailey Einon Wood lies on the banks of the River Ithon, a tributary of the Wye. The wood has many of the characteristics of the 'wild wood' that used to cover most of Wales thousands of years ago. Many of the woods that exist today are over-grazed or have been replaced by alien conifers. Both of these practices reduce habitats and therefore wildlife – making woods like Bailey Einon especially important.

Nature Trail The 2-km (1¼-mile) waymarked trail is accessible from a local beauty spot – the 'shaky bridge' and 13th-century church of Cefnllys. The path can be muddy so suitable footwear is essential. A second waymarked walk continues beyond the reserve to Alpine Bridge, providing the option of a 12.8-km (8-mile) circular walk. This optional extension is called 'A Trail of Two Bridges' and makes use of a public right of way maintained by Powys County Council. Nature Trail leaflets are available from a box at the reserve, or from the Tourist Information Centre in Llandrindod Wells, or from RWT.

Plants 100 recorded species, including Purple Orchid, Cranesbill.
Birds Buzzard, Pied Flycatcher, Redstart, Goosander.
Animals Polecat, Otter, Bank Vole, several species of Bats and Shrews.

Guide By prior arrangement with RWT (giving one month's notice)   **Disabled Access** No
School Parties By prior arrangement with RWT (giving one month's notice)   **Parking** In car park   **Toilets** No   **Food** No, but there is a picnic area with barbecue facilities and tables.

Further Information Contact RWT.

Powys

GLASLYN

OS Ref SN828942   Landranger Sheet 136
Nearest Town Machynlleth   **Size of Reserve** 216.5 hectares (535 acres)
Managed by Montgomeryshire Wildlife Trust (MWT)   **Access** Open all year

Situated on the Plinlimon Uplands, Glaslyn Nature Reserve is a remote area of heather moorland, rough grassland, lake, blanket bog, ravine and scree slope.

Nature Trail There is no waymarked trail but the whole reserve is a beautiful site for walking, with spectacular views over the surrounding Welsh countryside. Visitors must not enter the ravine because of the dangers of falling rock and unstable scree slopes. It can be seen from above.

Glaslyn is exciting for its birdlife, with birds of prey a speciality. Diving ducks can be seen on the lake in winter.
Plants Heather moorland and blanket bog of special interest with 3 species of Heather, Sundew, Ivy-leaved Bellflower, etc.
Birds Red Kite, Peregrine, Merlin, Kestrel, Buzzard, Raven, Wheatear, Red Grouse, Golden Plover, Ring Ouzel, Goldeneye, Tufted Duck, Pochard, Whooper Swan (occasionally), Sandpiper.

Under Threat Moorland habitat of this type has been rapidly disappearing in Wales, both through reclamation to grass pasture and afforestation with conifers. Bogs and rough grassland are now also very scarce.

Guide For groups only, by prior arrangement with MWT   **Disabled Access** No
School Parties By prior arrangement with MWT   **Parking** For about 6 cars. It is sometimes best to park on the road and walk down the track   **Toilets** No   **Food** No

Further Information There is an interpretative board and a leaflet dispenser at the reserve entrance.

Powys

PRIORY GROVES

OS Ref SO047292   Landranger Sheet 146
Nearest Town Brecon   **Size of Reserve** 1.5 km (1 mile) long
Managed by Brecknock Wildlife Trust (BWT) in association with Brecknock
Borough Council   **Access** Open all year

The Priory Groves stretch about 1.5 km (1 mile) up the west bank of the River Honddu and provide attractive and varied walks on paths through woodland, by water-side, across meadow and with occasional glimpses of the Brecon Beacons.

Nature Trail About 3 km (2 miles). Lettered markers along the path refer to the Nature Trail leaflet available from BWT. The path can be muddy at times. The trail begins at the boundary of the Cathedral grounds in Brecon.

Plants Bluebell, Violet and other woodland spring flowers.
Trees Oak, Beech, Wellingtonia, Ash, Hazel, Western Hemlock, Sycamore, Holly, Alder, Hawthorn.
Birds Woodland birds (eg. Pied Flycatcher) and river birds (Dipper, Grey Wagtail, Kingfisher).
Animals Fox, Wood Mouse, Otter, Feral Mink, Badger.

Under Threat The River Usk which flows through Brecon is threatened by increased incidence of farm pollution. Badger setts in the area are being disturbed by digging and baiting.

Guide By prior arrangement with the Conservation Officer at BWT
Disabled Access No   **School Parties** Arrangements must be made with the Conservation Officer (as above) at least 3 weeks in advance.   **Parking** In Brecon, 100 metres (110 yards) away   **Toilets** Near beginning of trail   **Food** No

Further Information Contact BWT.

Powys

ROUNDTON HILL

OS Ref SO293947   Landranger Sheet 137
Nearest Town Montgomery   **Size of Reserve** 35 hectares (87 acres)
Managed by Montgomeryshire Wildlife Trust (MWT)   **Access** Open all year

Roundton is a volcanic hill topped by an Iron Age fort surrounded by ancient hill grassland, open woodland, rock outcrops, scree, scrub and a stream. It provides a superb viewpoint on the Welsh Borders.

Nature Trail There is no waymarked trail but there are tracks and paths round the reserve.

The ancient hill grassland, which has never been ploughed and reseeded, is of great botanical interest. Spring and early summer are the best times to visit for birds and plants.

Plants Ancient hill grassland supports 'Spring Ephemerals', such as Lady's Bed Straw, Tormentil, Mountain Pansy, etc. Lichens and mosses are a feature of the reserve with over 100 species recorded, including several rarities.

Trees Ash, Wych Elm, Sycamore, Oak, Hawthorn, Rowan, Holly. There are extensive areas of new tree planting.

Birds Wheatears breed in disused rabbit burrows, Redstar and Pied Flycatcher in the nest boxes. Also Buzzard, Raven, Warblers, Woodpeckers, Tawny Owl, etc.

Animals Large Rabbit warren, Polecat, Fox, Stoat, Badger.

Other Roundton is an important hibernation site for rare bats, including Lesser Horseshoe, Daubenton's, Natterer's and Long-eared. (There is no access to the hibernation site.)

Under Threat Surrounding areas are continually under threat from agricultural 'improvement', afforestation and pollution.

Guide For groups only, by prior arrangement with MWT   **Disabled Access** No
School Parties By prior arrangement with MWT   **Parking** For about 30 cars
Toilets No   **Food** No

Further Information There is an interpretative board and a leaflet dispenser at the reserve entrance.

Powys

SEVERN FARM POND

OS Ref SJ228068   Landranger Sheet 126
Nearest Town Welshpool   **Size of Reserve** 1.2 hectares (3 acres)
Managed by Montgomeryshire Wildlife Trust (MWT)   **Access** Open all year

An 'urban fringe' site on the edge of Welshpool, providing a mixture of habitats, including pond, wetland and scrub. A butterfly area has also been planted. It is very much a community and educational reserve with maximum access encouraged.

Nature Trail There is no waymarked trail, but there are well-surfaced paths through the reserve.

This is a good site for aquatic insects, especially dragonflies and damselflies. There is a birdwatching hide and a special scrape has been developed for pond-dipping.

Plants Extensive reed swamp with Reedmace, Yellow Flag, Bur-reed; aquatic plants include Amphibious Bistort, Spiked Water Milfoil, Soft Rush, Gipsywort, Watermint, Common Water Plantain, Water Pepper, Bittersweet, Willowherbs, Angelica, Field Horsetail, Meadowsweet, Hogweed, Marsh Bedstraw, Water Forget-me-not.

Trees Oak, Grey Willow, Hawthorn, Ash, Sycamore.
Birds Warblers, Reed Bunting, Coot, Moorhen, Heron, Finches, Swifts, Swallows, Swans, Ducks, Snipe (in winter).
Insects Dragonflies and damselflies.
Other Frogs and newts; fish species present include Pike and Tench.

Under Threat Surrounding areas of natural habitat are continually under threat from urban development, agricultural 'improvement', afforestation, pollution and canalisation (eg. the River Severn).

Guide For groups only, by prior arrangement with MWT   **Disabled Access** Paths are suitable for wheelchair users and the birdwatching hide has been specially adapted.
School Parties Please contact MWT in advance   **Parking** For about 10 cars
Toilets No   **Food** No

Further Information There is an interpretative board and a leaflet dispenser at the reserve.

1 Begwary Brook Marsh
2 Felmersham Gravel Pits
3 Sewell Cutting
4 Blackwater Reach Meadow
5 Bowdown Woods
6 Inkpen Common
7 Moor Copse
8 Northerams Wood
9 Owlsmoor Bog and Heath
10 Aston Clinton Ragpits
11 Bernwood Meadows
12 Boarstall Duck Decoy
13 Buckingham Canal
14 Buttler's Hangings
15 Calvert Jubilee
16 Chequers
17 Dancersend
18 Deep Mill Lane Pond
19 Gomm Valley
20 Grangelands
21 Little Linford Wood
22 Millfield Wood
23 Pilch Field
24 Pitstone Hill
25 Rushbeds Woods
26 Stony Stratford
27 Weston Turville Reservoir
28 Black Lake
29 Danes Moss
30 Swettenham Meadows
31 Cromford Canal
32 Chedworth
33 Edward Richardson
34 Silk Wood
35 Slimbridge Wildfowl Reserve
36 Clay Vallets Wood
37 Knapp and Papermill
38 Lea and Pagets Wood
39 Leeping Stocks
40 Dimminsdale
41 Prior's Coppice
42 Gibraltar Point
43 Snipe Dales
44 Compstall
45 Dark Lane
46 Red Rocks Marsh
47 Attenborough Gravel Pits
48 Bunny Old Wood
49 Daneshill Gravel Pit
50 Eaton Wood
51 Martin's Pond
52 Sellers Wood
53 Spa Ponds

CENTRAL ENGLAND

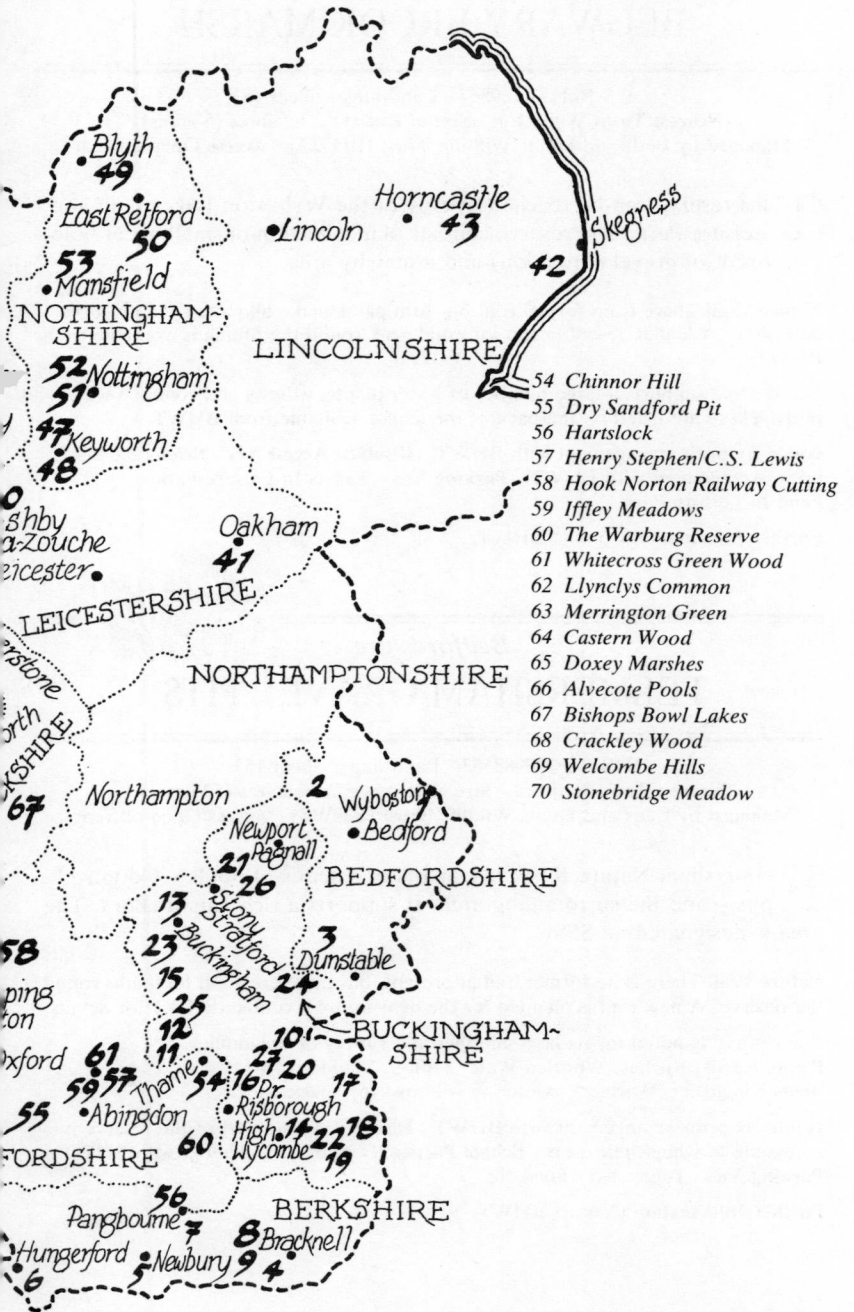

54 Chinnor Hill
55 Dry Sandford Pit
56 Hartslock
57 Henry Stephen/C.S. Lewis
58 Hook Norton Railway Cutting
59 Iffley Meadows
60 The Warburg Reserve
61 Whitecross Green Wood
62 Llynclys Common
63 Merrington Green
64 Castern Wood
65 Doxey Marshes
66 Alvecote Pools
67 Bishops Bowl Lakes
68 Crackley Wood
69 Welcombe Hills
70 Stonebridge Meadow

Bedfordshire
BEGWARY BROOK MARSH

OS Ref TL169564   Landranger Sheet 153
Nearest Town Wyboston   **Size of Reserve** 2 hectares (5 acres)
Managed by Beds and Hunts Wildlife Trust (BHWT)   **Access** Open all year

This reserve can be reached by way of the Wyboston Lakes Golf and Leisure Park. The reserve consists of a collection of small water holes (the result of gravel extraction) and a marshy area.

Nature Trail There is no formal trail but firm paths make all parts of the reserve accessible. A leaflet describing an informal walk round the Marsh is available from BHWT.

The reserve supports a large number of water plants, willows and common water birds. These are listed on the back of the leaflet available from BHWT.

Guide By prior arrangement with BHWT   **Disabled Access** Yes   **School Parties** By prior arrangement with BHWT   **Parking** Yes   **Toilets** In Leisure Park
Food In Leisure Park

Further Information Contact BHWT.

Bedfordshire
FELMERSHAM GRAVEL PITS

OS Ref SP988583   Landranger Sheet 153
Nearest Town Bedford   **Size of Reserve** 21 hectares (52 acres)
Managed by Beds and Hunts Wildlife Trust (BHWT)   **Access** Open all year

Felmersham Nature Reserve consists of a series of pools – old gravel pits – and the surrounding area. It supports a rich aquatic flora. The area is designated an SSSI.

Nature Trail There is no formal trail at present, but there are good footpaths round the reserve. A new trail is planned for the near future – contact BHWT for details.

The reserve is noted for its large number and variety of dragonflies.
Plants Reeds, Rushes, Whorled Water Milfoil, Bladderwort.
Birds Kingfisher, Warblers, wintering wildfowl (65 species).

Guide By prior arrangement with BHWT   **Disabled Access** Part of the reserve is accessible to wheelchair users   **School Parties** By prior arrangement with BHWT
Parking Yes   **Toilets** No   **Food** No

Further Information Contact BHWT.

Bedfordshire
SEWELL CUTTING

OS Ref SP995221 to TL005227   Landranger Sheet 165
Nearest Town Dunstable   **Size of Reserve** 3.2 hectares (8 acres)
Managed by Beds and Hunts Wildlife Trust (BHWT)   **Access** Open all year

S ewell Cutting is a unique site in Bedfordshire, since it is the only cutting of any size – road or rail – that lies east-west through chalk. With its length and steep, high banks, it is now a large area of chalk grassland, a habitat that is becoming increasingly rare in the country.

Nature Trail There is no formal trail, but the floor of the cutting gives easy access.

The chief interest of the reserve is its chalkland flora and butterflies – Chalkhill Blue, Comma, Holly Blue, Brown Argus, Small Blue.

Guide No   **Disabled Access** No   **School Parties** By prior arrangement with BHWT
Parking At Frenchs Avenue at the western end of the cutting   **Toilets** No   **Food** No

Further Information Reserve leaflets are available from BHWT.

Berkshire
BLACKWATER REACH MEADOW

OS Ref SU843608   Landranger Sheet 175
Nearest Town Bracknell   **Size of Reserve** 1 hectare (2.3 acres)
Managed by Berkshire, Buckinghamshire and Oxfordshire
Naturalists' Trust (BBONT)   **Access** Open all year. Please leave the area to the west of the ditch undisturbed during the nesting season

A rough wet meadow situated in a relatively unspoilt area of meadows, streams and hedgerows. The site is bordered by the River Blackwater.

Nature Trail The reserve is reached on foot from the Sandhurst Town Council Offices. It is a walk of about 1.5 km (1 mile) to the reserve.

The site is valuable for invertebrates. A ditch crossing the reserve is accessible for pond-dipping.
Plants Ragged Robin, Betony, Marsh Stitchwort, Sneezewort, Meadow Thistle, 5 species of sedge.

Guide Contact BBONT   **Disabled Access** No   **School Parties** By prior arrangement with BBONT; contact the Education Officer on Oxford (0865) 775476. A book entitled *Educational Opportunities on Nature Reserves* is available from BBONT   **Parking** Sandhurst Town Council Offices Car Park   **Toilets** No   **Food** No

Further Information Contact BBONT.

Berkshire
BOWDOWN WOODS

OS Ref SU504657 Landranger Sheet 174
Nearest Town Newbury **Size of Reserve** 20 hectares (50 acres)
Managed by Berkshire, Buckinghamshire and Oxfordshire
Naturalists' Trust (BBONT) **Access** Open all year

The reserve consists of a wide range of habitats, including dry heathland, woodland on high ground, wet valley woods, ash coppice, ponds and grassland. This ancient woodland supports a great variety of plants and is also good for looking for animal tracks (especially in the mud near the pond). The reserve is part of the Bowdown and Chamberhouse Woods SSSI.

Nature Trail Although there is no formal waymarked trail, well-defined paths give easy access.

Trees Oak, Birch, Hazel, Rowan, Cherry, Alder, Willow.
Animals Roe and Muntjac Deer.
Insects Dragonflies.

Guide Contact BBONT **Disabled Access** No **School Parties** By prior arrangement with BBONT; contact the Education Officer on Oxford (0865) 775476. A book entitled *Educational Opportunities on Nature Reserves* is available from BBONT
Parking There is a small car park which is inaccessible to coaches **Toilets** No
Food No

Further Information Contact BBONT.

Berkshire
INKPEN COMMON

OS Ref SU382641 Landranger Sheet 174
Nearest Town Hungerford **Size of Reserve** 10.4 hectares (26 acres)
Managed by Berkshire, Buckinghamshire and Oxfordshire
Naturalists' Trust (BBONT) **Access** Open all year

The reserve is a remnant of the former Inkpen Great Common now turned to heathland, bog, a pond and areas of woodland.

Nature Trail There is no formal waymarked trail but public footpaths run through the reserve.

Plants Bog Asphodel, Meadow Thistle, Pale Heath Violet, Dwarf Gorse.
Trees Birch, Oak.
Birds Over 50 species nest.
Other The small pond provides a habitat for amphibians and aquatic invertebrates.

Guide Contact BBONT   **Disabled Access** No   **School Parties** By prior arrangement with BBONT; contact the Education Officer on Oxford (0865) 775476. A book entitled *Educational Opportunities on Nature Reserves* is available from BBONT **Parking** In lane or layby   **Toilets** No   **Food** No

Further Information A Reserve Information Sheet is available from the Reserve Manager through the BBONT office.

Berkshire

MOOR COPSE

OS Ref SU635742   Landranger Sheet 175
Nearest Town Pangbourne   **Size of Reserve** 28 hectares (70½ acres)
Managed by Berkshire, Buckinghamshire and Oxfordshire Naturalists'
Trust (BBONT)   **Access** Open all year but restricted to Hogmoor Copse
and Park Wood areas

M oor Copse is part of a larger SSSI and is divided into several sections: Hogmoor Copse, a wet wood; Park Wood, an old wet wood traditionally managed as coppice with standards; a field; Moor Copse, mainly ash coppice with oak and ash standards; the River Pang; an island in the River Pang. The varied structure of the woodland makes it ideal for doing studies of the woodland habitat.

Nature Trail There is no formal waymarked trail, but well-defined paths provide access to Hogmoor Copse and Park Wood. The riverside path is very narrow so please take care.

Plants The reserve has an impressive show of Bluebells, Primroses and other woodland flowers in May. 270 species of plants have been recorded.
Insects 300 species of butterfly and moth have been recorded.
Other Brown Trout in the River Pang.

Guide Contact BBONT   **Disabled Access** No   **School Parties** By prior arrangement with BBONT; contact the Education Officer on Oxford (0865) 775476. A book entitled *Educational Opportunities on Nature Reserves* is available from BBONT **Parking** In layby   **Toilets** No   **Food** No

Further Information Contact BBONT.

Berkshire
NORTHERAMS WOOD

OS Ref SU856682   Landranger Sheet 175
Nearest Town Bracknell   **Size of Reserve** 3 hectares (7½ acres)
Managed by Berkshire, Buckinghamshire and Oxfordshire
Naturalists' Trust (BBONT)   **Access** Open all year

This reserve is a remnant of the old Northerams Wood, most of which has disappeared under housing and industrial development. It is a mixed deciduous woodland with small areas of damp meadow, improved grassland and scrub. It is a useful reserve for educational purposes, providing a variety of habitats in a very small area.

Nature Trail There is no formal waymarked trail but the reserve has a good network of footpaths.

Plants There is a good show of wild flowers in spring.
Trees Oak, Hazel, Birch, Aspen, Holly, Hawthorn, Crab Apple, Alder, Willow, Sweet Chestnut, Elder, Cherry, Sycamore.
Birds The reserve supports good numbers of birds.
Other A pond is in the process of being established in order to provide a habitat for freshwater invertebrates and amphibians.

Guide Contact BBONT   **Disabled Access** No   **School Parties** By prior arrangement with BBONT; contact the Education Officer on Oxford (0865) 775476. Some teachers' notes are available on request from the BBONT office. A book entitled *Educational Opportunities on Nature Reserves* is available from BBONT
Parking Yes   **Toilets** No   **Food** No

Further Information Contact BBONT.

Berkshire
OWLSMOOR BOG AND HEATH

OS Ref SU845632   Landranger Sheet 175
Nearest Town Bracknell   **Size of Reserve** 26 hectares (64 acres)
Managed by Berkshire, Buckinghamshire and Oxfordshire
Naturalists' Trust (BBONT)   **Access** Open all year

The site is part of the Sandhurst and Owlsmoor Bogs and Heaths SSSI, and includes areas of bog, wet heath, dry heathland and woodland.

Nature Trail Access to the reserve is on foot via Edgbarrow Woods. The path then continues along a bridleway through the reserve. There is no formal waymarked trail. Please do not walk over the boggy areas as this habitat is extremely delicate.

Plants Sundews, various Sedges, Bog Asphodel, Cross-leaved Heath, Purple Moor Grass, Heathers.
Trees Pine, Birch.
Insects The bog area is good for dragonflies and the heath areas support a wide variety of insects and spiders.
Other The dry heath supports a number of reptiles, including the Common Lizard and the Adder.

Guide Contact BBONT **Disabled Access** No **School Parties** By prior arrangement with BBONT; contact the Education Officer on Oxford (0865) 775476. A book entitled *Educational Opportunities on Nature Reserves* is available from BBONT
Parking In Edgbarrow Woods car park (Bracknell District Council) **Toilets** No
Food No

Further Information Contact BBONT.

Buckinghamshire

ASTON CLINTON RAGPITS

OS Ref SP888108   Landranger Sheet 165
Nearest Town Aston Clinton   **Size of Reserve** 2.2 hectares (6 acres)
Managed by Berkshire, Buckinghamshire and Oxfordshire
Naturalists' Trust (BBONT)   **Access** Open all year

This small but diverse site, including old pits which were formerly worked for chalk freestone ('rag'), is situated at the foot of the Chiltern escarpment. A rich variety of plants and animals occurs amongst the following habitats: woodland, grassland, scrub.

Nature Trail There is no formal trail but a public footpath runs the length of the reserve.

Plants Fragrant Orchid (late June), Pyramidal Orchid (early July), Cowslip, Chalk Milkwort, Autumn Gentian, Horseshoe Vetch, Knapweeds, Marjoram, St. John's Wort.
Trees Beech, Corsican Pine, Yew, Hawthorn, Dogwood.
Butterflies 30 species recorded (most numerous in August).

Guide Contact BBONT **Disabled Access** No **School Parties** By prior arrangement with BBONT; contact the Education Officer on Oxford (0865) 775476. A book entitled *Educational Opportunities on Nature Reserves* is available from BBONT
Parking On roadside   **Toilets** No   **Food** No

Further Information Large scale maps of the site are available from BBONT.

Buckinghamshire
BERNWOOD MEADOWS

OS Ref SP606110   Landranger Sheet 164
Nearest Town Brill   **Size of Reserve** 7.3 hectares (18½ acres)
Managed by Berkshire, Buckinghamshire and Oxfordshire
Naturalists' Trust (BBONT)   **Access** Open all year but keep to the footpaths from
mid-April until the hay has been harvested

T he reserve consists of two neutral grassland meadows bordered by
hedges, some of which are ancient. There is a pond in each meadow.

Nature Trail There is no formal waymarked trail but public footpaths cross the
reserve.

Over 100 plant species have been recorded, including 23 grasses, Green-winged
Orchid and Adderstongue Fern. There are abundant invertebrates and both Fallow
and Muntjac Deer frequent the site.

Guide Contact BBONT.   **Disabled Access** No   **School Parties** By prior arrangement
with BBONT; contact the Education Officer on Oxford (0865) 775476. A book
entitled *Educational Opportunities on Nature Reserves* is available from BBONT
Parking There is a small car park suitable for cars and minibuses   **Toilets** No
Food No

Further Information A set of interpretative panels is situated near the reserve
entrance.

Buckinghamshire
BOARSTALL DUCK DECOY

OS Ref SP623151   Landranger Sheet 164
Nearest Town Brill   **Size of Reserve** 7.3 hectares (18 acres)
Managed by Berkshire, Buckinghamshire and Oxfordshire
Naturalists' Trust (BBONT)   **Owned by** The National Trust   **Access** The reserve
can be used by school parties on Wednesdays throughout the summer months, and
also during January, February and March. The site is also open to the public at
weekends and bank holidays in the summer. Please keep to the paths in April and
May when the bluebells are out and birds are nesting

T his is one of only three working duck decoys in the country (see also
page 164). This decoy consists of a pond with 4 'pipes' leading off into
which the ducks swim. They are caught for ringing and then released. The
pond is surrounded by woodland rich in wildlife.

Nature Trail There is a circular waymarked nature trail round the wood.

Duck decoying demonstrations are given at 11.00 and 15.00 at weekends and bank holidays when the Warden is available. The woodland supports a varied ground flora and there are good populations of various birds and mammals.

Information Centre There is a small Information Centre.

Guide Contact BBONT **Disabled Access** The footpath round the woods is suitable for disabled visitors in dry weather **School Parties** By prior arrangement with BBONT; contact the Education Officer on Oxford (0865) 775476. A book entitled *Educational Opportunities on Nature Reserves* is available from BBONT
Parking Yes **Toilets** No **Food** No

Further Information Contact BBONT.

Buckinghamshire

BUCKINGHAM CANAL

OS Ref SP725352 Landranger Sheet 152
Nearest Town Buckingham **Size of Reserve** 1 hectare (2.6 acres)
Managed by Berkshire, Buckinghamshire and Oxfordshire
Naturalists' Trust (BBONT) **Access** Open all year

T he reserve covers both banks of the disused canal which closed in 1961. The reserve is bounded by overgrown hedgerows. The western end of the canal is dry but pools of water are more frequent towards the east until just beyond the lock, when the overflow from a gravel pit forms open water.

Nature Trail There is no formal waymarked trail, but a public footpath runs the length of the reserve along the canal towpath. The sides of the lock are very high and dangerous so children must be kept away from them.

The main interest of the site is the aquatic fauna, including grass snakes, toads, frogs, and newts, and invertebrates including dragonflies and damselflies. Some unusual birds, such as Bittern and Water Rail, have been recorded here.

Guide Contact BBONT **Disabled Access** No **School Parties** By prior arrangement with BBONT; contact the Education Officer on Oxford (0865) 775476. A book entitled *Educational Opportunities on Nature Reserves* is available from BBONT
Parking In field **Toilets** No **Food** No

Further Information Contact BBONT.

Buckinghamshire
BUTTLER'S HANGINGS

OS Ref SU818962   Landranger Sheet 165
Nearest Town High Wycombe   **Size of Reserve** 4 hectares (10 acres)
Managed by Berkshire, Buckinghamshire and Oxfordshire
Naturalists' Trust (BBONT)   **Access** Open all year

B uttler's Hangings is a sloping area of chalk grassland with a small strip of beech wood stretching down the reserve from the woods above. The slope faces south west and gets very warm on summer afternoons.

Nature Trail There is no formal waymarked trail but a public footpath, part of the West Wycombe Farm Trail, crosses the reserve.

The main interest of the site is invertebrate fauna; 26 species of butterfly are recorded regularly and 108 species of spider have been identified. The ground flora is rich but has no rarities.

Guide Contact BBONT   **Disabled Access** No   **School Parties** By prior arrangement with the Reserve Manager through the BBONT office. A book entitled *Educational Opportunities on Nature Reserves* is available from BBONT   **Parking** On roadside verge   **Toilets** No   **Food** No

Further Information A West Wycombe Farm Trail leaflet is available from the West Wycombe Caves entrance.

Buckinghamshire
CALVERT JUBILEE

OS Ref SP684250   Landranger Sheet 165
Nearest Town Buckingham   **Size of Reserve** 37 hectares (94½ acres)
Managed by Berkshire, Buckinghamshire and Oxfordshire
Naturalists' Trust (BBONT)   **Access** By prior arrangement with BBONT

C alvert Jubilee is the site of an old claypit now filled with water and used as a winter sanctuary by wildfowl. The reserve has been extended to include a length of disused railway line and is an interesting example of how industrial activities can lead to the creation of valuable wildlife habitats if managed sympathetically. Habitats include open water, neutral grassland, a callow-covered area and scrub.

Nature Trail A footpath runs right round the lake and to a birdwatching hide.

Plants Mosses and bryophytes with Barren Strawberry, Mouse-eared Hawkweed, Fairy Flax, Centaury and Blue Fleabane.

Birds Wildfowl, especially Mallard, Tufted Duck and Pochard, plus Nightingale, Treecreeper, Woodpeckers, etc.

Guide Contact BBONT   **Disabled Access** The birdwatching hide is designed primarily for disabled watchers with a concrete path leading directly from the car park to the hide   **School Parties** By prior arrangement with BBONT; contact the Education Officer on Oxford (0865) 775476. A book entitled *Educational Opportunities on Nature Reserves* is available from BBONT   **Parking** Small car park (SP682250)   **Toilets** No   **Food** No

Further Information Contact BBONT.

Buckinghamshire
CHEQUERS

OS Ref SP830055   Landranger Sheet 165
Nearest Town Princes Risborough   **Size of Reserve** 33.2 hectares (83 acres)
Managed by Berkshire, Buckinghamshire and Oxfordshire Naturalists'
Trust (BBONT)   **Access** Open all year but coombe area is not open to the public

T he Chequers Reserve is an area of rich chalk grassland situated on the scarp face of the Chiltern Hills. An old sunken way traverses the site, providing an example of the erosive power of human and livestock trampling. There are fine views over the Vale of Aylesbury. The reserve forms part of the Ellesborough and Kimble Warren SSSI.

Nature Trail There is no formal waymarked trail but public footpaths provide access to the area. Grangelands and Pulpit Hill Reserve (page 127) is adjacent and could be included in a walk.

Plants Thyme, Cowslip, Squinancywort, Viper's Bugloss, Musk Orchid, Twayblade.

Guide Contact BBONT   **Disabled Access** No   **School Parties** By prior arrangement with BBONT; contact the Education Officer on Oxford (0865) 775476. A book entitled *Educational Opportunities on Nature Reserves* is available from BBONT **Parking** In layby   **Toilets** No   **Food** No

Further Information Contact BBONT.

Buckinghamshire
DANCERSEND

OS Ref SP900095   Landranger Sheet 165
Nearest Town Wendover   **Size of Reserve** 30 hectares (79 acres)
Managed by Berkshire, Buckinghamshire and Oxfordshire
Naturalists' Trust (BBONT)   **Access** Open all year

Dancersend is mostly woodland with some unimproved grassland areas. Dancersend is a valuable site for looking at succession and also for relating vegetation to soils since the soil composition varies greatly on the reserve.

Nature Trail There is a waymarked circular trail which takes in most of the habitats in the area. Public footpaths also provide access to the reserve.

Plants Over 270 species of flowers, including 10 orchids.
Butterflies Duke of Burgundy, Dark Green Fritillary.
Other The site is good for invertebrates.

Guide Contact BBONT **Disabled Access** No **School Parties** By prior arrangement with BBONT; contact the Education Officer on Oxford (0865) 775476. A book entitled *Educational Opportunities on Nature Reserves* is available from BBONT
Parking On roadside verge. Suitable for cars and minibuses, but not coaches
Toilets No **Food** No

Further Information Contact BBONT.

Buckinghamshire

DEEP MILL LANE POND

OS Ref SU907995 Landranger Sheet 165
Nearest Town High Wycombe **Size of Reserve** 1.6 hectares (4 acres)
Managed by Berkshire, Buckinghamshire and Oxfordshire
Naturalists' Trust (BBONT) **Access** Open all year

The reserve includes a pond and adjacent spinney with a hazel hedge forming the boundary with the road. The pond is rich in aquatic life.

Nature Trail A walk of some 100 metres (110 yards) runs alongside the pond.

The pond is accessible for dipping during the early summer before the emergent vegetation grows too tall.
Plants Common Reed, Yellow Flag Iris.

Guide Contact BBONT **Disabled Access** No **School Parties** By prior arrangement with BBONT; contact the Education Officer on Oxford (0865) 775476. A book entitled *Educational Opportunities on Nature Reserves* is available from BBONT
Parking On roadside at SU907995. Not suitable for coaches **Toilets** No **Food** No

Further Information Contact BBONT.

Buckinghamshire

GOMM VALLEY

OS Ref SU898922   Landranger Sheet 175
Nearest Town High Wycombe   **Size of Reserve** 4 hectares (10 acres)
Managed by Berkshire, Buckinghamshire and Oxfordshire
Naturalists' Trust (BBONT)   **Access** Open all year

G omm Valley Reserve was an area of herb-rich chalk grassland but is now in an advance stage of reversion to scrub and pioneer woodland.

Nature Trail There is a walk of about 400 metres (¼ mile) from the parking area to the reserve, then visitors may wander through the reserve at will.

The reserve is noted as a good over-wintering site for several bird species. It is also good for butterflies and moths.

Plants Many of the chalk grassland herbs are still to be found, including Carline and Stemless Thistles, Centaury, Common and Greater Knapweeds and a number of Orchids – Common Spotted, Fragrant, Pyramidal and Twayblade.

Other Common Lizard, Slow-worm.

Guide Contact BBONT   **Disabled Access** No   **School Parties** By prior arrangement with BBONT; contact the Education Officer on Oxford (0865) 775476. A book entitled *Educational Opportunities on Nature Reserves* is available from BBONT

Parking Yes   **Toilets** No   **Food** No

Further Information Contact BBONT.

Buckinghamshire

GRANGELANDS and PULPIT HILL

OS Ref SP827049   Landranger Sheet 165
Nearest Town Princes Risborough   **Size of Reserve** 20 hectares (50 acres)
Managed by Berkshire, Buckinghamshire and Oxfordshire Naturalists'
Trust (BBONT)   **Access** Open all year. Much of the Pulpit Hill area is inaccessible

G rangelands is an area of species-rich chalk grassland with a good display of plants and butterflies. There are also areas of scrub. Pulpit Hill is mostly beech woodland but also includes an area of chalk downland that is gradually being colonised. There are good views over the Vale of Aylesbury.

Nature Trail The reserve is covered by a good network of public footpaths and bridleways. The reserve is adjacent to Chequers Reserve (page 125) which could be included in a walk.

With its rich variety of habitats, this site provides good opportunities for studying succession.
Plants Dogwood, Juniper.
Trees Beech, Yew, Whitebeam.

Guide Contact BBONT   **Disabled Access** No   **School Parties** By prior arrangement with BBONT; contact the Education Officer on Oxford (0865) 775476. A book entitled *Educational Opportunities on Nature Reserves* is available from BBONT
Parking In car park   **Toilets** No   **Food** No

Further Information Contact BBONT.

Buckinghamshire
LITTLE LINFORD WOOD

OS Ref SP832455   Landranger Sheet 152
Nearest Town Newport Pagnell   **Size of Reserve** 42.5 hectares (105 acres)
Managed by Berkshire, Buckinghamshire and Oxfordshire
Naturalists' Trust (BBONT)   **Access** Open all year

This is an ancient woodland marked on a map dated 1766; it may have existed as woodland since trees first colonised Britain after the recession of the last Ice Age. There is also a small pond in the centre of the wood.

Nature Trail There is no formal waymarked trail but there are woodland rides through the wood, providing easy access.

Plants 130 species of higher plants have been recorded, including 23 species which indicate the wood's ancient woodland status.
Trees Oak, Ash, Field Maple.

Guide Contact BBONT   **Disabled Access** No   **School Parties** By prior arrangement with BBONT; contact the Education Officer on Oxford (0865) 775476. A book entitled *Educational Opportunities on Nature Reserves* is available from BBONT
Parking In car park   **Toilets** No   **Food** No

Further Information Contact BBONT.

Buckinghamshire
MILLFIELD WOOD

OS Ref SU870954   Landranger Sheet 165
Nearest Town High Wycombe   **Size of Reserve** 7.3 hectares (19 acres)
Managed by Berkshire, Buckinghamshire and Oxfordshire
Naturalists' Trust (BBONT)   **Access** Open all year

M illfield Wood is a rare example of a semi-natural Chiltern beechwood on chalk. There are good views from the reserve over the
Hughenden Valley.

Nature Trail There is a nature trail in the wood. Trail leaflets are available from
BBONT.

A chalk bank adjacent to the reserve supports a species-rich chalk grassland; over
190 species of flowering plant have been recorded and the area is good for butterflies.
Plants The ground flora is richer than is usual in beechwoods and includes Bluebell,
Wood Sanicle, Wood Anemone and Pignut, plus a few rarities, including Herb Paris
and Lily of the Valley.
Trees Beech, Ash, Cherry, Hazel, Holly, Maple, Whitebeam.

Guide Contact BBONT   **Disabled Access** No   **School Parties** By prior arrangement
with BBONT; contact the Education Officer on Oxford (0865) 775476. A book
entitled *Educational Opportunities on Nature Reserves* is available from BBONT
Parking Yes   **Toilets** No   **Food** No

Further Information Contact BBONT.

Buckinghamshire
PILCH FIELD

OS Ref SP747322   Landranger Sheet 152/165
Nearest Town Buckingham   **Size of Reserve** 11.8 hectares (29 acres)
Managed by Berkshire, Buckinghamshire and Oxfordshire
Naturalists' Trust (BBONT)   **Access** Open all year

T his reserve consists of two ancient meadows including both neutral and
calcareous grassland types, and surrounded by hedgerows. There are
many wet flushes which support a fen community. It provides a good
example of unimproved meadows. The fields are grazed by cattle.

Nature Trail There is no formal waymarked trail, but a footpath runs down one side
of the reserve.

Plants The drier areas contain some interesting grasses and the flowers include
Green-winged Orchid, Common Spotted Orchid, Salad Burnet, Cowslip, Spiny
Rest-harrow and Dropwort.

Guide Contact BBONT   **Disabled Access** No   **School Parties** By prior arrangement
with the Reserve Manager through the BBONT office. A book entitled *Educational
Opportunities on Nature Reserves* is available from BBONT   **Parking** On roadside
verge   **Toilets** No   **Food** No

Further Information Contact BBONT.

PITSTONE HILL

OS Ref SP950145   Landranger Sheet 165
Nearest Town Aylesbury   **Size of Reserve** 21.8 hectares (54 acres)
Managed by Berkshire, Buckinghamshire and Oxfordshire
Naturalists' Trust (BBONT)   **Access** Open all year

S ituated within the Chilterns Area of Oustanding Natural Beauty, Pitstone Hill comprises the scarp face southwards to Aldbury Nowers Wood. It is a very good tract of grazed chalk grassland. A stretch of Grimm's Ditch runs most of the length of the site.

Nature Trail A footpath runs right round the reserve, providing good access. There is no formal waymarked trail.

Plants Wild Carrot, Pasque Flower, Squinancywort, Carline Thistle, Rockrose, Horseshoe Vetch, Kidney Vetch.
Birds Meadow Pipit, Skylark.
Butterflies 26 species recorded.
Other Numerous anthills made by the Yellow Hill Ant.

Guide Contact BBONT   **Disabled Access** No   **School Parties** By prior arrangement with BBONT; contact the Education Officer on Oxford (0865) 775476. A book entitled *Educational Opportunities on Nature Reserves* is available from BBONT
Parking In car park   **Toilets** No   **Food** No

Further Information Contact BBONT.

RUSHBEDS WOODS and LAPLAND FARM

OS Ref SP668157   Landranger Sheet 164/165
Nearest Town Brill   **Size of Reserve** 45 hectares (114 acres)
Managed by Berkshire, Buckinghamshire and Oxfordshire
Naturalists' Trust (BBONT)   **Access** Open all year

R ushbeds Woods is ancient oak-dominated mixed woodland. The reserve also includes two narrow paddocks and some fields (Lapland Farm) adjacent to the woodland. The woodland is damp throughout the year; a small stream meanders through the site.

Nature Trail Although there is no formal waymarked trail, there are well-defined paths through the wood.

The woodland has a very rich ground flora and good populations of butterflies, including some rare species.

Guide Contact BBONT **Disabled Access** No **School Parties** By prior arrangement with BBONT; contact the Education Officer on Oxford (0865) 775476. A book entitled *Educational Opportunities on Nature Reserves* is available from BBONT **Parking** There is a car park but it is not suitable for coaches, which can park in the adjacent layby **Toilets** No **Food** No

Further Information Contact BBONT.

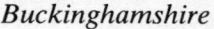

Buckinghamshire
STONY STRATFORD

OS Ref SP785412   Landranger Sheet 152
Nearest Town Stony Stratford   **Size of Reserve** 23 hectares (57 acres)
Managed by Berkshire, Buckinghamshire and Oxfordshire
Naturalists' Trust (BBONT)   **Access** The reserve is a sanctuary for wildfowl so
public access must be restricted to the public footpath and the birdwatching hide in
the northern part of the reserve

S tony Stratford has recently been reinstated as a wildfowl sanctuary after much of it had been excavated for gravel. It now consists of a series of lakes with islands which have been sympathetically treated to provide habitats for nesting waders and waterfowl. The birdwatching hide at the eastern end provides an excellent view of the site.

Nature Trail A public footpath runs round the northern end of the reserve and to the hide.

The pond in the outer section of the reserve, near the car park, is suitable for dipping.

Guide Contact BBONT **Disabled Access** Yes **School Parties** By prior arrangement with BBONT; contact the Education Officer on Oxford (0865) 775476. A book entitled *Educational Opportunities on Nature Reserves* is available from BBONT **Parking** In car park **Toilets** No **Food** No

Further Information Contact BBONT.

Buckinghamshire
WESTON TURVILLE RESERVOIR

OS Ref SP862096   Landranger Sheet 165
Nearest Town Princes Risborough   **Size of Reserve** 4.8 hectares (12 acres)
Managed by Berkshire, Buckinghamshire and Oxfordshire Naturalists'
Trust (BBONT)   **Access** Open to the public along the north and east banks

T he BBONT reserve consists of the reedbed, marshy fen, hedge and woodland of the area surrounding this 'disused' reservoir. The open water is leased to local sailing and angling clubs. There are good views over the open water from the dam bank and the path on the west bank. It is a good place to see many of the commoner wildfowl.

Nature Trail A footpath runs round the reservoir, through the reserve area, providing access to all habitats.

Birds The reserve is good for wintering wildfowl and passage migrants and has good breeding colonies of Reed Warbler and Ruddy Duck. It is also renowned as an autumn roost for Swallow and Martin.

Guide Contact BBONT **Disabled Access** No **School Parties** By prior arrangement with BBONT; contact the Education Officer on Oxford (0865) 775476. A book entitled *Educational Opportunities on Nature Reserves* is available from BBONT **Parking** In layby **Toilets** No **Food** No

Further Information Contact BBONT.

Cheshire
BLACK LAKE

OS Ref ST537709   Landranger Sheet 117
Nearest Town Northwich   **Size of Reserve** 0.4 hectares (1 acre)
Managed by Cheshire Conservation Trust (CCT)   **Access** Open access all year to the margin of the lake to Trust members. No access to Sphagnum basin because of safety considerations and its delicate structure

B lack Lake lies within Delamere Forest and shows a good example of early 'schwingmor' or floating bog development. It supports a rich variety of mossland species.

Nature Trail There is no formal trail but the reserve is reached along numerous forest trails through Delamere Forest. Visitors are warned that underneath the Sphagnum raft there is a fair depth of water.

Plants Cotton Grass, Cranberry, Sundew, Cross-leaved Heath, Liverworts.
Birds The surrounding area of Delamere Forest is rich in woodland birds.
Insects Dragonflies, including White-faced Darter.

Information Centre There is a Forestry Commission Interpretative Centre at Linmere. The reserve can be reached from Linmere, using forest paths.

Guide Contact CCT **Disabled Access** No **School Parties** No **Parking** At Barnesbridge Gates Car Park (SJ542716) or in the County Council Car Park by the Interpretative Centre at Linmere **Toilets** No **Food** No

Further Information A collection of reserve cards, with maps, is available from CCT (price £1.20).

Cheshire

DANES MOSS

OS Ref SJ908704   Landranger Sheet 118
Nearest Town Macclesfield   **Size of Reserve** 12.5 hectares (31 acres)
Managed by Cheshire Conservation Trust (CCT)   **Access** Open all year

D anes Moss Reserve is an area of broadleaved woodland, coniferous plantation, heathland, open water and regenerating mossland.

Nature Trail A public footpath passes through the reserve.

Plants Purple Moor Grass.
Trees Most of the moss woodland consists of Corsican Pine. The broadleaved woodland contains both Sessile and Pedunculate Oak.
Birds Over 75 species recorded. The open water area attracts wildfowl during winter and early spring.
Animals Most of the small mammals have been observed, together with Badger, Brown Hare and Grey Squirrel.
Insects Several species of damselfly.

Guide Contact CCT   **Disabled Access** No   **School Parties** Contact CCT
Parking On roadside at start of public footpath (SJ903701)   **Toilets** No   **Food** No

Further Information A collection of reserve cards, with maps, is available from CCT (price £1.20).

Cheshire

SWETTENHAM MEADOWS

OS Ref SJ804674   Landranger Sheet 118
Nearest Town Congleton   **Size of Reserve** 3.6 hectares (9 acres)
Managed by Cheshire Conservation Trust (CCT)   **Access** Open all year

S wettenham Meadows Reserve consists of semi-natural broadleaved woodland and species-rich grassland. Many interesting species of flowering plant are present in the grassland, and the woodland provides nesting areas for many bird species in spring and summer.

Nature Trail A public footpath runs through the reserve.

Birds Winter visitors include Brambling, Fieldfare and Redwing.

Guide Contact CCT   **Disabled Access** No   **School Parties** Contact CCT   **Parking** Yes
Toilets No   **Food** No

Further Information A collection of reserve cards, with maps, is available from CCT (price £1.20).

Derbyshire
CROMFORD CANAL

OS Ref SK340532   Landranger Sheet 119
Nearest Town Belper   **Size of Reserve** 3.2 km (2 miles) long
Managed by Derbyshire Wildlife Trust (DWT)   **Access** Open all year

C romford Canal was in use as a waterway up to 1944. Since it fell into disuse the canal has become an important refuge for a rich and diverse collection of plants. These range from those of open water, through swamp vegetation to meadow and woodland species beside the towpath. Many are becoming increasingly uncommon elsewhere in the country. Insects, birds and other animals also find it an ideal haven.

Nature Trail The towpath which runs along the whole 3-km (2-mile) stretch is a public footpath.

Plants Over 250 species recorded, including Flowering Rush, a canal speciality which is quite rare in the region.
Birds The best time of year is from mid-April to early June – Willow Warbler, Wren, Chaffinch. Mallard and Moorhen breed on the canal.
Insects Dragonflies, damselflies, hoverflies.
Butterflies Small Tortoiseshell, Peacock, Meadow Brown, Wall Brown, Green Veined White, Orange-tip.
Other Frogs, toads, grass snake.

Under Threat Wetland wildlife habitats, such as this reserve, have declined rapidly throughout Britain. Derbyshire has few wetland areas where wildlife has priority. Wetlands are not just attractive to wildlife – many plants and animals actually depend upon them for their survival.

Guide By prior arrangement with DWT   **Disabled Access** The towpath is flat
School Parties Yes   **Parking** There are car parks at Crich Chase Bridge (SK340532) and at Whatstandwell   **Toilets** No   **Food** No

Further Information Reserve leaflets are available from DWT.

Gloucestershire
CHEDWORTH

OS Ref SP051138   Landranger Sheet 163
Nearest Town Northleach   **Size of Reserve** 5 hectares (12½ acres)
Managed by The Gloucestershire Trust for Nature Conservation (GTNC)
Access Open all year to GTNC members only. A public footpath runs through the woods to the west of the reserve

T he Chedworth Reserve consists of 2 km (1¼ miles) of disused railway line through the Chedworth Woods, in the heart of the Cotswolds. The principal interest of the reserve lies in its geology which is well displayed in the railway cuttings. For this reason, the site has been designated an SSSI. Also of considerable interest, however, is the way in which vegetation is colonising the cuttings, embankments and the trackway itself. A walk along the length of the reserve and back will provide a good sample of the animal, bird and plant life of a Cotswold woodland.

Nature Trail 2 km (1¼ miles), waymarked. Good strong footwear is essential for walking on the ballast that covers the trackway.

Plants Over 200 species recorded, many lime-loving.
Trees Oak, Ash, Hazel (coppice), Beech, planted conifers.
Birds Over 70 species recorded, including Buzzard, Sparrowhawk, Warblers, Woodcock (roding displays), Tawny Owl.
Animals 4 species of Deer – Fallow, Roe, Sika, Muntjac.

Guide No   **Disabled Access** No   **School Parties** No   **Parking** For GTNC members only   **Toilets** No   **Food** No

Further Information Introductory booklets are available from GTNC, as well as more specialised booklets on geology, deer, birds, fossils and molluscs.

Gloucestershire

EDWARD RICHARDSON and PHYLLIS AMEY

OS Ref SP215008   Landranger Sheet 163
Nearest Town Lechlade   **Size of Reserve** 5.6 hectares (14 acres)
Managed by The Gloucestershire Trust for Nature Conservation (GTNC)
Access Open all year

T his reserve consists of two flooded gravel pits and peripheral land of unusually high wildlife value. As well as the open water, other habitats include species-rich grassland, and willow carr.

Nature Trail 800 metres (½ mile), waymarked. The circular trail runs around the southern pond. A Nature Trail Guidebook is available from GTNC. Part of the trail can be flooded in winter – Wellingtons are recommended throughout the year.

The site supports a number of local plant species. Dragonfly interest is particularly high – 15 species recorded. Overwintering waterfowl and Warblers are also very well represented. There is a birdwatching hide.

Under Threat The entire reserve is threatened by development of surrounding land and the proposed construction of a new bypass which would bisect the site. At present it is designated a proposed SSSI.

Guide No   **Disabled Access** The viewing hide and a short section of the trail are accessible to disabled visitors   **School Parties** No   **Parking** For 7 cars   **Toilets** No **Food** No

Further Information Contact GTNC.

Gloucestershire

SILK WOOD

OS Ref ST839892   Landranger Sheet 162
Nearest Town Tetbury   **Size of Reserve** 8.5 hectares (21 acres)
Managed by The Gloucestershire Trust for Nature Conservation (GTNC)
Access Open all year. Access is from the Westonbirt Arboretum

S ilk Wood is a typical example of damp oak woodland. Traditional management with oak standards over hazel coppice has now been reintroduced on part of the reserve, a second part is managed as high forest and the remainder has been left to develop untouched.

Nature Trail 2 km (1¼ miles), unmarked – along woodland rides which can be very wet after rain.

It is of interest to compare the different management methods. There is a typical field-layer flora and the rides can be good for butterflies.
Plants Primrose, Bluebell, Bugle, Wood Spurge, Woodruff, Yellow Archangel, plus a rich variety of lichens.
Birds 34 species recorded, incuding Green Woodpecker and Tawny Owl.
Butterflies Speckled Wood, Meadow Brown.

Guide No   **Disabled Access** No   **School Parties** No   **Parking** 250 metres (275 yards) from the reserve   **Toilets** No   **Food** No

Further Information Reserve leaflets are available from GTNC.

Gloucestershire

SLIMBRIDGE WILDFOWL RESERVE

OS Ref S07105   Landranger Sheet 162
Nearest Town Stroud   **Size of Reserve** 404 hectares (1,000 acres)
Managed by The Wildfowl Trust (WT)   **Access** Open daily from 9.30–17.00 in summer or 16.00 in winter. Closed 24th and 25th December. There is an admission charge but there are reductions for children, senior citizens and groups

S limbridge is the headquarters of The Wildfowl Trust and incorporates a wild bird reserve as well as the largest and most varied collection of wildfowl in the world. Slimbridge lies in the Berkeley Vale, a lowland area between the Cotswold Hills and the Severn estuary. Much of it is land reclaimed from the river by tidal defences built over hundreds of years. Part of the reserve has been progressively developed, by the creation of ponds, planting and landscaping, to make a home for a large and varied population of tame waterfowl from all over the world, and many rare birds are bred here. Facilities on the reserve include an exhibition, research centre, education centre, information desk, cinema and a unique Tropical House.

Nature Trail 1.5 km (1 mile), waymarked. WT Walkabout Guides are available. There are 2 optional shorter routes and extra paths lead out to the observation hides.

The reserve is home to a specialist wildfowl collection of over 2,500 birds of 180 different kinds. In summer there are resident wildfowl with their young and at all times of the year visitors can walk among these tame birds and feed them. All six kinds of flamingo can be seen on the reserve. The Tropical House exhibits Hartlaub's Touracos, hummingbirds and sunbirds. There is a working duck decoy used to catch ducks for ringing. Birds are grouped in pens according to their country of origin.

Information Centre There is an Information Desk in the Entrance Hall.

Guide Yes **Disabled Access** All paths are firm and level and access to the observation hides is good. Taped commentaries are available for visually handicapped visitors and some labelling is in braille **School Parties** Welcomed. A Teacher's Pack of Information Sheets, Theme Sheets and other resources, is available **Parking** Yes **Toilets** Yes, including for the disabled. **Food** Self-service restaurant **Shop** Selling gifts and books

Further Information Contact The Wildfowl Trust, Slimbridge, Gloucestershire GL2 7BT (tel. 045 389 333).

Hereford and Worcester
CLAY VALLETS WOOD

OS Ref SO353678   Landranger Sheet 148
Nearest Town Lingen   **Size of Reserve** 3.2 hectares (8 acres)
Managed by Herefordshire Nature Trust (HNT)   **Access** Open all year

The reserve is situated on west and south-west facing slopes and is an area of oak-dominated ancient semi-natural woodland with a rather sparse understorey. On the steepest slopes, the thin acid soils support heather and bilberry.

Nature Trail About 800 metres (½ mile), waymarked with blue-topped posts. The path is very steep in places.

Plants Cow Wheat, Golden Rod, Devil's Bit Scabious.
Birds Buzzard, Pied Flycatcher, Warblers.
Other Woodland butterflies.

Guide By prior arrangement with HNT **Disabled Access** No **School Parties** By prior arrangement with HNT **Parking** Limited **Toilets** No **Food** No

Further Information Contact HNT.

Hereford and Worcester

KNAPP and PAPERMILL

OS Ref SO746520   Landranger Sheet 150
Nearest Town Worcester   **Size of Reserve** 25 hectares (62 acres)
Managed by The Worcestershire Nature Conservation Trust (WNCT)
Access Open all year

T he Knapp and Papermill Reserves combine a wide diversity of
habitats in a relatively small area. These habitats include mixed
deciduous woodland, meadows, ponds and orchard. The reserves are
situated in the Leigh Brook valley and have been designated an SSSI.

Nature Trail 2.4 km (1½ miles), waymarked. Paths can be muddy after rain so
suitable footwear is essential. The circular trail begins and ends at Knapp House.
Booklets about the reserves and detailing the nature trail are available on site.

There is a birdwatching hide overlooking a Kingfisher nesting site. The diversity of
habitats is reflected in the botanical diversity of the reserve – over 1,500 species
recorded.

Information Centre There is a small unstaffed Information Centre which is open
whenever the reserves are open.

Guide By prior arrangement with Wardens through WNCT   **Disabled Access** No
School Parties By prior arrangement with Wardens   **Parking** For 10–15 cars
Toilets At Information Centre   **Food** Sweets and drinks available

Further Information Contact WNCT.

Hereford and Worcester

LEA AND PAGETS WOOD

OS Ref SO598343   Landranger Sheet 149
Nearest Town Hereford   **Size of Reserve** 11.3 hectares (28 acres)
Managed by Herefordshire Nature Trust (HNT)   **Access** Open all year

L ea and Pagets Wood is ancient semi-natural woodland on Silurian
limestone. It includes a fine diversity of tree species, many of them
associated with ancient woodland, together with a rich understorey. The
wood is managed by traditional methods and examples of recent and
derelict coppice may be seen.

Nature Trail 2 km (1¼ miles), waymarked with numbered blue-topped posts. The
trail can be muddy and is steep in places, with steps in the steepest parts. Nature
Trail leaflets (for children and adults) are available at the reserve.

The reserve supports a very rich woodland ground flora and is excellent for butterflies and birds.

Plants Spurge Laurel, Herb Paris, Common Twayblade, and Early Purple, Butterfly and Common Spotted Orchids.

Trees Wild Service.

Birds Pied Flycatcher, Warblers, 3 species of Woodpecker.

Animals Badger, Fallow Deer, Dormouse, Yellow-necked Mouse, Wood Mouse.

Guide By prior arrangement with HNT   **Disabled Access** No   **School Parties** By prior arrangement with HNT   **Parking** Limited   **Toilets** No   **Food** No

Further Information Contact HNT.

Hereford and Worcester

LEEPING STOCKS

OS Ref SO552160   Landranger Sheet 142
Nearest Town Ross-on-Wye   **Size of Reserve** 7.8 hectares (19 acres)
Managed by Herefordshire Nature Trust (HNT)   **Access** Open all year

The reserve is situated on the west-facing slopes of the Great Doward carboniferous limestone massif. It consists of a mosaic of habitats – beech and oak woodland, mixed scrub and limestone grassland. A network of ancient beech boundary hedges, raised on low piles of stones, demark the old field and woodland units. The reserve has an excellent limestone flora and is good for butterflies and birds.

Nature Trail The nature trail is marked by blue-topped posts. Nature Trail leaflets are available from the HNT head office.

Plants Bird's Nest Orchid, Meadow Saffron, Deadly Nightshade, Columbine, Twayblade, Broadleaved Helleborine.

Birds Pied Flycatcher, Warblers.

Animals Wood Mouse, Dormouse, Badger, Fallow Deer.

Butterflies Brimstone.

Guide By prior arrangement with HNT   **Disabled Access** No   **School Parties** By prior arrangement with HNT   **Parking** Very limited   **Toilets** No   **Food** No

Further Information Contact HNT.

Leicestershire
DIMMINSDALE

OS Ref SK376219   Landranger Sheet 128
Nearest Town Ashby de la Zouch   **Size of Reserve** 6.5 hectares (16 acres)
Managed by Leicestershire and Rutland Trust for Nature Conservation (LRTNC)
Access Open all year to Trust members. Members of the public wishing to visit
should contact LRTNC in advance to make arrangements

D imminsdale Reserve comprises a series of flooded lead/limestone
quarries and surrounding area, with an interesting mix of calcareous/
acid plant communities. Scenically, it is a very beautiful reserve and is
designated an SSSI.

Nature Trail A waymarked trail of about 2 km (1¼ miles) runs round the reserve,
mostly through mixed woodland.

Of interest to industrial archaeologists are old lime kilns and an old tramway.
Plants Giant Bellflower, Cowslip, Primrose, Hartstongue Fern, fine show of
Snowdrops in February.
Birds Kingfisher, Heron, Coot, Mallard, Blackcap.

Guide By prior arrangement with the Conservation Officer at LRTNC
Disabled Access No   **School Parties** By prior arrangement with the Conservation
Officer at LRTNC (giving at least one month's notice)   **Parking** Car park
200 metres (218 yards) away   **Toilets** No   **Food** No

Further Information A reserves booklet is available from LRTNC (price £2.00 inc.
p & p).

Leicestershire
PRIOR'S COPPICE

OS Ref SK831052   Landranger Sheet 141
Nearest Town Oakham   **Size of Reserve** 28 hectares (69 acres)
Managed by Leicestershire and Rutland Trust for Nature Conservation (LRTNC)
Access Open all year

P rior's Coppice is an area of ancient woodland predominantly of ash,
maple and oak.

Nature Trail 2 km (1¼ miles), waymarked. Nature Trail leaflets and maps are
available from LRTNC. The trail is generally wet so suitable footwear is advised.

Plants The very rich ground flora includes 3 species of Orchid, Yellow Archangel,
Ragged Robin, Herb Paris and Bluebell.

Guide By prior arrangement with the Conservation Officer at LRTNC
Disabled Access No   **School Parties** By prior arrangement with the Conservation
Officer at LRTNC (giving at least one month's notice)   **Parking** For 10–15 cars,
at gate   **Toilets** No   **Food** No

Further Information Contact LRTNC.

Lincolnshire

GIBRALTAR POINT

OS Ref TF556581   Landranger Sheet 122
Nearest Town Skegness   **Size of Reserve** 404.7 hectares (1,000 acres)
Managed by Lincolnshire and South Humberside Trust for Nature
Conservation (LSHTNC)   **Access** Open all year

The reserve consists of a 4.8-km (3-mile) stretch of coastline and
includes sandy and muddy seashore, sand-dune, saltmarsh and freshwater habitats. The reserve is designated an SSSI because of its importance
to wildlife.

Nature Trail An extensive network of paths enables visitors to pass through major
habitats without disturbing the wildlife. A variety of routes can be taken. Numbered
posts beside paths correspond to a map in the 'Walkabout Guide' available from the
reserve, or from LSHTNC.

Exceptional facilities at this reserve include a Visitor Centre, Field Station and two
viewpoints, as well as an observation hide. The Wash Viewpoint, converted from
an old military building, offers excellent views over the Wainfleet Marshes and the
Wash beyond. It also contains displays about the natural features and wildlife of the
Wash. There is an observation platform on one of the highest points of the reserve,
offering views all round. The hide overlooks the recently-dug freshwater mere,
which attracts many species of duck and wader. There is a ringing laboratory at
the Gibraltar Point observatory.
Plants The reserve supports a very varied flora, including Pyramidal Orchid,
Cowslip, Marsh Samphire, Sea Lavender, Sea Aster, Sea Spurrey, Sea Buckthorn.
Birds Little Tern (a colony nests on the beach), Ringed Plover, Redshank,
Oystercatcher, Long-eared Owl, Short-eared Owl, plus large numbers of migrants
passing through.
Animals Grey and Common Seals.

Under Threat On the landward side, the area is under threat from draining and
arable agriculture. There are also threats of development along the coastline, either
for tourism (eg. caravan sites) or housing. The Wash is constantly under threat from
pollution.

Visitor Centre Open daily during the summer but only at weekends during the
winter. Includes interpretative displays and a shop.
Field Station Open to individual naturalists, organised groups from schools, colleges
or universities, natural history societies, etc. Includes laboratories, a classroom,
common room, library and residential accommodation for up to 28 people. Further
details are available from the Warden, through LSHTNC.

Guide By prior arrangement with LSHTNC. Guided walks are advertised during the summer months **Disabled Access** Some of the reserve is accessible, eg. a ramp allows access for wheelchair users to the Wash Viewpoint **School Parties** By prior arrangement with LSHTNC **Parking** There are 2 car parks – one large (paying) and one small (free) **Toilets** Yes, including for the disabled **Food** No

Further Information As well as the 'Walkabout Guide', various maps and posters are available from the reserve or LSHTNC headquarters.

Lincolnshire

SNIPE DALES

OS Ref TF320863 Landranger Sheet 122
Nearest Town Louth **Size of Reserve** 48.5 hectares (120 acres);
Country Park 36.4 hectares (90 acres) **Managed by** Lincolnshire and South
Humberside Trust for Nature Conservation (LSHTNC) **Access** Open all year

Snipe Dales is divided into two parts. The Nature Reserve consists of two main valleys fretted by streams. The higher slopes are rough grassland, the lower areas damp grassland. There is some young woodland. The Country Park is mainly coniferous woodland with a series of new ponds. Many broadleaved trees and shrubs have been planted recently.

Nature Trail There are 6 trails of varying lengths. The shortest are just under 1.6 km (1 mile), the longest is 5 km (3 miles). Only the longest trail covers both the Reserve and the Country Park. All trails are marked by coloured posts. Routes are marked on a map in a leaflet available from LSHTNC.

Plants Many wild flowers, including Marsh Marigold, Yellow Flag, Water Avens, Ragged Robin.
Birds Blackcap, Sedge Warbler, Snipe, Meadow Pipit, Grasshopper Warbler, Barn Owl.
Butterflies 18 species recorded.
Other Frogs and toads colonizing new ponds.

Under Threat Most of the surrounding area is under threat from the plough, or already arable. Much of the traditional management of wet valleys such as this (eg. woodland or rough grazing) has been converted to arable land, making Snipe Dales a true wildlife 'oasis' in the midst of farmland.

Guide By prior arrangement with LSHTNC **Disabled Access** No **School Parties** By prior arrangement with LSHTNC **Parking** Yes **Toilets** No **Food** No

Further Information Contact LSHTNC.

Manchester, South
COMPSTALL

OS Ref SJ975915   Landranger Sheet 109
Nearest Town Stockport   **Size of Reserve** 15.5 hectares (38 acres)
Managed by Cheshire Conservation Trust (CCT)   **Access** Open at all times to Trust members and to public by permit, obtainable from Country Park Ranger's Office at the car park

C ompstall lies within Etherow Country Park and consists of semi-natural broadleaved woodland, wetland and open water on one side of the River Etherow. The site is classified as an SSSI.

Nature Trail A footpath of about 1.5 km (1 mile) runs from the car park to the reserve entrance, and then to the birdwatching hide. The path crosses a weir on the River Etherow.

Plants Several ferns and 3 species of Horsetail are present in the wetter areas, whilst the marshy areas are dominated by Sweet Flag, amongst others.
Birds Tufted Duck, Mallard, Dipper, Grey Wagtail, plus woodland species during spring migration.

Information Centre There is a Country Park Ranger's Office at the car park.

Guide Contact CCT   **Disabled Access** No   **School Parties** Contact CCT   **Parking** In Country Park Car Park (paying)   **Toilets** No   **Food** No

Further Information A collection of reserve cards, with maps, is available from CCT (price £1.20).

Manchester
DARK LANE

OS Ref SJ739906   Landranger Sheet 109
Nearest Town Trafford   **Size of Reserve** 4 hectares (10 acres)
Managed by Cheshire Conservation Trust (CCT)   **Access** Open all year but permit required to leave footpath. Available from the Conservation Officer at CCT

D ark Lane Reserve is an area of scrub woodland with ground flora characteristic of rough grassland. The area attracts a wide variety of bird species, many of which breed on the reserve.

Nature Trail There is a walk of about 400 metres (¼ mile) from the road to the reserve, then a public footpath continues through the reserve.

On sheltered days during the summer, the site is well frequented by butterflies and other insects.

Trees Hawthorn, Elder.

Guide Contact CCT   **Disabled Access** No   **School Parties** Contact CCT
Parking On roadside   **Toilets** No   **Food** No

Further Information A collection of reserve cards, with maps, is available from CCT
(price £1.20).

Merseyside
RED ROCKS MARSH

OS Ref SJ206880   Landranger Sheet 108
Nearest Town West Kirby   **Size of Reserve** 4 hectares (10 acres)
Managed by Cheshire Conservation Trust (CCT)   **Access** Open all year along
foreshore and boardwalk. Visitors should not enter the reedbed

R ed Rocks is a coastal site consisting of sand dunes, reedbeds and
grassland. The reserve lies within the Red Rocks SSSI.

Nature Trail There is no formal trail but the foreshore and marked paths provide
access.

The main interest of the reserve is that it supports the only breeding colony of
Natterjack Toads on the Wirral. This species is extremely limited in Britain and is
now protected.
Plants Over 50 species of flowering plants recorded, including Parsley Piert, Danish
Scurvey Grass and Wild Asparagus.

Guide Contact CCT   **Disabled Access** No   **School Parties** Contact CCT
Parking In West Kirby   **Toilets** No   **Food** No

Further Information A collection of reserve cards, with maps, is available from CCT
(price £1.20).

Nottinghamshire
ATTENBOROUGH GRAVEL PITS

OS Ref SK523343   Landranger Sheet 129
Nearest Town Nottingham   **Size of Reserve** 145.6 hectares (360 acres)
Managed by Nottinghamshire Wildlife Trust (NWT) and Butterley Aggregates Ltd
Access Open to the public at all times. Visitors are asked to keep to the main
footpaths

T he reserve comprises a series of disused gravel pits excavated between
1929 and 1951. There is now a wide range of aquatic and waterside
habitats, including open water, scrub, grassland and areas of native willow
and old stream courses. The site is designated an SSSI.

Nature Trail 2.4 km (1½ miles), waymarked. A series of cards forms a Nature Trail Guide, available at the reserve or from NWT.

The site is best known for its birds. A birdwatching hide overlooks an area frequented by passage waders. Keys are available from the Visitor Centre at weekends.

Plants A large number of plant species are to be found and more species are continually being recorded as recolonisation takes place.

Birds Winter wildfowl – Ducks in large numbers, Cormorants, breeding Common Tern, passage Waders. A bird checklist is available.

Other Wide range of fish and invertebrates, including Great Diving Beetle, dragonflies and damselflies.

Visitor Centre Currently open at weekends only.

Guide By prior arrangement with NWT (giving at least one week's notice)

Disabled Access No   **School Parties** By prior arrangement with NWT (giving at least one week's notice)   **Parking** For about 50 cars   **Toilets** No   **Food** A refreshment caravan is often parked in the main car park

Further Information Fact sheets are available at the reserve or from NWT on receipt of an s.a.e.

Nottinghamshire
BUNNY OLD WOOD (WEST)

OS Ref SK579283   Landranger Sheet 129
Nearest Town Keyworth   **Size of Reserve** 15.5 hectares (38½ acres)
Managed by Nottinghamshire Wildlife Trust (NWT)   **Access** Open all year

B unny Wood is of ancient origin and is situated on a steep north-facing slope. Dutch Elm disease has severely affected the wood and much felling and replanting is taking place with the eventual aim of restoring the wood to its former status. The reserve has been denotified as an SSSI following the effects of Dutch Elm disease.

Nature Trail A formal trail is planned for the future. At present, footpaths and woodland rides provide good access. These are shown on the map on the reserve fact sheet available from NWT.

Plants Dog's Mercury, Bluebell, Wood Anemone, Moschatel, Sanicle, Common Twayblade.

Birds A good variety of woodland bird species is present, including Great and Lesser Spotted Woodpeckers and Tawny Owl.

Animals Fox, Grey Squirrel.

Butterflies 10 species recorded, including White Letter Hairstreak.

Guide By prior arrangement with NWT (giving at least one week's notice)

Disabled Access No   **School Parties** By prior arrangement with NWT (giving at least one week's notice)   **Parking** Limited to roadside   **Toilets** No   **Food** No

Further Information Fact sheets are available from NWT on receipt of an s.a.e. A guide book is also available – contact NWT for details.

Nottinghamshire
DANESHILL GRAVEL PIT

OS Ref SK666867   Landranger Sheet 110
Nearest Town East Retford   **Size of Reserve** 16 hectares (40 acres)
Managed by Nottinghamshire Wildlife Trust (NWT)   **Access** Open to the public
throughout the year. Visitors should keep to the path

D esignated a Local Nature Reserve (LNR), Daneshill is a former
gravel working. The vegetation has had 20 years to develop although
excavation has recently taken place in an area of deep water on the eastern
side, allowing the banks to be graded. The site has a range of habitats,
including open water, wet grassland, drier areas of gorse and willow/birch
scrub. The reserve consists of the northern area only. Daneshill (South) is
managed by Nottinghamshire County Council as a conservation area with
recreational facilities.

Nature Trail There is no formal trail but a footpath runs right round the reserve,
providing good access. This path is shown on a map on the fact sheet available
from NWT.

Plants Common Spotted and Southern Marsh Orchids, Celery-leaved Buttercup,
Weld and Goat's Rue.
Birds Breeding Warblers include Willow, Sedge and Reed Warblers, Whitethroat
and Blackcap. Winter wildfowl in good numbers as well as Water Rail, Siskin,
Goldcrest and Finch flocks.
Butterflies Brimstone, Common Blue, Meadow Brown, Gatekeeper, Ringlet.
Other Dragonflies and damselflies.

Guide No   **Disabled Access** No   **School Parties** By prior arrangement with NWT
(giving at least one month's notice)   **Parking** Large car park at Daneshill South
Toilets No   **Food** No

Further Information Fact sheets (for northern section only), with maps,
are available from NWT on receipt of an s.a.e.

Nottinghamshire
EATON WOOD

OS Ref SK727772   Landranger Sheet 120
Nearest Town East Retford   **Size of Reserve** 24.2 hectares (60 acres)
Managed by Nottinghamshire Wildlife Trust (NWT)   **Access** Open to the public all
year. Visitors must keep to the rides and paths

E aton Wood is an area of ancient woodland which is particularly
important for its rich ground flora. It is designated an SSSI.

Nature Trail There is no formal waymarked trail, but woodland rides and public footpaths provide good access. Maps showing these paths are included on the reserve fact sheet available from NWT.

The best time to visit the reserve is between mid-April and the end of June.
Plants Primrose, Wood Anemone, Bluebell, Early Purple Orchid, Common Spotted and Butterfly Orchids, Broadleaved Helleborine, Moschatel, Herb Paris, Wood Sorrel, Yellow Archangel, Ladies Mantle, Sweet Woodruff (some of which are indicative of ancient woodland).
Trees Ash, Elm, Hazel (coppice), Oak, Field Maple, Sallow, Silver Birch.
Butterflies At least 12 species recorded.

Guide No   **Disabled Access** No   **School Parties** No   **Parking** There is a little car parking space at the entrance. Otherwise, cars should be parked in minor road to the west of Gamston Wood   **Toilets** No   **Food** No

Further Information Fact sheets are available from NWT on receipt of an s.a.e.

Nottinghamshire
MARTIN'S POND

OS Ref SK527401   Landranger Sheet 129
Nearest Town The reserve is in Nottingham   **Size of Reserve** 4.4 hectares (11 acres)
Managed by Nottinghamshire Wildlife Trust (NWT) and Nottingham City Council
Access Open all year

M artin's Pond is an urban wetland area situated about 4.8 km (3 miles) west of the City Centre. It comprises some open water, reed swamp and a small central wooded island. The site is designated a Local Nature Reserve (LNR). The adjacent woodland of Harrison's Plantation is also managed by NWT and is accessible from Martin's Pond.

Nature Trail A waymarked circular path allows good views of the reedbeds and open water areas. This path is shown on the map on the fact sheet available from NWT. A formal Nature Trail is planned for the future – contact NWT for details.

Plants Over 150 flowering plants recorded, including Marsh Arrow Grass, Skullcap, Ragged Robin, Marsh Marigold.
Birds Breeding Willow, Sedge and Reed Warblers, Ruddy Duck, Great Crested and Little Grebes.
Animals Water Vole, Water Shrew, Fox.
Other Frogs, toads and newts breed.

Under Threat The adjacent allotments are currently threatened by development.

Guide By prior arrangement with NWT (giving at least one week's notice)
Disabled Access No   **School Parties** No   **Parking** On adjacent roads
Toilets No   **Food** No

Further Information Fact sheets are available from NWT on receipt of an s.a.e.

Nottinghamshire
SELLERS WOOD

OS Ref SK524454   Landranger Sheet 129
Nearest Town Nottingham   **Size of Reserve** 14.1 hectares (35 acres)
Managed by Nottinghamshire Wildlife Trust (NWT) and Nottingham City Council
Access The Nature Trails are open to the public

S ellers Wood is a fine example of broadleaved semi-natural woodland on varying Permian soils, which support a very varied flora, making the site one of regional importance. It is designated an SSSI and a Local Nature Reserve (LNR).

Nature Trail There are 2 waymarked trails – 800 metres (½ mile) and 1.2 km (¾ mile). Nature Trail leaflets are available from NWT or from Nottingham City Council Information Office.

The reserve stands on a geological fault which is responsible for the striking differences in flora which occur on the differing soil types. A number of well-vegetated ponds provide drinking areas for the birds.
Plants A wide ranging flora includes Giant Bellflower, Early Purple Orchid, Yellow Archangel and Wood Anemone.
Birds Most common woodland species.

Guide No   **Disabled Access** No   **School Parties** No   **Parking** On adjacent public roads   **Toilets** No   **Food** No

Further Information Fact sheets are available from NWT on receipt of an s.a.e.

Nottinghamshire
SPA PONDS

OS Ref SK570634   Landranger Sheet 120
Nearest Town Mansfield   **Size of Reserve** 6.4 hectares (16 acres)
Managed by Nottinghamshire Wildlife Trust (NWT)   **Access** Open all year.
Visitors must keep to the main footpaths

T his reserve comprises three medieval ponds and one modern pond, all fed by a spring. The reserve runs adjacent to the River Mann. On the edge of the river a swamp has developed due to subsidence; this has been planted with osier with a view to managing the area as a withy bed.

Nature Trail There is no formal trail but a public footpath running through the reserve provides access. There is a map, showing the route of the path, on the fact sheet available from NWT.

Birds Kingfisher, Little Grebe.

Insects The reserve is an important site for dragonflies, many species being recorded.

Guide No   **Disabled Access** No   **School Parties** No   **Parking** Not on site
Toilets No   **Food** No

Further Information Fact sheets are available from NWT on receipt of an s.a.e.

Oxfordshire

CHINNOR HILL

OS Ref SP766005   Landranger Sheet 165
Nearest Town Thame   **Size of Reserve** 28 hectares (70 acres)
Managed by Berkshire, Buckinghamshire and Oxfordshire
Naturalists' Trust (BBONT)   **Access** Open all year

C hinnor Hill Reserve is situated on the Chiltern escarpment and consists of ash and oak woodland, beech woodland, chalk downland and mixed scrub. The hill provides views over the Vale of Aylesbury and towards Oxford.

Nature Trail There is a nature trail and a good network of public footpaths and bridleways, including a section of the Icknield Way.

The reserve supports a large number of bird species. The muddy tracks are often good places to look for animal tracks.

Guide Contact BBONT   **Disabled Access** No   **School Parties** By prior arrangement with BBONT; contact the Education Officer on Oxford (0865) 775476. A book entitled *Educational Opportunities on a Nature Reserve* is available from BBONT **Parking** In car park   **Toilets** No   **Food** No

Further Information Contact BBONT.

Oxfordshire

DRY SANDFORD PIT

OS Ref SU467995   Landranger Sheet 164
Nearest Town Abingdon   **Size of Reserve** 8 hectares (20 acres)
Managed by Berkshire, Buckinghamshire and Oxfordshire Naturalists'
Trust (BBONT)   **Access** Open all year

T he reserve consists of an old stone and sand quarry excavated in the 1930s. Habitats found on the reserve include a spring-fed lake and calcareous fen, ponds, woodland, mixed scrub, calcareous grassland, Sandford Brook and lichen heath.

Nature Trail There is no formal waymarked trail but a good network of footpaths provides access. The fen is a very delicate habitat so please do not walk over it. Please keep clear of the quarry face as rock falls can occur.

The reserve is a good example of the way in which wildlife habitats can be created by industrial activity.

Guide Contact BBONT   **Disabled Access** No   **School Parties** By prior arrangement with BBONT; contact the Education Officer on Oxford (0865) 775476. A book entitled *Educational Opportunities on Nature Reserves* is available from BBONT **Parking** Car park suitable for cars, not coaches   **Toilets** No   **Food** No

Further Information Contact BBONT. An information board with coloured photographs of the reserve's wildlife is situated near the entrance.

Oxfordshire

HARTSLOCK

OS Ref SU618795   Landranger Sheet 175
Nearest Town Goring   **Size of Reserve** 4.4 hectares (11 acres)
Managed by Berkshire, Buckinghamshire and Oxfordshire Naturalists'
Trust (BBONT)   **Access** The reserve is open to the public but please do not cross
the temporary fencelines which mark where research work is undertaken

A rich chalk grassland area on south and south-west facing slopes overlooking the Goring Gap towards the north-east end of the Berkshire Downs; a very useful place to look at the view and to study landscape and land use. There is also a small area of woodland and scrub.

Nature Trail There is no formal waymarked trail. There are usually sheep on the reserve; please do not disturb them.

Plants The grassland supports a wide variety of flowers including Cowslip, Harebell, Clustered Bellflower, Autumn Gentian, Birdsfoot Trefoil and Horseshoe Vetch. **Butterflies** Over 20 species recorded.

Guide Contact BBONT   **Disabled Access** No   **School Parties** By prior arrangement with BBONT; contact the Education Officer on Oxford (0865) 775476. A book entitled *Educational Opportunities on Nature Reserves* is available from BBONT **Parking** On roadside or at Goring Station   **Toilets** No   **Food** No

Further Information Contact BBONT.

Oxfordshire

HENRY STEPHEN/C.S. LEWIS RESERVE

OS Ref SP560065   Landranger Sheet 164
Nearest Town Oxford   **Size of Reserve** 3 hectares (7½ acres)
Managed by Berkshire, Buckinghamshire and Oxfordshire Naturalists'
Trust (BBONT)   **Access** Open all year

T he focal point of this reserve is the pond which is rich in aquatic flora and fauna and provides an ideal site for pond-dipping. Behind the pond, a mixed woodland extends up the hill, and is thought to be a remnant of the ancient royal forest of Shotover. It supports a good population of woodland birds and small mammals. The reserve was once owned by C.S. Lewis and it is said that he and his friend, J.R.R. Tolkien, dreamed up the worlds of Narnia and Middle Earth on this site.

Nature Trail There is no waymarked trail but well-defined paths cross the reserve, providing access to all habitats.

Plants Giant Horsetail.
Trees Oak, Beech, Birch, Elder, Alder, Sycamore, Horse Chestnut, Larch.
Birds Moorhen, Little Grebe.
Insects Good populations of dragonflies and damselflies.

Guide Contact BBONT   **Disabled Access** No   **School Parties** By prior arrangement with BBONT. Advance booking of this reserve is especially important in the summer term. Contact the Education Officer on Oxford (0865) 775476. A book entitled *Educational Opportunities on Nature Reserves* is available from BBONT
Parking Yes   **Toilets** No   **Food** No

Further Information Contact BBONT.

Oxfordshire

HOOK NORTON RAILWAY CUTTING

OS Ref SP360320   Landranger Sheet 151
Nearest Town Chipping Norton   **Size of Reserve** 7.7 hectares (19 acres)
Managed by Berkshire, Buckinghamshire and Oxfordshire Naturalists'
Trust (BBONT)   **Access** Open all year

T he reserve consists of two sections of a disused railway line. Habitats include developing woodland and limestone grassland with developing scrub. The remains of a large viaduct can be seen adjacent to the northern end of the reserve.

Nature Trail The two sections of reserve can be visited separately or treated as one long walk. The floor of the cutting provides easy walking.

Plants Mosses and Ferns, including the Male Fern and Hartstongue Fern. The limestone grassland is rich in herbs.
Trees Oak, Maple, Ash, Willow.
Insects There are good populations of bees and butterflies, including Marbled White.

Guide Contact BBONT **Disabled Access** No **School Parties** By prior arrangement with BBONT; contact the Education Officer on Oxford (0865) 775476. A book entitled *Educational Opportunities on Nature Reserves* is available from BBONT
Parking For both sections of reserve **Toilets** No **Food** No

Further Information Contact BBONT.

Oxfordshire
IFFLEY MEADOWS

OS Ref SP524037 Landranger Sheet 164
Nearest Town The reserve is in Oxford **Size of Reserve** 33 hectares (82 acres)
Managed by Berkshire, Buckinghamshire and Oxfordshire Naturalists'
Trust (BBONT) **Access** The reserve is open to the public but is liable to flooding in
wet weather

The reserve consists of an ancient wet meadow lying between two arms of the River Thames in Oxford.

Nature Trail There is no formal trail but a public footpath runs the length of the reserve. Please take utmost care not to trample the Fritillaries, especially when they are in flower.

The main interest of the site is the Snakeshead Fritillary which used to grow in profusion over the whole area. They are now concentrated around the centre of the northern section, the numbers having been decimated by picking and mismanagement. This is one of the few sites where these rare and beautiful flowers can still be found in the wild. The best time to see them is April to mid-May.

Guide Contact BBONT **Disabled Access** No **School Parties** By prior arrangement with BBONT; contact the Education Officer on Oxford (0865) 775476. A book entitled *Educational Opportunities on Nature Reserves* is available from BBONT
Parking By Donnington Bridge **Toilets** In Oxford City Centre **Food** In Oxford City Centre

Further Information Contact BBONT.

Oxfordshire
THE WARBURG RESERVE

OS Ref SU720880   Landranger Sheet 175
Nearest Town Henley-on-Thames   **Size of Reserve** 102.8 hectares (257 acres)
Managed by Berkshire, Buckinghamshire and Oxfordshire Naturalists'
Trust (BBONT)   **Access** Open all year

The reserve lies in a dry valley and consists of a complex mixture of woodland, scrub and grassland. The reserve has an interesting climate and can get frosts throughout the year because of the pooling of cold air in the valley bottom.

Nature Trail There is a nature trail. Trail Guides and lists of plants and animals are available.

Plants The mixed deciduous woodland supports a rich variety of woodland wild flowers, including several rare orchids.
Trees Oak, Ash, Beech, Birch, Field Maple, Yew, Spruce, Larch, Douglas Fir, Hazel, Wayfaring Tree, Spindle, Buckthorn, Wild Privet, Corsican Pine.
Animals Fallow and Muntjac Deer, Badger, Fox.
Other Adder, Grass Snake, Slow-worm, Lizard.

Information Centre There is a small Information Centre.

Guide Contact BBONT   **Disabled Access** No   **School Parties** Contact the resident Warden on Nettlebed (0491) 641727 in advance. A book entitled *Educational Opportunities on Nature Reserves* is available from BBONT   **Parking** In car park
Toilets No   **Food** No

Further Information Contact the resident Warden (as above), or BBONT.

Oxfordshire
WHITECROSS GREEN WOOD

OS Ref SP603145   Landranger Sheet 164
Nearest Town Oxford   **Size of Reserve** 62 hectares (156 acres)
Managed by Berkshire, Buckinghamshire and Oxfordshire Naturalists'
Trust (BBONT)   **Access** Open all year

The reserve straddles the county boundary between Oxfordshire and Buckinghamshire and consists of an ancient woodland, the whole of which is shown on a map dated 1590. The area has possibly been under forest cover for some 8,000 years. As the wood has developed over so many years, it supports a large number of plants and their associated invertebrates. There is a pond in the middle of the site. In the 1960s, much of the wood was planted with conifers, which the Trust is now removing.

Nature Trail There is no formal trail but forest rides run through the wood.

The reserve is adjacent to Warren Farm (The Oxfordshire Agricultural Education Centre) which is open to the public.

Guide Contact BBONT **Disabled Access** No **School Parties** Schools wishing to use the reserve and/or the farm should contact the Schools' Liaison Officer for the farm on Stanton St. John (086 735) 794, as well as informing the BBONT office. A book entitled *Educational Opportunities on Nature Reserves* is available from BBONT **Parking** In Warren Farm car park **Toilets** No **Food** No

Further Information Contact BBONT.

Shropshire

LLYNCLYS COMMON

OS Ref SJ270230 Landranger Sheet 126
Nearest Town Oswestry **Size of Reserve** 41 hectares (101 acres)
Managed by Shropshire Wildlife Trust (SWT) **Access** Open all year

---

L lynclys Common is a large wild area of gorse and bracken heath, with fine views over the Shropshire Plain and the hills of the Welsh Border. Along the western edge is a clearly recognisable section of Offa's Dyke, the ancient boundary between England and Wales. There are also areas of grass and woodland.

Nature Trail A network of tracks and footpaths covers the reserve.

Plants The reserve supports a good limestone grassland flora with several Orchids, including both species of Butterfly Orchid.
Birds Scrub woodland has a wide range of bird species, especially in summer – at least 6 Warbler species, Redstart, Pied Flycatcher.

Guide No **Disabled Access** No **School Parties** Only by prior arrangement with the Trust's WATCH group **Parking** In layby **Toilets** No **Food** No

Further Information Reserve leaflets are available from SWT.

Shropshire

MERRINGTON GREEN

OS Ref SJ465209 Landranger Sheet 126
Nearest Town Shrewsbury **Size of Reserve** 12 hectares (29 acres)
Managed by Shropshire Wildlife Trust (SWT) **Access** Open all year

M errington Green is an area of old common land which has developed into scrubby woodland. It rises some 15 metres (50 feet) above the surrounding plain. A lower area of the common contains three pools.

Nature Trail 2 km (1¼ miles), waymarked by numbered posts. The figure-of-eight trail starts and finishes at the car park. The trail can be muddy in places so suitable footwear is essential. Detailed Nature Trail Guides, with maps, are available from SWT.

Plants Rosebay Willowherb, Bracken, Gorse, Rushes, Brooklime, Bramble, Marsh Thistle, Marsh Horsetail, Water Plantain.
Trees Birch, Sallow, Oak, Elder, Hawthorn, Sycamore.
Birds Bullfinch, Kestrel, Curlew, Coot.
Animals Badger.
Insects Dragonflies and damselflies.
Butterflies Red Admiral, Small Tortoiseshell, Peacock, Comma.

Guide No   **Disabled Access** The first part of the trail (500 metres/⅓ mile) is accessible to disabled visitors   **School Parties** No   **Parking** In car park   **Toilets** No   **Food** No

Further Information Contact SWT.

Staffordshire
CASTERN WOOD

OS Ref SK116538   Landranger Sheet 119
Nearest Town Leek   **Size of Reserve** 20.6 hectares (51 acres)
Managed by Staffordshire Nature Conservation Trust (SNCT)   **Access** Open all year.
The more southerly section of the reserve is not open to visitors

C astern Wood is in two parts and consists of deciduous woodland, scrub and grassland in a steep-sided valley sloping down to a meander of the River Manifold. It was designated an SSSI in 1972. The reserve provides excellent views over the Manifold Valley.

Nature Trail There is no formal trail but paths round the reserve are marked, providing a walk of about 3 km (2 miles). Steps allow access to steep slopes but the walk is still very strenuous.

Plants Limestone plants such as Orchids, Cowslip, Dovesfoot Cranesbill, Rockrose, Wild Thyme, etc.
Birds Woodland birds, including Redstart, Pied Flycatcher and Owls.
Animals Bats, Fox.
Trees Ash, Sycamore, Field Maple, Lime.
Butterflies Of particular interest is the Northern Brown Argus.

Guide By prior arrangement with SNCT   **Disabled Access** Only to enjoy views from car park   **School Parties** Yes   **Parking** For about 40 cars on grass   **Toilets** No **Food** No

Further Information Reserve leaflets are available from SNCT.

Staffordshire
DOXEY MARSHES

OS Ref SJ912242   Landranger Sheet 127
Nearest Town Stafford   **Size of Reserve** 687 hectares (170 acres)
Managed by Staffordshire Nature Conservation Trust (SNCT)   **Access** Open all year

D oxey Marshes Reserve is bordered on three sides by the town of
Stafford and its suburbs, and on the fourth by the M6. The Marshes
show a complete progression from dry meadows, through damp meadows,
ditches and marshes, to reedbeds and open water. An observation hide
overlooks three artificial scrapes specially created to encourage various
species of bird to the reserve.

Nature Trail There is no formal trail but paths round the reserve are marked,
providing a walk of about 3 km (2 miles). The Marshes can be wet and muddy and
are liable to flood after heavy rain. Wellingtons are a must!

Main interest is to see waterfowl and waders (especially on migration). The hide
and a viewing platform provide good viewing facilities.

Guide By prior arrangement with SNCT   **Disabled Access** Most parts of the reserve
are accessible to disabled visitors   **School Parties** Yes – both for visits and practical
work. Contact SNCT for details   **Parking** For about 20 cars   **Toilets** No   **Food** No

Further Information Reserve leaflets are available from SNCT.

Warwickshire
ALVECOTE POOLS

OS Ref SK250043   Landranger Sheet 140
Nearest Town Atherstone   **Size of Reserve** 225 hectares (555 acres)
Managed by Warwickshire Nature Conservation Trust (WARNACT)   **Access** Open
all year. Public access is to the southern part of the reserve only (Pooley Fields)

T his reserve comprises a series of shallow freshwater pools along the
River Anker. The pools were formed as a result of mining
subsidence and together make a valuable habitat for aquatic plants and
insects. The area is also of outstanding importance as a wildfowl refuge,
with large overwintering flocks.

Nature Trail 800 metres (½ mile), waymarked with numbered posts which
correspond to the reserve guide available from WARNACT. Part of the trail is called
the Miners' Path because it was used by coal miners travelling to and from work.

The reserve exhibits many good examples of the ways in which nature has taken over and colonised an industrial landscape.

Plants Sphagnum, Bladderwort, Tussock Sedge, Common and Southern Marsh Orchids.
Birds Wildfowl – Swans, passage Waders, Kingfisher, Terns, Warblers.
Insects 14 species of dragonfly, 20 species of butterfly.
Other Fungi, including Fly Agaric.

Guide By prior arrangement with WARNACT **Disabled Access** No
School Parties By prior arrangement with WARNACT **Parking** For 30 cars
Toilets No **Food** No

Further Information Contact WARNACT.

Warwickshire
BISHOPS BOWL LAKES

OS Ref SP385588 Landranger Sheet 151
Nearest Town Leamington Spa **Size of Reserve** 50 hectares (123½ acres)
Managed by Warwickshire Nature Conservation Trust (WARNACT) in co-operation with the owners, Bishops Bowl Lakes Ltd **Access** Open all year. All fishing is by day ticket, and further information can be obtained at the Lakes' office

B ishops Bowl Lakes are operated as a commercial fishery formed round a disued lime quarry. Although the Lakes are not within a nature reserve, the owners are anxious to preserve the natural beauty of the area and the unique flora and fauna that it supports. Habitats include scrub/woodland and typical limestone grassland as well as open water.

Nature Trail About 2.4 km (1½ miles), unmarked. The route is marked on a map in the Nature Guide available from the Lakes' office or from WARNACT.

The area is visually very attractive. The sides of the lakes are steep rock faces of quarried limestone and the water in them is a bright blue green due to the clay particles suspended in the water.
Plants Limestone grassland flora, including Bee, Great Butterfly and Common Spotted Orchids, Autumn Gentian.
Birds Kingfisher, Reed and Sedge Warblers, Blackcap, Garden Warblers and wildfowl.
Butterflies Marbled White, Small Blue, Grizzled Skipper, Dingy Skipper, Green Hairstreak.

Under Threat A large area adjacent to Bishops Bowl Lakes was bulldozed in October 1988 to make way for a £50 million development – despite its being a proposed SSSI.

Information Centre A small office acts as an information centre.

Guide By prior arrangement with WARNACT **Disabled Access** No
School Parties By prior arrangement with WARNACT **Parking** For about 50 cars **Toilets** At site office **Food** Snacks available

Further Information Contact WARNACT.

Warwickshire

CRACKLEY WOOD

OS Ref SP290738   Landranger Sheet 139
Nearest Town Kenilworth   **Size of Reserve** 25 hectares (62 acres)
Managed by Warwickshire Nature Conservation Trust (WARNACT)
Access Open all year

C rackley Wood Reserve is an area of semi-natural woodland typical of woodland on acid soils. It was once part of the Forest of Arden.

Nature Trail About 1.2 km (¾ mile), unmarked. Nature Guide leaflets, showing the route, are available from WARNACT.

Plants Bluebell, Wood Sage, Wood Sorrel, Dog's Mercury, Yellow Pimpernel, Wood Anemone.
Birds Treecreeper, Willow Warbler, Chiffchaff, Tits, Siskin, Redpoll, 3 species of Woodpecker.
Animals Fox, Muntjac Deer, Badger.
Other Fungi, including Fly Agaric.

Guide By prior arrangement with WARNACT   **Disabled Access** No
School Parties By prior arrangement with WARNACT   **Parking** For 10-15 cars in laybys along Crackley Lane   **Toilets** No   **Food** No, but there are picnic tables in the wood.

Further Information Contact WARNACT.

Warwickshire

WELCOMBE HILLS

OS Ref SP208567   Landranger Sheet 151
Nearest Town Stratford-upon-Avon   **Size of Reserve** 135 hectares (333 acres)
Managed by Warwickshire Nature Conservation Trust (WARNACT). The site is owned and maintained by Stratford-upon-Avon District Council
Access Open all year

W elcombe Hills consists of undulating cattle-grazed pasture with scrub and woodland. Part of the hillside is scarred by many ridges and furrows which were created by ox-drawn ploughs in mediaeval times. The top of the ridge provides a panoramic view of the Avon Valley.

Nature Trail About 1.2 km (¾ mile), unmarked. Nature Guide leaflets are available from Stratford-upon-Avon District Council, or from WARNACT.

Plants Typical neutral grassland with Cowslip, Yarrow, Selfheal, Birdsfoot Trefoil,

Spotted Medick, Meadow Woodrush, Cuckoo-pint, Lesser Celandine, Ivy-leaved Toadflax, Wild Clematis, Lady's Bedstraw.
Trees Walnut, Beech, Ash, Sycamore, Pine, Oak, Horse Chestnut, Larch, Hornbeam, Lime.
Birds Kestrel, Wood Pigeon, Magpie, Great Spotted and Green Woodpeckers, Nuthatch, Owls, Thrushes (in winter).
Butterflies Gatekeeper, Meadow Brown, Small Heath.

Guide By prior arrangement with WARNACT   **Disabled Access** No
School Parties By prior arrangement with WARNACT   **Parking** For 20 cars
Toilets No   **Food** No, but there are picnic tables

Further Information Contact WARNACT or the Chief Planning Officer, Stratford-upon-Avon District Council, 5 Tyler Street, Stratford-upon-Avon, Warwickshire (tel. 0789 67575).

West Midlands
STONEBRIDGE MEADOW

OS Ref SP347756   Landranger Sheet 139
Nearest Town Coventry   **Size of Reserve** 7.7 hectares (19 acres)
Managed by Warwickshire Nature Conservation Trust (WARNACT) and Coventry City Council   **Access** Open all year

S tonebridge Meadow is an area of horse-grazed unimproved pasture and wet alder woodland by the River Sowe. The abundant wildlife led to its designation as a Local Nature Reserve (LNR) in 1987.

Nature Trail Just under 1.5 km (1 mile), unmarked. Nature Trail leaflets are available from WARNACT.

Plants Harebell, Tormentil, Betony, Lady's Bedstraw, Great Hairy Willow Herb, Yellow Flag Iris, Marsh Marigold, Marsh Speedwell (locally rare), Purple Loosestrife, Valerian, Meadow-rue.
Birds Sparrowhawk and typical scrub birds.
Trees Field Maple, Ash, Alder, Willow.
Butterflies Meadow Brown, Skipper.

Under Threat The reserve is constantly under threat from the urban spread of Coventry.

Guide By prior arrangement with WARNACT   **Disabled Access** No
School Parties By prior arrangement with WARNACT   **Parking** For 5 cars in layby on A45   **Toilets** No   **Food** No

Further Information Contact WARNACT.

1 Ely Nature Trail
2 Fulbourn
3 Grafham Water
4 Peakirk Waterfowl Gardens
5 Wicken Fen
6 The Backwarden
7 Fingringhoe Wick
8 John Weston
9 Warley Place
10 Cassiobury Park
11 Fir and Pond Woods
12 Stocker's Lake
13 Tring Reservoirs
14 Verulamium Park
15 Cley Marshes
16 Cockshoot Broad
17 East Wretham Heath
18 Filby Broad
19 Hickling Broad
20 Holme Dunes
21 Honeypot Wood
22 How Hill
23 Narborough Railway Line
24 Ranworth
25 Roydon Common
26 Thompson Common
27 Upton Fen
28 Wayland Wood
29 Welney Wildfowl Refuge
30 Bradfield Woods
31 Carlton Marshes
32 Redgrave and Lopham Fens

Hunstanto

K
Lyn

Wisbech

4

Peterborough

29
Welr

Ely
1

CAMBRIDGESHIRE

3   Huntingdon   5

Cambridge • Fulbo
2

HERTFORDSHIRE

13 Tring   St Albans

14 Potters 11
Watford   Bar

10 Brentu

12

Rickmansworth

EAST ANGLIA AND REGIONS

15

Holt

NORFOLK

Wroxham. 22 19
Woodbastwick. 16 Ludham
21 East 24 18
Dereham 27 Filby
Swaffham Norwich Acle
Vatton 28
26
17
Thetford Diss 31 Lowestoft
32

Bury St Edmunds

30 SUFFOLK

Colchester
8
SSEX 7 Walton-on-the-Naze

msford
6

Cambridgeshire
ELY NATURE TRAIL/ROSWELL PITS

OS Ref TL547805   Landranger Sheet 143
Nearest Town Ely   **Size of Reserve** 32 hectares (80 acres)
Managed by Cambridgeshire Wildlife Trust (CWT)   **Access** Open all year

This is a varied site around some old clay pits with open water, reedswamp, woodland, scrub and grassland areas which are rich in plant, insect and bird life. The reserve is situated on the outskirts of Ely on the high ground which formed the medieval 'Isle of Ely'. It overlooks former fenland now drained and cultivated.

Nature Trail 5 km (3 miles) or 1.5 km (1 mile), waymarked. Ely Nature Trail booklets are available from CWT. Some of the banks of Roswell Pits are very steep, the soil may slip, and the water is deep. Take good care of children.

Plant life is rich and varied with one or two rarities.
Birds Kingfisher, Grebes, Wildfowl, Warblers, Reedbed birds, Waders, Terns.
Butterflies Gatekeeper, Ringlet, Large Skipper, Whites, Small Tortoiseshell, Peacock, Red Admiral.
Other Dragonflies.

Guide No   **Disabled Access** No   **School Parties** No   **Parking** On roadside only
Toilets No   **Food** No

Further Information Contact CWT.

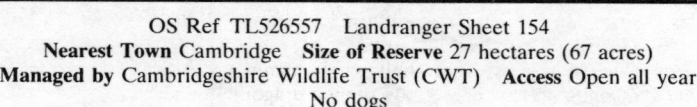

Cambridgeshire
FULBOURN

OS Ref TL526557   Landranger Sheet 154
Nearest Town Cambridge   **Size of Reserve** 27 hectares (67 acres)
Managed by Cambridgeshire Wildlife Trust (CWT)   **Access** Open all year
No dogs

Fulbourn is an Educational Nature Reserve consisting of drained fen with peaty chalk-rich soil, grassland and woodland. It provides a variety of wildlife habitats, including a pond.

Nature Trail There is an unmarked nature trail on the reserve. Leaflets are available from CWT. Many of the paths are fairly boggy after rain.

Plants Primrose, Wood Avens, Bugle, Wood Violet, Salad Burnet, Lady's Bedstraw, Quaking Grass, Bee Orchid, Adderstongue Fern, Birdsfoot Trefoil, Silverweed, Common Spotted and Southern Marsh Orchids.

Trees Norway Spruce, Scots Pine, Oak, Beech, Ash, Sycamore, Larch, Grey Poplar.
Birds Over 60 species recorded, including Yellowhammer, Spotted Flycatcher,
3 Woodpeckers, many species of Tit, Finch and Warbler, Kestrel, Tawny Owl.
Animals Stoat, Rabbit, Hare, Fox, Mole.
Butterflies 15 species recorded, including Yellow Brimstone, Peacock.

Guide By prior arrangement with CWT   **Disabled Access** No   **School Parties** A
prime function of the reserve is to serve as an educational resource for local schoolchildren and students   **Parking** On roadside verge   **Toilets** No   **Food** No

Further Information Information sheets are available form CWT.

Cambridgeshire
GRAFHAM WATER

OS Ref TL143672   Landranger Sheet 153
Nearest Town Huntingdon   **Size of Reserve** 150 hectares (370 acres)
Managed by Beds and Hunts Wildlife Trust (BHWT)   **Access** Open all year

G rafham Water is a large reservoir designated an SSSI. Only the
western and north-western shores are within the BHWT reserve. The
reserve is accessible from Mander Car Park on the south shore of the
reservoir. It is noted for its wintering wildfowl, and consists of creeks and
two areas of ancient woodland, as well as more recent plantations. The rest
of the reserve consists of rough grassland and arable farmland. There is
also a specially designed dragonfly pond.

Nature Trail There are 3 waymarked trails of varying lengths: the Mander Nature
Trail and Hide (about 1 hour), the Woodland Walk (about 2 hours), and the Savages
Spinney Nature Trail (about 2 hours). A booklet describing the trails and called
'Discover Grafham Water's Wildlife' is produced by the Cambridge Division of
Anglian Water and is available from them at Great Ouse House, Clarendon Road,
Cambridge CB2 2BL, or from BHWT.

Birds Osprey, large numbers of wintering wildfowl – Widgeon, Teal, Tufted Duck,
etc. Also Cormorant and woodland birds.
Animals Fox, Muntjac Deer, Rabbit, small mammals.
Other Dragonfly on new horse-shoe shaped dragonfly pond.

Guide By prior arrangement with BHWT   **Disabled Access** At Phimner Park (not
within the reserve but overlooking Grafham Water), there is a special hide for
disabled visitors   **School Parties** Contact Grafham Water Residential Centre
(AWB), Perry, Huntingdon, Cambridgeshire PE18 0BX   **Parking** At Mander and
at Hill Farm on the reserve   **Toilets** Yes   **Food** Yes

Further Information Contact the Cambridge Division of Anglian Water (tel. 0223
61561) or BHWT.

Cambridgeshire
PEAKIRK WATERFOWL GARDENS

OS Ref TF168065   Landranger Sheet 142
Nearest Town Peterborough   **Size of Reserve** 6.9 hectares (17 acres)
Managed by The Wildfowl Trust (WT)   **Access** Open daily from 9.30–17.30 in
summer or 1 hour before dusk in winter. Closed 24th and 25th December. No dogs
are allowed into the reserve. There is an admission charge for all visitors over 4 years
old but there are reductions for children, senior citizens and groups

Occupying the site of an old osier bed through which passed the ancient
Car Dyke, these peaceful gardens are a beautiful combination of
woodland and water. There is a 'wild' area, a wader scrape and a secluded
area to attract as wide a variety of birds as possible.

Nature Trail There is a trail of about 1 km (⅔ mile). WT Walkabout Guides are
available.

Plants Characteristic of fen waterside habitats – Purple Loosestrife, Meadowsweet,
Figwort, Great Willow-herb, etc.

Birds About 650 individual waterfowl of 110 species are kept, some very rare.
Among the special attractions are the Chilean Flamingos, the Black-necked and
Coscoroba Swans, the Andean Geese, and the Trumpeter Swans. Wild birds include
Goldfinch, Kingfisher, Pied and Yellow Wagtails and Cuckoo.

Animals In the Education Centre can be seen live displays of small animals
indigenous to wetland areas (mainly during the warmer months).

Other The WT at Peakirk is also responsible for maintenance of the famous Borough
Fen Duck Decoy. This is the largest decoy in the world, and the wetland area there
has been preserved since the 17th century. For details of Open Days, contact the WT
at Peakirk.

Under Threat Several areas of wetland and woodland close to the City of
Peterborough are under threat from development.

Guide Yes   **Disabled Access** All paths are tarmac-surfaced and level and wheelchairs
are available on loan   **School Parties** Welcomed. Arrangements should be made in
advance with the Education Officer at the Gardens. A set of slides with
accompanying notes can be borrowed by schools in advance of a visit, and topic
sheets are available for use during the visit. The Education Centre contains a
classroom and there are facilities for showing films and slide shows, plus other
activities such as pond-dipping and brass-rubbing. Schools are encouraged to bring
the same group of children at different times of the year to observe seasonal changes

Parking Yes   **Toilets** Yes, including for the disabled   **Food** Restaurant
open April to October, vending machines at other times   **Shop** Selling gifts and
books

Further Information Contact The Wildfowl Trust, The Waterfowl Gardens,
Peterborough, Cambridgeshire PE6 7NP (tel. 0733 252271).

Cambridgeshire

WICKEN FEN

OS Ref TL563705   Landranger Sheet 143
Nearest Town Cambridge   **Size of Reserve** 244.8 hectares (605 acres)
Managed by The National Trust (NT)   **Access** Open daily (except Christmas Day).
Access is by permit available from The William Thorpe Building (£1.50 or 50p for
children under 17) on arrival. NT members admitted free. Mosquitoes can be a
hazard between June and September.

W icken Fen is one of the oldest nature reserves in Britain. The main
part of the reserve is the only remnant of the once extensive fens of
the Great Level remaining undrained and readily accessible to the public.
The variety of fenland habitats can be found, ranging from open water to
woodland, making it particularly rich in plant and invertebrate life and very
attractive to birds.

Nature Trail The 3-km (2-mile) circular trail runs round the main part of the
reserve, Sedge Fen. There are several bench seats sited round the trail. The Fen can
be very wet underfoot at all times of the year so waterproof footwear is
recommended. There is also a 1.2-km (¾-mile) Boardwalk Trail, specifically
designed for wheelchair users, but also providing an all-weather circuit for those with
limited time or inadequate footwear. Trail Guides are available from the William
Thorpe building.

Plants Comfrey, Ragged Robin, Meadow Rue, Marsh Orchid, Bladderwort, Lesser
Reedmace, Marsh Marigold, Brooklime, Bog Myrtle, Guelder Rose.
Trees Ash, Oak, Bay Willow, Birch, Alder.
Birds Great and Lesser Spotted Woodpeckers, Long-tailed Tit, Bullfinch, Bearded
Tit, Swallow, Sand Martin, Wildfowl, Waders, Hen Harrier.
Butterflies Yellow Brimstone, Large Skipper.
Other Dragonfly.

Under Threat The major threat to the reserve is the general lowering of the area's
water-table due to improved drainage of the surrounding farmland. This leads to the
Fen drying out and becoming unsuitable for the characteristic plants of damp
conditions.

Information Centre The William Thorpe Building houses a comprehensive display
about the reserve's history and present-day management.

Guide Contact the Head Warden, Warden's House, Lode Lane, Wicken, Ely,
Cambridgeshire CB7 5XP (tel. 0353 720274)   **Disabled Access** The Boardwalk Trail
is specially designed for wheelchair users and at least 2 of the observation hides are
accessible   **School Parties** By prior arrangement with the Education Team on Ely
(0353) 723095, or at the address above   **Parking** For 100 cars, with space for coaches
Toilets Yes, including for the disabled   **Food** No, but picnic tables are provided
round the edge of the car park

Further Information Contact the Head Warden (as above), or the National Trust.

Essex
THE BACKWARDEN

OS Ref TL781041   Landranger Sheet 167
Nearest Town Chelmsford   **Size of Reserve** 12 hectares (30 acres)
Managed by The Essex Naturalists' Trust (ENT)   **Access** Open all year

The Backwarden is an area of relic heathland owned by The National Trust. Habitats include relic heath, woodland, blackthorn thicket, pools formed from old marl workings, bogs and a marsh. The area is part of Danbury Common SSSI. The considerable variety of habitats means the reserve still supports a rich and varied wildlife.

Nature Trail A circular trail of about 1.2 km (¾ mile) begins from the car park and is marked by a series of yellow discs on trees, and arrows at certain points. Nature Trail Guides are available from ENT (25p).

Plants Germander Speedwell, Herb Bennet, Herb Robert, Black and White Bryony, Betony, Wood Mellick, Butcher's Broom, Enchanter's Nightshade.
Trees Silver Birch, Aspen, Holly, Alder Buckthorn, Crab Apple, Oak, Ash, Hazel, Hornbeam, Field Maple.
Birds Blackcap, Garden Warbler, Lesser Whitethroat, Nightingale, Mallard, Long-tailed Tit, Reed Bunting.
Animals Dormouse, Rabbit.
Butterflies Comma, Gatekeeper, Small Heath, Small Copper, Common Blue, Essex Skipper, Brimstone.
Other Fungi.

Guide By prior arrangement with ENT   **Disabled Access** No   **School Parties** No
Parking Yes   **Toilets** No   **Food** No

Further Information Contact ENT.

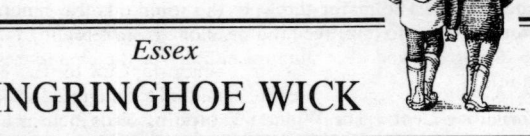

Essex
FINGRINGHOE WICK

OS Ref TM041195   Landranger Sheet 168
Nearest Town Colchester   **Size of Reserve** 50.5 hectares (125 acres)
Managed by The Essex Naturalists' Trust (ENT)   **Access** Open daily (except Monday) 9.00–16.30. Open Bank Holiday Mondays but closed following Tuesday. Closed 25th and 26th December. Organised party visits are welcome on Tuesday, Thursday, Friday and Saturday. Visitors are asked to make a donation

Nature Trail There are 3 waymarked trails, including one for disabled visitors. Nature Trail leaflets (25p) are available for all 3 trails. Highlights include bird hides, a route through plant and butterfly-rich heathland, several rich ponds and superb views over the Colne estuary. There are seats at places of special interest.

Fingringhoe Wick is protected as part of the Colne Estuary SSSI.
Birds Nightingales may be heard/seen in spring or early summer. In all, 200 bird species have been recorded.
Animals Fox, Stoat, Weasel, Badger (occasionally).
Insects Dragonfly.

Information Centre The Fingringhoe Centre is the headquarters of ENT. It houses an Interpretative Area, an illuminated display and a reference library, as well as an information and sales counter.

Guide Yes   **Disabled Access** Yes   **School Parties** By prior arrangement with the Secretary, ENT. Both indoor and outdoor projects and activities can be arranged for school groups   **Parking** Yes   **Toilets** Yes   **Food** No

Further Information Contact The Secretary or Warden at ENT. Flora and fauna check-lists are also available (25p).

Essex
JOHN WESTON

OS Ref TM265235   Landranger Sheet 169
Nearest Town Walton-on-the-Naze   **Size of Reserve** 3.6 hectares (9 acres)
Managed by The Essex Naturalists' Trust (ENT)   **Access** Open all year

The reserve consists of an area of blackthorn and bramble thickets, rough grassland and ponds, and is part of Hamford Water SSSI. The whole Naze area is a public open space owned by the Tendring District Council. The John Weston Reserve area is an example of a small natural habitat which is fast disappearing elsewhere. The reserve is named after the late John Weston, a leading naturalist in Essex and in the ENT.

Nature Trail A circular waymarked trail runs round the Naze, including the John Weston Reserve. Marker posts and directions are placed along the route. The path runs along the cliff top and walkers should take care not to approach the cliff edge. Naze Nature Trail leaflets are available from ENT.

The Essex coast is internationally important for birds.
Birds John Weston has become a landfall for migrant birds, such as the Firecrest, and a wide variety of winter migrants. Nesting birds include Lapwing, Redshank, Sedge and Reed Warblers.
Butterflies Common Blue, Meadow Brown, Essex Skipper, Painted Lady, Red Admiral, Peacock, Small Tortoiseshell.
Other Fossils.

Guide No   **Disabled Access** No   **School Parties** No   **Parking** Yes   **Toilets** Yes
Food From shop. There is also a picnic area

Further Information Contact ENT.

Essex
WARLEY PLACE

OS Ref TQ583906   Landranger Sheet 177
Nearest Town Brentwood   **Size of Reserve** 6.5 hectares (16 acres)
Managed by The Essex Naturalists' Trust (ENT)   **Access** By prior arrangement with
the Warden, Phil Butler, 218 Lodge Lane, Collier Row, Romford (tel. 0708 754391)

Warley Place is an old garden that was once owned by Miss Ellen Willmott who died in 1934. As a keen horticulturalist, she was responsible for introducing to Warley (and to Britain) many exotic plants, some of which are still to be found on the reserve. Habitats include woodland and pond.

Nature Trail 5 km (3 miles), waymarked. Some parts of the trail are dangerous because of hidden cellars and decaying walls. Please keep to the footpaths and follow the waymarked trail. Nature Trail Guides are available from ENT (25p).

An observation hide overlooks the wettest surviving area of the artificial ponds.
Plants Marsh Marigold, Lesser Celandine, Male Fern, Periwinkle, Abraham, Isaac and Jacob, Ramson, Three-cornered Leek, Nettle-leaved Bellflower, Hartstongue Fern, Rosebay Willowherb, Purple Toothwort, Himalayan Balsam.
Trees Copper Beech, Indian Cedar, Sycamore, Ash, Tree of Heaven, Oak, Walnut, Sweet Chestnut.
Birds Woodpeckers, Treecreeper, Nuthatch, Tawny Owl, Wren, Song Thrush, Goldfinch.
Animals Badger.
Butterflies Comma, Peacock, Common Blue, Holly Blue, Orange-tip, Small Heath, Meadow Brown, Gatekeeper.

Guide No   **Disabled Access** No   **School Parties** By prior arrangement with the Warden (as above)   **Parking** Adjacent to Thatchers Arms Public House   **Toilets** No **Food** No

Further Information Contact the Warden (as above) or ENT.

Hertfordshire
CASSIOBURY PARK

OS Ref TQ090970   Landranger Sheet 166
Nearest Town Watford   **Size of Reserve** 5 hectares (12 acres) but the
whole of Cassiobury Park covers 50 hectares (123 acres)
Managed by Herts and Middlesex Wildlife Trust (HMWT)   **Access** Open all year

Cassiobury Park Nature Reserve is a small and fairly inaccessible area of a large park situated between the River Colne and the Grand

Union Canal on the edge of a large urban area. The park provides excellent birdwatching, especially in winter. There are several old watercress beds, and one still in use.

Nature Trail A waymarked trail of about 2 km (1¼ miles) is in preparation. Contact HMWT for details.

Birds Winter birds are outstanding – Water Rail, Water Pipit, Siskin, Redpoll, Snipe, Teal.
Other Excellent for dragonflies and other invertebrates.

Guide No **Disabled Access** There are good, level, hard-surfaced public footpaths to the best areas **School Parties** No special arrangements **Parking** Yes **Toilets** In park **Food** No

Further Information Information leaflets are currently in preparation. Contact HMWT for details.

Hertfordshire

FIR AND POND WOODS

OS Ref TL276011 and TL278005   Landranger Sheet 166
Nearest Town Potters Bar   **Size of Reserve** 27 hectares (67 acres)
Managed by Herts and Middlesex Wildlife Trust (HMWT)   **Access** Open all year

An area of oak-hornbeam woodland occupying a south-facing slope with Turkey Brook at its foot. At the lower end of the slope is an area of rough acid grassland known as The Meadow, and there is also a large woodland pond. The whole area is a remnant of the once-extensive Enfield Chase forest.

Nature Trail There is no formal waymarked trail but attractive woodland footpaths provide good access to the woods.

Birds Almost all woodland species occur as well as water birds, including Little Grebe.
Animals Muntjac Deer.
Trees Oak, Hornbeam, Birch, Beech, Field Maple, Alder.
Insects Over 150 species of moth and 19 butterflies.
Other Frogs, toads, newts. Excellent for fungi.

Guide By prior arrangement with HMWT **Disabled Access** No **School Parties** By prior arrangement with HMWT **Parking** In Coopers Lane Road **Toilets** No **Food** No

Further Information Reserve leaflets are available form HMWT.

Hertfordshire

STOCKER'S LAKE

OS Ref TQ044931   Landranger Sheet 166
Nearest Town Rickmansworth   **Size of Reserve** 38 hectares (94 acres)
Managed by Herts and Middlesex Wildlife Trust (HMWT)   **Access** There is a public
footpath at the north-eastern end, but access to the reserve itself is by free permit
from HMWT (send s.a.e). There is free access to public lakes – Bury Lake
(Aquadrome) and Batchworth Lake.

S tocker's Lake is a flooded shallow gravel pit, with many refuge islands, situated in the Colne Valley. It is designated a Local Nature Reserve (LNR) and is an important site for wildfowl.

Nature Trail A trail of about 2 km (1¼ miles) is being prepared. Meanwhile, good views of all the species of interest can be obtained from the public footpath. A leaflet is also being prepared. Contact HMWT for details.

Plants Marginal vegetation is very important for invertebrates.
Birds Nearly 170 species recorded. Good numbers and variety of most wildfowl species at all times of the year, but especially winter. Small heronry.

Guide For groups only, by prior arrangement with HMWT   **Disabled Access** No
School Parties By prior arrangement with HMWT   **Parking** Follow street signs to
Aquadrome car park   **Toilets** In Aquadrome grounds   **Food** In Rickmansworth

Further Information Contact HMWT.

Hertfordshire

TRING RESERVOIRS

OS Ref SP905132 and SP920135   Landranger Sheet 166
Nearest Town Tring   **Size of Reserve** 150 hectares (370 acres)
Managed by Herts and Middlesex Wildlife Trust (HMWT)
Access Almost all open access

T he reserve comprises a series of man-made lakes constructed in the 19th century for the Grand Union Canal. The area is famous for birds, but other species are well represented, especially fish and invertebrates. It is designated an SSSI and (currently) a National Nature Reserve (NNR). Almost all the banks are accessible, and there are public viewing hides on the west side of Tringford Reservoir.

Nature Trail 3 km (2 miles), unmarked. A new Nature Trail leaflet is in preparation. Currently available is an old leaflet produced by The Nature Conservancy Council (NCC) and available from HMWT.

Plants Special wetland species.

Birds Very attractive during migration, and for wintering wildfowl. Osprey occur annually.

Information Centre At Tring Museum.

Guide No   **Disabled Access** No   **School Parties** No special arrangements
Parking Three main areas with other smaller car parking places   **Toilets** Nearby in Tring   **Food** Nearby in Tring

Further Information Contact HMWT.

Hertfordshire
VERULAMIUM PARK

OS Ref TL136072   Landranger Sheet 166
Nearest Town The park is in St. Albans   **Size of Reserve** 100 hectares (247 acres)
Managed by Herts and Middlesex Wildlife Trust (HMWT)   **Access** Open all year

Verulamium Park is a public park with a lake and Roman remains. Wildfowl can easily be seen on the ornamental lake.

Nature Trail 2 km (1¼ miles), unmarked. Nature Trail leaflets are available from the nearby Roman Museum or from HMWT at Grebe House in St. Albans.

Guide For groups only, by prior arrangement with HMWT
Disabled Access Yes   **School Parties** By prior arrangement with HMWT
Parking Two public car parks   **Toilets** Yes   **Food** Yes

Further Information New leaflet being prepared. Contact HMWT for details.

Norfolk
CLEY MARSHES

OS Ref TG054441   Landranger Sheet 133
Nearest Town Holt   **Size of Reserve** 312 hectares (776 acres)
Managed by Norfolk Naturalists' Trust (NNT)   **Access** Open daily from April–October, 10.00–17.00. Closed Mondays (except Bank Holidays). Permits may be obtained in advance from the Warden, Watcher's Cottage, Cley-next-the-Sea, Holt – tel. Cley (0263) 740380 – or from the Visitors' Centre at the main car park. Annual and winter permits are available at the Warden's discretion. Please keep to the paths at all times. No dogs

The Cley Marshes Nature Reserve is situated on the North Norfolk Coast and consists of a shingle bank, saltmarsh, pools and dykes of varying degrees of salinity. It is an exceptional site for bird life. Large numbers of migrating waders and summer visitors may be seen. The area is also of considerable interest for coastal and saltmarsh flora.

Nature Trail There is no formal trail – boardwalks provide access to numerous observation hides.

The bird life is the chief interest of the reserve. There are 11 hides, including one for the disabled and 2 public hides.
Plants Sea Aster, Sea Lavender, Sea Sandwort, Sea Pea, Sea Plantain, Mud Rush, Water Crowfoot, Reed, False Fox Sedge, Sea Club-rush, Yellow-horned Poppy.
Birds Spring and winter migrants – numerous waders and wildfowl. Breeding birds include Avocet, Common Tern, Bittern, Bearded Tit.

Information Centre There is an Information Centre on the main road (A149).

Guide By prior arrangement with the Warden (as above)   **Disabled Access** One hide is suitable   **School Parties** By prior arrangement with the Warden (as above)
Parking Plenty
Toilets At beach car park   **Food** Beach café

Further Information Reserve leaflets, with maps, are available from NNT.

Norfolk
COCKSHOOT BROAD

OS Ref TG345157   Landranger Sheet 134
Nearest Town Wroxham   **Size of Reserve** The Broad is included in the Ranworth Nature Reserve of 130 hectares (320 acres)
Managed by Ranworth Reserve is owned by Norfolk Naturalists' Trust (NNT) but the Cockshoot Broad conservation project, including the construction of a boardwalk giving public access, was carried out by the Broads Authority (BA)
Access Open all year

C ockshoot Broad is part of the Bure Marshes National Nature Reserve (NNR) and is within an area known as Ranworth Reserve (see page 178) which is owned by NNT. Cockshoot has been the subject of a conservation project carried out by the BA, involving removal of its surface mud and isolation of the Broad from the River Bure. Cockshoot Broad and Dyke now have crystal clear water teeming with wildlife. The Broad is surrounded by fen and carr woodland.

Nature Trail The ony public access to the Broad is by way of a boardwalk running alongside Cockshoot Dyke, arriving at an observation hide positioned on the edge of Cockshoot Broad. This walk is about 1.2 km (¾ mile) long and starts from the car park at Woodbastwick. There is a sign at the start of the walkway.

Plants Yellow and White Waterlilies.
Birds Heron, Ducks, Swans, Coots, Moorhens and other water birds.
Animals Invertebrates.

Guide For group visits, by prior arrangement with BA   **Disabled Access** Boardwalk is flat and suitable for wheelchair users   **School Parties** By prior arrangement with BA **Parking** For about 16 cars. There are also mooring facilities at the end of Cockshoot Dyke for people visiting by boat   **Toilets** In nearby villages of Ranworth and Salhouse   **Food** In nearby villages

Further Information Leaflets, with maps, are available from BA. Interpretative boards have been put up in the hide explaining the project and the wildlife that can be seen on the Broad.

Norfolk

EAST WRETHAM HEATH

OS Ref TL913887   Landranger Sheet 144
Nearest Town Thetford   **Size of Reserve** 147 hectares (363 acres)
Managed by Norfolk Naturalists' Trust (NNT)   **Access** Open 10.00–17.00 every day except Tuesdays. Permits are obtainable from the Warden. Please keep to the paths at all times. No dogs

E ast Wretham Heath is an area of breckland grassland and open heath with coniferous and deciduous woodland, meres and the now-crumbling runways of a wartime aerodrome. These features combined provide habitats for a wide variety of plants (over 250 species) and birds.

Nature Trail There are 2 waymarked trails with accompanying leaflets available from NNT at the reserve or from the Trust shop, Cathedral Close, Norwich.

Plants Mulleins, Hound's-tongue, Long-leaved Thyme, Dyer's Greenweed, Rue-leaved Saxifrage.
Birds Sparrowhawk, Crossbill, Nightjar. Occasional visitors include Wheatear, Stone Curlew, Stonechat and Whinchat, Grey Shrike.
Animals Roe Deer, Fox, Stoat, Weasel, Red Squirrel.

Information Centre Yes

Guide By prior arrangement with the Warden on Great Hockham (095 382) 339
Disabled Access One of the trails (about 1 km/⅔ mile) is suitable for visually handicapped visitors   **School Parties** By prior arrangement with the Warden on the above number   **Parking** For 30 cars   **Toilets** No   **Food** No

Further Information Reserve leaflets (price 40p) are available from NNT at the reserve or from the NNT shop, Cathedral Close, Norwich.

Norfolk
FILBY BROAD

OS Ref TG461137   Landranger Sheet 134
Nearest Town Acle
Managed by Broads Authority (BA)   **Access** Open all year

F ilby Broad provides a walk through fen and woodland to a birdwatching hide overlooking open water.

Nature Trail About 400 metres (¼ mile) of boardwalk. There is a sign at the beginning of the walkway.

Birds Duck and other water birds.

Guide By prior arrangement with BA   **Disabled Access** Boardwalk is flat and suitable for wheelchair users   **School Parties** By prior arrangement with BA
Parking For about 30 cars   **Toilets** No   **Food** Available in village of Filby

Further Information Contact BA. There will be interpretative panels in the hide.

Norfolk
HICKLING BROAD

OS Ref TG428222   Landranger Sheet 134
Nearest Town Ludham   **Size of Reserve** 532 hectares (1,308 acres)
Managed by Norfolk Naturalists' Trust (NNT)   **Access** Open April to October 9.00–18.00 every day except Tuesdays; November to March open Thursdays and Sundays only. Permits are needed. Available from the Warden's Office at the reserve. Please keep to the paths at all times. No dogs

H ickling Broad is the longest stretch of open water in Broadland, with surrounding large areas of sedge, reed and grazing marshes as well as woodland and artificial lakes (scrapes) for wildfowl. The area is designated a National Nature Reserve (NNR).

Nature Trail There are 2 land-based trails (4 km/2½ miles and 1.5 km/1 mile) and one Water Trail (2½ hours – May to September only). The Water Trail takes visitors to bird hides, reedbeds and an 18-metre (60-foot) observation tower in woodland. As the Water Trail is limited to 12 people, advance booking is essential. Telephone Hickling (069 261) 276.

Traditional reed and sedge management can be seen. The reserve is an important birdwatching area with a number of resident species as well as summer visitors and passage migrants. There are several observation hides.
Plants Milk Parsley, Crested Buckler Fern, Meadow Thistle, Cotton Grass, Marsh Orchids.

Birds Wintering wildfowl – Bewick's and Whooper Swans, Ducks (including Smew), Hen Harrier, Mergansers, Goosanders. Summer visitors – Terns and Warblers, passage migrants such as Waders.
Butterflies Early summer – Swallowtail. August – Purple Hairstreak.
Other Common Hawkmoths.

Information Centre Information is available from the Warden's Office.

Guide By prior arrangement with the Warden on Hickling (069 261) 276
Disabled Access No   **School Parties** By prior arrangement with the Warden
Parking For over 100 cars   **Toilets** At car park   **Food** No

Further Information Reserve leaflets, with maps, are available from the Warden's Office at the reserve, or from the NNT shop, Cathedral Close, Norwich.

Norfolk

HOLME DUNES

OS Ref TF697438   Landranger Sheet 132
Nearest Town Hunstanton   **Size of Reserve** 160 hectares (550 acres)
Managed by Norfolk Naturalists' Trust (NNT)   **Access** Open daily 10.00–17.00.
Please keep to paths at all times. No dogs. Permits are needed. Available from the Warden's House (The Firs) at the reserve – tel. Holme (048 525) 240. Visitors not wishing to purchase permits are requested to keep to the beach and waymarked public footpath

H olme Dunes Reserve is on the North Norfolk Coast and is part of the SSSI. It is predominantly sand dunes with saltmarsh, pine shelter-belt, grazing marsh and brackish pools. The site is important for spring and autumn bird migration, with seasonal rarities possible.

Nature Trail There is no formal trail but paths give access to birdwatching hides. The Norfolk Coast Path crosses the reserve.

The reserve incorporates Holme Bird Observatory (administered by the Norfolk Ornithologists' Association). There are several hides overlooking the wader pools, giving excellent opportunities for close observation.
Plants Plant life is typical of sandy beaches and saltmarsh, including several orchid species and the rare Grey Hair-grass. Other species include Hound's-tongue, Centaury and Sea Rocket.
Birds Winter – Snow Bunting, Twite, Brent Goose, Short-eared Owl, plus huge flocks of shore Waders. Spring – migrant Warblers and Chats. Autumn – Waders such as Greenshank, Little Ringed Plover and Green Sandpiper, plus passerines and seabirds.

Information Centre Information is available from the Warden at The Firs.

Guide By prior arrangement with the Warden   **Disabled Access** No   **School Parties** By prior arrangement with the Warden   **Parking** There are 3 parking areas, giving space for about 115 cars   **Toilets** At beach car park   **Food** No

Further Information Reserve leaflets, with maps, are available from the Warden's House or from the NNT shop, Cathedral Close, Norwich.

Norfolk
HONEYPOT WOOD

OS Ref TF934143   Landranger Sheet 132
Nearest Town East Dereham   **Size of Reserve** 9 hectares (23 acres)
Managed by Norfolk Naturalists' Trust (NNT)   **Access** Open all year. Please keep to the paths at all times. No dogs

Honeypot Wood is a small area of ancient woodland with a long history of traditional management of ash/oak standards with hazel/field maple coppice. This long history of coppicing has resulted in the development of a rich ground flora which is particularly attractive in spring. An adjacent wartime airfield has left the area with bunkers and concrete rides, adding further habitats to the wood.

Nature Trail There are unmarked paths round the wood which can be very wet in winter months. Special 'Honeypot Trail for Children' leaflets are available.

Honeypot Wood is coppiced on a 7-year cycle, about 3 acres per year, producing about 500 faggots used as mattressing for river banks and coastal erosion control by Anglian Water.
Plants Dog's Mercury, Bluebell, Wood Anemone, Twayblades, Herb Paris, Broad Helleborine.
Trees Hazel, Ash, Oak, Field Maple.
Birds Long-tailed, Blue and Great Tits, Yellowhammer, Chiffchaff, Willow Warbler, Great Spotted Woodpecker.

Guide No   **Disabled Access** Concrete paths and rides suitable for wheelchair users
School Parties Can be self-guided round wood with children's leaflet   **Parking** For 4 cars only in the wood – roadside parking unsatisfactory   **Toilets** No   **Food** No

Further Information Reserve leaflets are available from NNT.

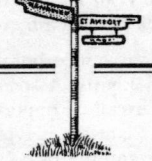

Norfolk
HOW HILL

OS Ref TG373190   Landranger Sheet 134
Nearest Town Ludham   **Size of Reserve** 148 hectares (365 acres)
Managed by Broads Authority (BA)   **Access** Open April, May and October weekends, bank holidays and local half-term; June to September every day

How Hill is described as The Environmental Centre for the Broads. It consists of a house, run by the How Hill Trust as a residential centre for children and adults, plus a nature reserve. The reserve provides examples of all the Broads habitats: open water (Cromes Broad, Reedham

Water, River Ant), fen (reed and sedge beds, managed in the traditional way), carr woodland and grazing marshes. The reserve is excellent for viewing all Broadland wildlife.

Nature Trail There is a land-based Nature Trail (1½–2 hours), and a Wildlife Water Trail (50 minutes) which includes a short walk to a birdwatching hide overlooking a flooded water meadow. As the boat takes only 8 people, advanced bookings are advised (tel. 069 262 763). Walking Nature Trail booklets, with maps, are available from How Hill. All interpretation of the Water Trail is done by the warden/guide who operates the boat.

How Hill Environmental Centre, run by the How Hill Trust, runs day and residential educational courses on environmental matters, as well as general residential courses open to the public. There are 3 windpumps and some ornamental Water Gardens (open occasionally) in the grounds.
Plants Yellow and white Waterlilies, Milk Parsley, Yellow Flag Iris.
Birds Marsh Harrier, Hen Harrier, Bearded Tit, Reed Bunting, Lapwing, Cormorant, Grebe, Heron, Common Tern.
Animals Invertebrates, living in dykes.
Other Swallowtail Butterfly, Norfolk Aeschna Dragonfly, Brown Hawker Dragonfly.

Information Centre Toad Hole Cottage Marshman's Museum acts as a mini-information centre as well as providing an impression of the home and working life of a marshman and his family about 100 years ago. The Museum is also a sales point for tickets for walking and water trails, books, maps, postcards and souvenirs.

Guide For group visits, by prior arrangement with the How Hill Trust, How Hill, Ludham, Gt. Yarmouth NR29 5PG. Tel. St. Benets (069 262) 555. On the Water Trail, all guidance is provided (see above) **Disabled Access** To Water Gardens only. Contact How Hill Trust (as above) for details **School Parties** By prior arrangement with the How Hill Trust (as above). The Water Trail boat can take as many as 10 small children (up to 10 years) **Parking** For about 30 cars. Camping facilities are available **Toilets** Yes **Food** Available in Ludham (2.4 km/1½ miles away)

Further Information Contact BA or the How Hill Trust.

Norfolk
NARBOROUGH RAILWAY LINE

OS Ref TF750118   Landranger Sheet 143
Nearest Town Swaffham   **Size of Reserve** 6 hectares (15 acres)
Managed by Norfolk Naturalists' Trust (NNT) and Norfolk branch of British Butterfly Society (BBS)   **Access** Open all year. Please keep to the footpaths at all times. No dogs

This reserve consists of a disused railway embankment supporting one of the best examples of chalk grassland in Norfolk.

Nature Trail There is no formal trail but the disused railway line provides easy access. Paths can be muddy.

The reserve supports a diversity of chalk grassland flora and 26 species of butterfly.
Plants Carline Thistle, Stemless Thistle, Purging Flax, Autumn Felwort, Eyebright, Small Scabious, Kidney Vetch, Ploughman's Spikenard, Twayblade, Southern Marsh Orchid, Common Spotted Orchid.
Butterflies Dingy Skipper, Grayling, Green Hairstreak, Purple Hairstreak, Brown Argus. Commoner species include Brimstone, Small Heath, Meadow Brown, Common Blue.

Guide No   **Disabled Access** No   **School Parties** No   **Parking** On roadside only
Toilets No   **Food** No

Further Information Reserve leaflets, with maps, are available from NNT.

Norfolk

RANWORTH

OS Ref TG357149   Landranger Sheet 134
Nearest Town Acle   **Size of Reserve** 130 hectares (320 acres)
Managed by Norfolk Naturalists' Trust (NNT)   **Access** Open all year. Please keep to the paths at all times. No dogs

R anworth Reserve lies within the middle reaches of the River Bure Valley and forms part of the Bure Marshes National Nature Reserve (NNR). Habitats include various stages of succession from open water to mature oak woodland. Large areas of unreclaimed fen extend from the edge of the broad to the river.

Nature Trail The trail takes the form of a 500-metre (⅓-mile) boardwalk with 8 interpretative boards along the route. The trail starts about 400 metres (¼ mile) from the car park along a minor road.

Plants Emergent plants – Lesser Reedmace, Burreed, Sweet Flag, Sedges. Open marsh plants – Marsh Pea, Milk Parsley, Cowbane, Bog Myrtle, Marsh Saw Thistle.
Birds Winter – Wigeon, Tufted Duck, Pochard, Shoveler, Gadwall, Mallard, Teal, Goldeneye, Bewick's Swan, Cormorant, Gull roosts. Spring – Heron, Grebe, Common Tern, Waders, Warblers. Summer – Marsh Harrier.
Animals Chinese Water Deer, Pipistrelle and Noctule Bats.
Insects Swallowtail Butterflies (May–June), 7 species of Dragonfly, 3 species of Damselfly.

Information Centre Broads Conservation Centre moored on Ranworth Broad. It is open daily April to October, 10.30–17.30, Saturdays 14.00–17.30. Closed on Fridays. There is mooring for small boats at the Centre.

Guide By prior arrangement, from April to October. Contact the Broads Conservation Centre on South Walsham (060 549) 479. At other times, contact the NNT   **Disabled Access** No   **School Parties** By prior arrangement as above
Parking For 40 cars   **Toilets** At car park   **Food** From shop near car park

Further Information Reserve leaflets are available from the Broads Conservation Centre or from the NNT Shop, Cathedral Close, Norwich.

Norfolk

ROYDON COMMON

OS Ref TF681230   Landranger Sheet 132
Nearest Town King's Lynn   **Size of Reserve** 109 hectares (270 acres)
Managed by Norfolk Naturalists' Trust (NNT)   **Access** Open all year. Please keep to
paths at all times. No dogs

T he wide range of plant species to be found on Roydon Common
reflects the habitat range from dry heath to mixed mire and alder
carr. The reserve has recently been extended to include habitats such as
woodland, marshland and open pools. The area has an attractive
'wilderness' quality and is a good site for viewing Hen Harrier and Merlin.

Nature Trail There is no waymarked trail but there are informal pathways and a
boardwalk (installed by end 1989) across the reserve.

Plants Heather, Bracken, Cross-leaved Heath, Purple Moor Grass, Common
Cotton-grass, Deargrass, Sphagnum Mosses, 3 species of Sundew, Bog Asphodel,
White Beak-sedge, Sweet Gale, Willow, Greater Tussock Sedge, Marsh Fern.
Birds Nightingale, Nightjar, Curlew and Tree Pipit breed on the reserve. In winter,
Merlin and Hen Harrier.
Insects Several Dragonflies, including Black Sympetrum and Four-spotted Chaser.
Other Common Lizard and Adder.

Guide No   **Disabled Access** No   **School Parties** No   **Parking** For 40 cars
Toilets No   **Food** No

Further Information Reserve leaflets, with maps, are available from NNT.

Norfolk

THOMPSON COMMON

OS Ref TL934967   Landranger Sheet 144
Nearest Town Watton   **Size of Reserve** 125 hectares (309 acres)
Managed by Norfolk Naturalists' Trust (NNT)   **Access** Open all year. Please keep to
the paths at all times. No dogs

T hompson Common is a mosaic of grasslands, pingos (shallow ponds
formed at the end of the last Ice Age), scrub, woodland and a large
shallow lake. It is an important site for aquatic flora and fauna, and
supports a range of grassland communities.

Nature Trail There is a waymarked trail. The reserve can be very waterlogged and
muddy so suitable footwear is essential.

Plants Greater Spearwort, Marsh Marigold, Marsh Orchids, Ragged Robin, Pondweeds, Amphibious Bistort, Bogbean. Water Violets in the pingos (especially mid–late May).
Birds Coot, Moorhen, various Ducks, wintering Wildfowl and Waders on passage. Sedge and Reed Warblers, Reed Bunting.
Animals Roe Deer.
Other Parts of the reserve are grazed throughout the year by a herd of Shetland ponies which have become an integral part of the management.

Guide No **Disabled Access** Being improved. Contact NNT for details
School Parties No **Parking** For about 30 cars on 2 sites which can be potholed and boggy **Toilets** No **Food** No

Further Information Reserve leaflets, with maps, are produced in association with the County Council and are available from NNT.

Norfolk

UPTON FEN

OS Ref TG379137   Landranger Sheet 134
Nearest Town Acle   **Size of Reserve** 50 hectares (120 acres)
Managed by Norfolk Naturalists' Trust (NNT)   **Access** Open all year. Please keep to paths at all times. No dogs

Upton Fen is one of the few fen and broad systems isolated from the main polluted river system and fed by clean spring water. It supports a high diversity of plants and several species of dragonfly and butterfly.

Nature Trail The trail round the reserve uses partly 'corduroy' track and partly mud/grass walkways. Tracks can be muddy.

Upton Fen is an exceptional site for dragonflies, damselflies and butterflies, including the rare Norfolk Hawker Dragonfly and Swallowtail Butterflies.
Plants Snowdrop, Primrose, Hop, Honeysuckle, Broad Buckler Fern, Milk Parsley, Marsh Thistle, Yellow Flag, Angelica, Hemp Agrimony, Bog Myrtle, Creeping Willow, many Orchids, Lesser Tussock Sedge, Black Bog Rush, Round-leaved Wintergreen, Marsh Fern.
Birds Sparrowhawk, Heron, Woodcock, Water Rail, Great and Lesser Spotted Woodpeckers.

Guide By prior arrangement with the Warden on Potter Heigham (0692) 670311
Disabled Access No **School Parties** By prior arrangement with the Warden on above number **Parking** On verge of road alongside reserve **Toilets** No **Food** No

Further Information Reserve leaflets, with maps, are available from NNT.

Norfolk
WAYLAND WOOD

OS Ref TL924995   Landranger Sheet 144
Nearest Town Watton   **Size of Reserve** 34 hectares (80 acres)
Managed by Norfolk Naturalists' Trust (NNT)   **Access** Open all year. Please keep to the paths at all times. No dogs

This is an ancient and historic wood managed in the traditional way as coppice with oak standards. The coppice is mainly a hazel/bird cherry mixture with some ash, field maple, dogwood, spindle, willow and holly. There is a magnificent show of springtime flowers and the wood supports a wide variety of birds.

Nature Trail There is no formal trail but signs indicate a suggested route along woodland rides.

Plants Bluebell, Primrose, Early Purple Orchid, Yellow Archangel.
Birds Woodcock, Great and Lesser Spotted Woodpeckers, Golden Pheasant.
Animals Roe Deer.

Guide No   **Disabled Access** No   **School Parties** No   **Parking** For about 7 cars only on verges and side of busy road   **Toilets** No   **Food** No

Further Information Reserve leaflets, with maps, are available from NNT.

Norfolk
WELNEY WILDFOWL REFUGE

OS Ref TL546945   Landranger Sheet 143
Nearest Town Welney   **Size of Reserve** 344 hectares (850 acres)
Managed by The Wildfowl Trust (WT)   **Access** Open daily from 10.00-17.00 in summer or 1 hour before dusk in winter. Closed 24th and 25th December. There is an admission charge for all visitors over 4 years old, but there are reductions for children, senior citizens and groups

Welney is a wetland area situated on the River Ouse Washes. It is extensively flooded in winter but usually dry grassland in summer with permanent lagoons, scrapes and splashes.

Nature Trail Summer Walk – open 1st June to 30th September. This walk is about 4 km (2½ miles) long and gives the visitor a closer look at the general ecology and management of the Washes, and at the plant life and abundant insects to be seen. Visitors get an elevated view of the flat vastness of the Washes. Numbered stations have been set up along the walk and information is given in The Welney Summer Walk leaflet.

Hides and a spacious observatory give views of wildfowl, waders and small bird life.
Plants The nature trail reveals a wealth of wild flowers and wetland plants. There are some natural or original fen vegetation areas.
Birds 5,000 Bewick's Swans winter at Welney. During autumn, winter and early spring, visiting birds include tens of thousands of Ducks, amongst them Wigeon, Mallard, Teal and Shoveller. In spring and summer, breeding birds include Snipe, Redshank, Ruff and Black-tailed Godwit.
Butterflies Peacock, Gatekeeper, Painted Lady, Common Blue, Red Admiral.
Other All the ditches abound with aquatic invertebrate life in the summer months – Great Diving Beetle, Water Boatman, Mayfly Nymph, Great Ramshorn Snail.

Guide For pre-booked groups only. From 1st June to 31st August and from 7th November to 1st March, escorted parties of 20 or more may visit at night to watch the birds by floodlight **Disabled Access** To the main hide only
School Parties Welcomed. There is a pond-dipping point for school use
Parking Yes **Toilets** Yes, including for the disabled **Food** Yes **Shop** Selling gifts

Further Information Contact The Wildfowl Trust, Welney, Wisbech, Cambridgeshire PE14 9TN (tel. 0353 860711).

Suffolk

BRADFIELD WOODS

OS Ref TM935575 Landranger Sheet 155
Nearest Town Bury St. Edmunds **Size of Reserve** 65 hectares (160 acres)
Managed by Suffolk Wildlife Trust (SWT) **Access** Open all year. Please keep to rides. Dogs must be kept on leads

B radfield Woods is an area of large coppice woodland which has been managed by traditional methods since the 13th century, and still is today. Its diverse ground flora reflects a variety of soil types – over 370 plant species have been recorded.

Nature Trail There is no formal trail but there is a network of rides and paths. These are shown on the reserve sign and on the leaflet available from SWT.

Plants Typical coppice flora – Herb Paris, Oxlip, Early Purple Orchid, Cow Wheat, Savicle, Primrose, Gromwell.
Trees Oak, Ash, Maple, Dogwood, Spindle, Guelder Rose.
Birds Nightingale, Blackcap and other Warblers, Woodcock, Tawny Owl, Great Spotted Woodpecker, Redpoll, Brambling, Long-tailed Tits (in winter).
Animals Roe Deer (common), Fox, Stoat, Weasel, Dormouse.
Insects 15 species of butterfly, 150 species of moth, 100 types of beetle.
Other Fungi.

Information Centre A small Information Centre is open at weekends only.

Guide By prior arrangement with the Warden at SWT address **Disabled Access** No
School Parties By prior arrangement with the Warden at SWT address **Parking** For about 20 cars **Toilets** No **Food** No

Further Information Reserve leaflets, with maps, are available from SWT.

CARLTON MARSHES

OS Ref TM508920   Landranger Sheet 134
Nearest Town Lowestoft   **Size of Reserve** 45 hectares (111 acres)
Managed by Suffolk Wildlife Trust (SWT)   **Access** Open all year. Please keep to paths. Dogs must be kept on leads and no dogs may enter the area of the reserve surrounding Sprats Water

Carlton Marshes is situated on the edge of Oulton Broad and Oulton Dyke in the Waveney Valley, and is a mini-Broadland. Habitats include grazing marsh, dyke, reed rond, fen and small broad. In an area which is rapidly being drained and turned over to agriculture, the reserve provides a haven for wetland plants, birds and insects.

Nature Trail There is an unmarked trail which can be walked in about 30 minutes. The route is shown on the main reserve signs.

Plants Marsh Pea, Milk Parsley, Greater and Lesser Spearwort, Southern Marsh Orchid, Bladderwort, Bogbean (in spring). Water Soldier, Flowering Rush and Water Violet in dykes.
Birds Marsh Harrier (summer), Hen Harrier (winter), Snipe, Sparrowhawk, Short-eared Owl, Reed, Sedge and Cetti's Warblers.
Insects Dragonflies and damselflies near dykes and open water.

Information Centre There is a Visitor Centre with an exhibition and information on the Waveney Valley.

Guide By prior arrangement with the Warden, Mr. R. Briggs, 51 Elmhurst Avenue, Oulton Broad   **Disabled Access** Yes   **School Parties** By prior arrangement with the Warden at the above address   **Parking** For about 100 cars   **Toilets** In Visitor Centre, including for the disabled   **Food** No

Further Information Reserve leaflets, with maps, are available from SWT.

Suffolk
REDGRAVE and LOPHAM FENS

OS Ref TM045801   Landranger Sheet 144
Nearest Town Diss   **Size of Reserve** 123 hectares (303 acres)
Managed by Suffolk Wildlife Trust (SWT)   **Access** Open all year. Please keep to
paths. Dogs must be kept on leads

Redgrave and Lopham Fens form a natural oasis for many wetland plants and animals now rapidly becoming so rare in East Anglia. Designated a Grade 1 SSSI, the area is the largest remaining example of the once extensive fens of the Waveney-Little Ouse Valley. It consists of a mosaic of different habitats including reedbed, sedgebed, waterways and pools, heath, woodland, old peat-digging and alder carr.

Nature Trail There are about 14.5 km (9 miles) of pathways around the reserve. The whole waymarked trail takes about 2½ hours but it can be divided into shorter mini-trails. Nature Trail leaflets are available from SWT.

This fen is the only known site in the country for the Great Raft Spider. Pools have been specially created on the reserve to provide an ideal habitat for this, the largest, British spider, which is most likely to be seen in the summer.
Plants Black Bog Rush, Devil's-bit Scabious, Butterwort, Grass of Parnassus, Cross-leaved Heath.
Birds Reed and Sedge Warblers, Nightingale, Snipe, Water Rail, wintering Bearded Tit.
Insects Great Raft Spider, Dragonfly, Damselfly.
Other Traditionally managed reed and sedge beds.

Under Threat This and some other valley fens are threatened by gradual drying out due to land drainage, water abstraction and scrub invasion.

Guide For visiting groups of 10 or more, by prior arrangement with the Warden on Bressingham (037 988) 618 (daytime)   **Disabled Access** A boardwalk crossing the fen to the River Waveney, known as Spider Pit Path, is accessible   **School Parties** By prior arrangement with the Warden on the above number   **Parking** For about 50 cars   **Toilets** No   **Food** No

Further Information General reserve leaflets are available from SWT.

1 Coatham Marsh
2 Cowpen Marsh
3 Saltburn Gill
4 Ash Landing
5 Field End Bridge Nature Trail
6 Hawcoat Nature Trail
7 Nether Wasdale Nature Trail
8 Blackhall
9 Haswell to Hart Walkway
10 Hawthorn Dene
11 Joe's Pond
12 Rosa Shafto
13 Witton-le-Wear
14 Spurn
15 Haskayne Cutting
16 The Irwell Valley Way
17 Mere Sands Wood
18 Penwortham Riverside Trail
19 Rossendale Nature's Ways
   Trail
20 Warton Crag
21 Alkrington Woods
22 Healey Dell
23 Hopwood Woods
24 Jubilee
25 Princess Park
26 Summit Circuit
27 Thornham Lane
28 Inner Farne
29 Shibdon Pond

30 Washington Waterfowl Park
31 Bridestones Moor
32 Caphouse Colliery
33 Garbutt Wood
34 Moorlands
35 Potteric Carr
36 Skipwith Common
37 Thorpe Marsh

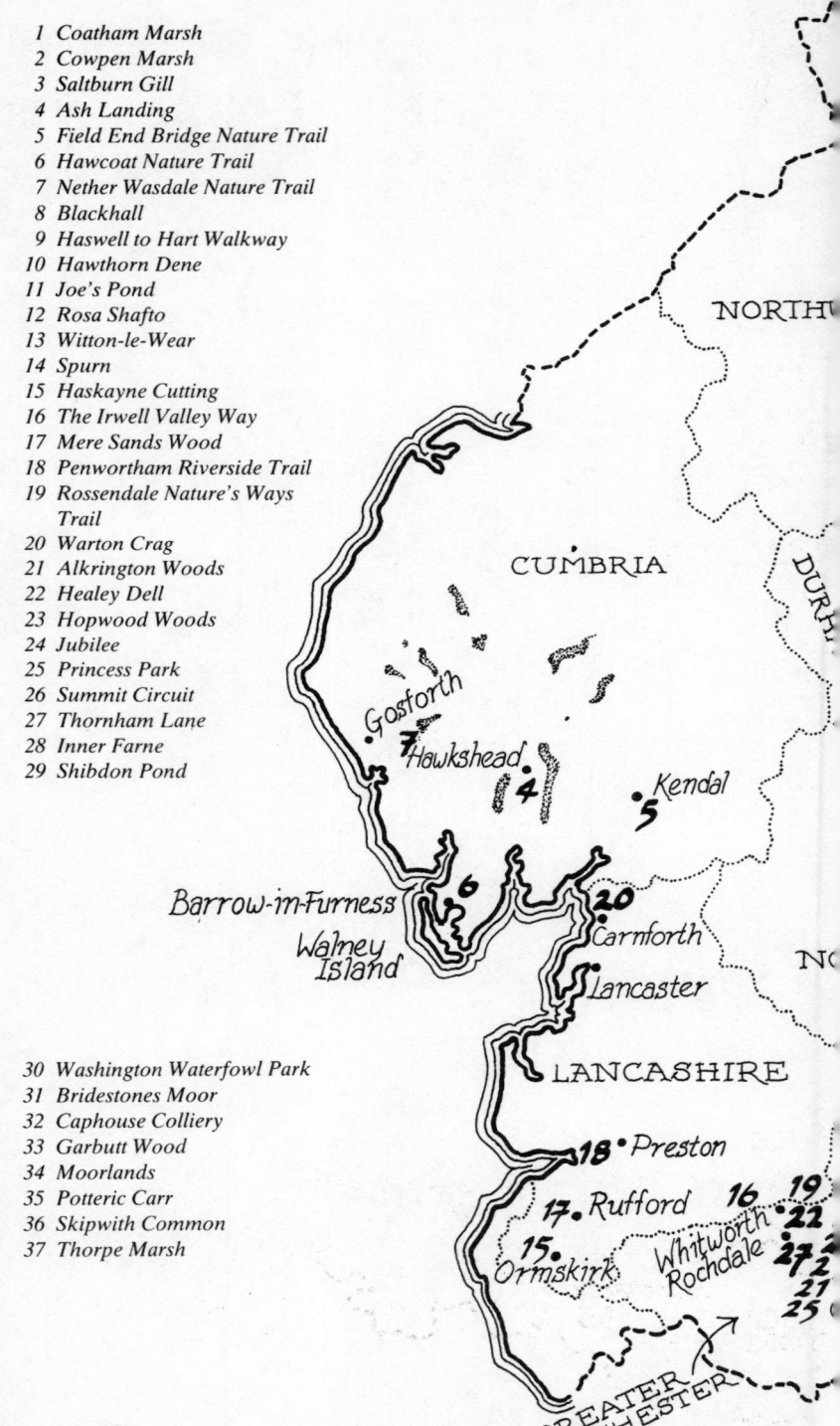

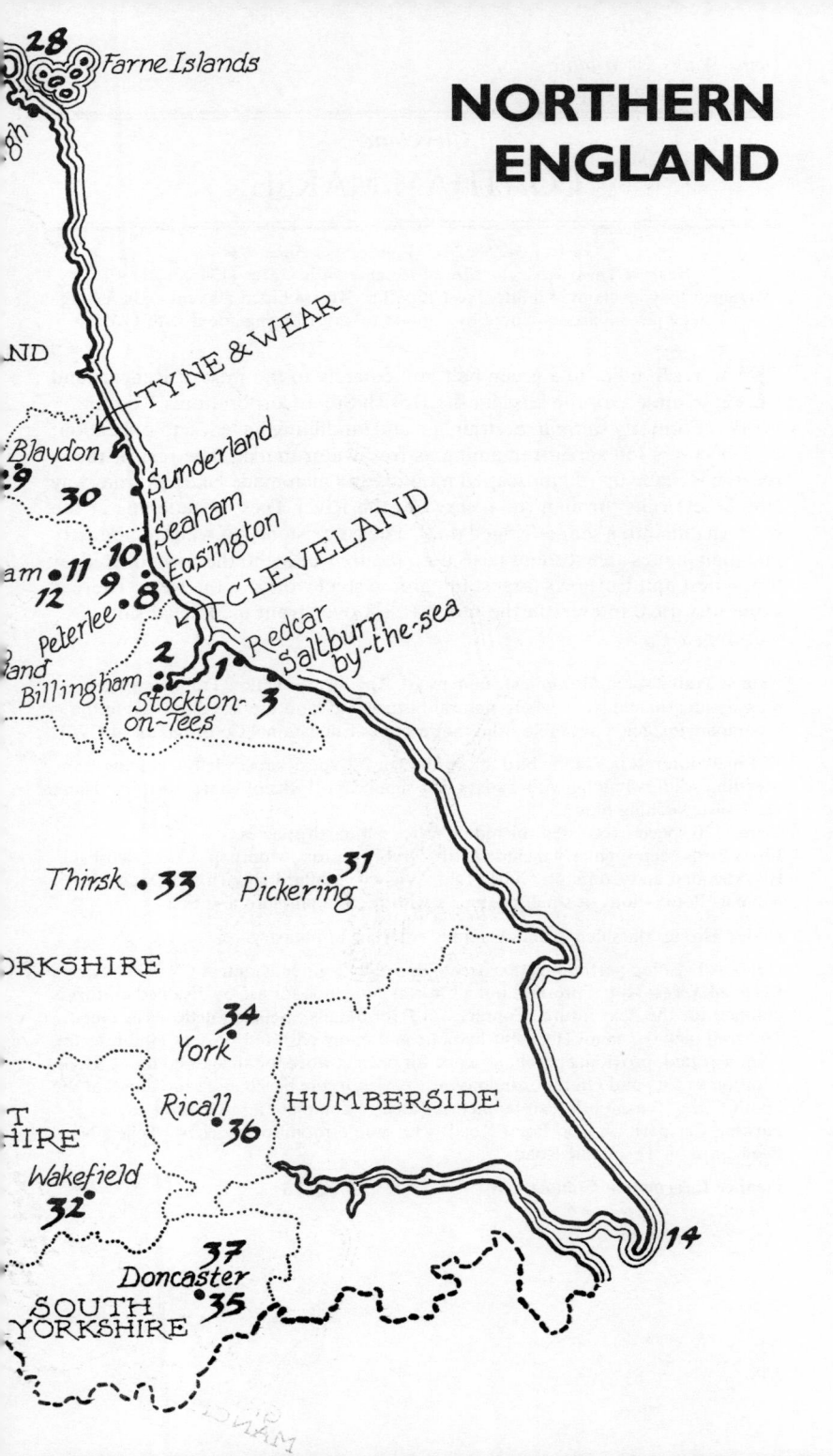

NORTHERN ENGLAND

Farne Islands

28

TYNE & WEAR

Blaydon

29 30 Sunderland

Seaham

Easington

CLEVELAND

am 11 10

12 9 8

Peterlee

2 Redcar Saltburn

Billingham 1 by-the-sea

Stockton- 3

on-Tees

Thirsk 33 Pickering 31

ORKSHIRE

34

York

Ricall HUMBERSIDE

HIRE 36

Wakefield

32

14

37

Doncaster

SOUTH 35

YORKSHIRE

Cleveland
COATHAM MARSH

OS Ref NZ586247   Landranger Sheet 93
Nearest Town Redcar   **Size of Reserve** 54 hectares (134 acres)
Managed by Cleveland Wildlife Trust (CWT)   **Access** Open all year. All visiting
parties must be accompanied by a guide by prior arrangement with CWT

The reserve lies in a green belt immediately to the west of Redcar, and is bounded on the east by the British Steel Corporation's Redcar Works. Formerly saltmarsh, drainage and landfilling have led to only about 20.2 hectares (50 acres) remaining as freshwater marsh. The rest of the reserve is made up of landscaped mounds and man-made lakes. A waterway (the Fleet) runs through the reserve to the River Tees, broadening at the western end into a sedge-fringed pool. The co-existence of wildlife, industry and man makes an excellent basis for a nature trail, with the town of Redcar to the east and Europe's largest integrated steel works to the west. There is some historical interest in the mounds left over from mediaeval salt workings.

Nature Trail 2.4 km (1½ miles), unmarked. This Conservation Trail comprises 6 easily-identifiable stops where natural history and land use are discussed in the accompanying guide available from the reserve's Educational Co-ordinator at CWT.

The main interest lies in the bird life, with over 200 species recorded, including many breeding wildfowl along with waders and significant flocks of winter visitors. There are 3 birdwatching hides.
Plants 170 species recorded, including relict saltmarsh species.
Birds Birds seen regularly include Little Grebe, Heron, Moorhen, Coot, Redshank, Blackheaded and Common Gulls, Teal, Wigeon, Mallard and Tufted Duck.
Animals Populations of small mammals with occasional Hare and Fox.

Under Threat Marshlands and wetlands adjacent to industry.

Guide All visiting parties must be accompanied by a guide. Contact CWT in advance
Disabled Access Not at present, but a birdwatching hide for use by disabled visitors is planned for the near future. Contact CWT for details   **School Parties** Welcomed. The trail includes many different habitats and many past and present land uses are demonstrated, providing excellent scope for project work for all ages up to GCSE, in addition to City and Guilds examinations. A visit to the beach and sand dunes at the South Gare, Teesmouth, can be incorporated to complete a fascinating day
Parking Car park off Tod Point Road, with ample room for coaches   **Toilets** No
Food Café on Tod Point Road

Further Information Contact CWT.

Cleveland

COWPEN MARSH

OS Ref NZ508251   Landranger Sheet 93
Nearest Town Billingham   **Size of Reserve** 65 hectares (160 acres)
Managed by Cleveland Wildlife Trust (CWT)   **Access** Open all year

C owpen Marsh Reserve is an SSSI consisting of freshwater marsh, largely used for grazing, and several 'fleets' which are popular with wildfowl and waders. A small, but valuable, part of the reserve is the only significant area of intertidal saltmarsh between the Humber and Lindisfarne. The reserve is situated slightly inland from Teesmouth and almost adjacent to Seal Sands SSSI. Also nearby is the Teesmouth Field Centre.

Nature Trail A walk of about 1.5 km (1 mile) can include Cowpen Marsh and Seal Sands. This is part of a longer 9.6-km (6-mile) trail which extends from the River Tees to the Teesmouth Field Centre.

Plants Saltmarsh species.
Birds Wildfowl and Waders a speciality throughout the year; Terns and other seabirds in summer; Raptor in winter.
Animals A small colony of Atlantic Grey and Common Seals.

Under Threat The intertidal mudflats and marshlands of the Tees estuary have been dramatically reduced over the last 100 years by reclamation for industry. It is to be hoped that the remaining areas can now be saved and improved for wildlife. On both sides of the estuary, the sand dunes are suffering from human erosion (including off-road motorcycles).

Information Centre Teesmouth Field Centre acts as an information centre for the area. A smaller information centre is planned for the reserve itself.

Guide By prior arrangement with the Warden at the Field Centre (address below). Visiting parties *must* be accompanied by a guide   **Disabled Access** Only to Teesmouth Field Centre   **School Parties** Welcomed. Bookings must be made with the Warden, Teesmouth Field Centre, Hartlepool Power Station, Tees Road, Hartlepool, Cleveland TS25 2BZ   **Parking** Both at Cowpen Marsh and at the Field Centre (also room for coaches)   **Toilets** At Teesmouth Field Centre   **Food** Hot drinks available at Teesmouth Field Centre

Further Information Contact the Warden at the Field Centre (as above), or CWT. Teesmouth Field Centre leaflets (including details of the Nature Trail) are available from the Field Centre.

Cleveland

SALTBURN GILL

OS Ref NZ673210 to NZ675203   Landranger Sheet 94
Nearest Town Saltburn-by-the-Sea   **Size of Reserve** 21 hectares (52 acres)
Managed by Cleveland Wildlife Trust (CWT)   **Access** Open all year. Visitors must
remain on public rights of way at all times

T he main part of the reserve consists of broadleaved woodland running north/south on the eastern banks of Saltburn Gill, with two smaller lateral valleys running into the Griff. A gorse and scrub covered slope and a flat area of bracken and regenerating oak woodland also occur. The woodland is designated an SSSI.

Nature Trail A public footpath provides good access to the reserve, starting from the Saltburn promenade area. A formal nature trail is planned for the future; contact CWT for details. The reserve is also within a few hundred yards of the Cleveland Way Coastal Path.

Plants There is a good ancient semi-natural woodland flora, with some interesting species of Lichen.
Trees Oak, Ash, Holly, Hazel.
Birds Warblers, Tits, Tawny Owl, Great Spotted Woodpecker, Woodcock, Finches, Grey Wagtail.
Animals Usual range of mammals.
Other The reserve is also close to Huntcliff Nature Reserve, a short stretch of coastal cliff through which the Cleveland Way runs. The cliffs support a colony of breeding Kittiwake, plus Cormorant and Fulmar. The seashore is rich in littoral fauna and has considerable geological interest (fossil-rich Lias clays).

Guide By prior arrangement with CWT   **Disabled Access** No   **School Parties** Yes
Parking At Saltburn promenade (Cat Nab) car park   **Toilets** In car park   **Food** Ship Inn Public House (nearby on promenade) and Beach Café (summer only)

Further Information Reserve Data Sheets are available to Trust members from CWT. For other information, contact CWT.

Cumbria

ASH LANDING

OS Ref SD3897   Landranger Sheet 96
Nearest Town Hawkshead
Managed by Cumbria Wildlife Trust (CWT)   **Access** Open all year

A sh Landing comprises a wide variety of habitats, including woodland, hedgerow, hay meadows, bogs and ponds. Part of the reserve still has remains of its previous use as a garden nursery.

Nature Trail There is a good network of footpaths around the reserve with interpretative boards indicating various habitats and the wildlife to be seen there.

The main interest is the wide variety of habitats that can be seen together on one reserve.
Animals Mice, Voles.
Insects Damselflies.
Other Frogs and toads.

Guide Contact CWT   **Disabled Access** Contact CWT for details
School Parties Welcomed. Various leaflets, available from CWT, are produced specially for visiting schoolchildren   **Parking** In car park   **Toilets** No   **Food** No

Further Information A large selection of leaflets and books on wildlife is available at the CWT Shop, The Badger's Paw, Church Street, Ambleside.

Cumbria

FIELD END BRIDGE to STAINTON NATURE TRAIL

OS Ref SD526850 (Stainton)   Landranger Sheet 97
Nearest Town Kendal   **Size of Reserve** 1 km (⅔ mile) long
Managed by Cumbria Wildlife Trust (CWT)
Access Open all year

This canal bank trail runs beside the Lancaster Canal from Field End Bridge to Stainton. This section of the canal is considered to be of natural history interest as it is a fine example of nature's adaptation of a man-made waterway habitat. The walk passes near-stagnant water, wooded banks, scrub, reeds, open fields and hedgerows.

Nature Trail The trail follows the canal towpath. A Nature Trail Official Guide is available from CWT (price 20p).

Plants Bur Reed, Horsetail, Cowslip, Lesser Celandine, Herb Robert, Maindenhair Fern, Dog's Mercury, Bluebell, Curly Pondweed, Canadian Pondweed, Spineless Hornwort.
Trees Larch, Silver Birch, Oak, Ash, Cherry, Willow.
Birds Redwing, Fieldfare, Sparrowhawk, Coot, Moorhen, Mute Swan, Redshank, Sandpiper, Curlew, Lapwing, Blackheaded Gull, Common Gull, Swallow, Housemartin, Warblers.
Animals Field Mouse, Mole, Mink.
Insects Caddis Fly, Damselfly, Pond Skater.
Butterflies Small Tortoiseshell, Peacock, Red Admiral, Orange-tip, Meadow Brown.

Guide Contact CWT   **Disabled Access** Contact CWT   **School Parties** Contact CWT
Toilets No   **Food** No

Further Information Contact CWT. A large selection of leaflets and books is available from the CWT shop, the Badger's Paw in Church Street, Ambleside.

Cumbria
HAWCOAT to ORMSGILL
URBAN NATURE TRAIL

OS Ref SD1969   Landranger Sheet 96
Nearest Town The walk is in Barrow-in-Furness   **Size of Reserve** About 1.5 km
(1 mile) long   **Managed by** Cumbria Wildlife Trust (CWT) Urban Wildlife Project
Access Open all year

The Hawcoat to Ormsgill Trail covers an area of Barrow-in-Furness and was designed by the CWT Urban Wildlife Project to promote the theme of 'Wildlife Where You Live'. It includes habitats such as a churchyard, hedgerows, an old quarry and the open water of Ormsgill Lake. Part of the walk provides fine views over the Duddon estuary, Sandscale Haws and Walney Island – all important sites for wildlife.

Nature Trail The walk takes about 2 hours to complete. Directions and a map showing the route are included in the Nature Trail Leaflet available from CWT.

Plants Wild flowers.
Birds Great Crested Grebe.

Guide By prior arrangement with CWT   **Disabled Access** Contact CWT
School Parties Contact CWT   **Parking** At Barrow Football Club on Holker Street
Toilets In Barrow-in-Furness   **Food** At local pubs en route

Further Information Contact CWT. A large selection of leaflets and books is available from the CWT shop, the Badger's Paw, Church Street, Ambleside.

Cumbria
NETHER WASDALE NATURE TRAIL

OS Ref NY147048   Landranger Sheet 96
Nearest Town Gosforth   **Size of Reserve** 5.6 km (3½ miles) long
Managed by Cumbria Wildlife Trust (CWT)   **Access** Open all year

The Nether Wasdale Nature Trail is situated at the southern end of Wast Water and provides an opportunity to study lakeland wildlife. Habitats include woodland, damp meadow, lake shore, scree, riverside and open water.

Nature Trail The main circular walk is about 5.6 km (3½ miles) long. Directions and a map showing the route are included in the Nature Trail Guide available from CWT (price 8p). A shorter route is also marked.

Plants Bracken, Male Fern, Violet, Wood Anemone, Bugle, Bilberry, Ling, Wood Sorrel, Golden Rod, Angelica, Wood Sage, Meadowsweet, Valerian, Figwort, Spearwort, Willow Herb, Flag Iris, Sphagnum Moss, Bog Asphodel, Sundew.
Trees Oak, Birch, Ash, Holly, Hazel, Lime, Sycamore, Willow, Spruce, Scots Pine, Larch
Birds Mallard, Red Breasted Merganser, Black-headed Gull, Common Sandpiper, Grey Wagtail, Dipper, Redstart, Wood Warbler, Pied Flycatcher, Stonechat, Redpoll, Buzzard, Sparrowhawk, Green and Great Spotted Woodpeckers, Raven, Peregrine.

Guide Contact CWT   **Disabled Access** No   **School Parties** Contact CWT
Parking In parking bays along roadside by lakeshore   **Toilets** No   **Food** No

Further Information Contact CWT. A large selection of leaflets and books is available from the CWT shop, The Badger's Paw in Church Street, Ambleside.

Durham
BLACKHALL

OS Ref NZ473387   Landranger Sheet 93
Nearest Town Peterlee   **Size of Reserve** 32 hectares (79 acres)
Managed by Durham Wildlife Trust (DWT)   **Access** Open all year to Trust members. Public access is by permit only from DWT.

The reserve is a splendid expanse of reef limestone. There are 18.2-metre (60-foot) cliffs of which the upper 6 metres (20 feet) are made up of two boulder clays separated by a bed of gravel. The cliff tops are covered by limestone-loving plants with a series of hollows and gullys containing wetland species.

Nature Trail There are 4 waymarked trails of varying lengths. A Nature Trail leaflet is available from DWT.

Plants Bloody Cranesbill, Sea Pink, Meadowsweet, False Fox Sedge, Burnet Rose, Sea Club Rush, Sea Spleenwort, Quaking Grass, Cowslip.
Birds Skua, Terns, Lapwing, Bunting, Seabirds (in winter). During spring and autumn, many migrating birds pass through.
Butterflies 15 species recorded, including Castle Eden Argus, Common Blue.
Other Frogs, Newts, Toads, Seals, rock pool creatures such as Crabs, Shrimp and Anemone.

Under Threat The reserve and surrounding area are under threat from sewage pollution on the beach, agricultural run-off, colliery waste dumping and fly tipping.

Guide The County Council car park and picnic site is wardened at weekends. Otherwise, contact DWT to make arrangements   **Disabled Access** No
School Parties No   **Parking** In County Council car park   **Toilets** At Crimdon Caravan Park (Easter to end of September only)   **Food** No, but there is a picnic site
Further Information Contact DWT.

Durham

HASWELL to HART
COUNTRYSIDE WALKWAY

OS Ref NZ3744 (Haswell)   Landranger Sheet 93
Nearest Town Peterlee   **Size of Reserve** 14.5 km (9 miles) long
Managed by East Durham Groundwork Trust (EDGT) **Owned by** Easington
District Council   **Access** Open all year

The Haswell to Hart Walkway runs between Haswell and Hart Station, along the old railway route designed by George Stephenson. The Walkway has largely been created by Easington District Council but is managed and promoted by a Ranger Service provided by EDGT. Along most of its lengh, the walk is a flat dolomite path bordered by rich varied limestone vegetation, providing an excellent habitat for many species of birds and animals. Some areas have been converted to wetland or ponds, creating a contrasting community of hydrophytic plants and pond life.

Nature Trail The Walkway is about 14.5 km (9 miles) long and is waymarked. Leaflets about the Walkway are available from EDGT.

Plants Various stages of rich limestone flora communities.
Birds Woodland species, including Raptor.
Other All British Newt species in pond areas.

Information Centre The EDGT Ranger Service has a cabin at the Recreation Ground, Station Road, Shotton Colliery, where there is a display.

Guide By prior arrangement with EDGT   **Disabled Access** Some parts of the Walkway are accessible to wheelchair users. Contact EDGT for details or see map in leaflet available from EDGT   **School Parties** Yes. Contact EDGT for details
Parking At various sites along the route   **Toilets** Not on the Walkway but available nearby   **Food** In nearby pubs. There are also picnic sites at several points along the route

Further Information Contact EDGT.

Durham
HAWTHORN DENE

OS Ref NZ433457   Landranger Sheet 88
Nearest Town Easington   **Size of Reserve** 66.7 hectares (165 acres)
Managed by Durham Wildlife Trust (DWT)   **Access** Open all year to Trust members.
Public access is by permit from DWT

This reserve lies in one of the steeply incised valleys which dissect the coastal magnesium plateau of East Durham, which is overlain by boulder clay. The area is deciduous woodland which has been very much influenced by its previous management. The coastal section of the reserve includes a limestone cliff with calcareous grassland on the top and exposures within the gorge on which a number of rare rock plants grow. The coal shale at the foot of the cliffs has also been colonised by a number of interesting limestone plants. The reserve is designated an SSSI.

Nature Trail There are 3 trails – the North Wood Nature Trail, the Short Nature Trail and the Long Nature Trail. Leaflets are available for all three from DWT. The points referred to in the texts are indicated along the routes by means of numbers painted on trees. Paths can be very slippery, particularly after rain.

Plants Early Purple and Spotted Orchids, False Oxlip, Giant Horsetail, Hartstongue Fern.
Trees Walnut, Norway Maple, Lawson's Cypress, Austrian Pine, Beech, Horse Chestnut, Larch, Sycamore, Large-leaved Lime.
Birds Common woodland birds; breeding Treecreepers and Tits; sea birds on coast.
Animals Roe Deer, Badger, Fox, Stoat, Hare, Common Shrew, Pipistrelle Bat, small rodents.
Other Jew's Ear Fungus.

Under Threat The reserve is threatened by the dumping of waste from a nearby coal pit.

Guide By prior arrangement with DWT   **Disabled Access** Much of the North Wood Nature Trail is accessible to wheelchair users   **School Parties** Yes. Contact DWT for details   **Parking** In car park   **Toilets** No   **Food** No

Further Information Contact DWT.

Durham
JOE'S POND

OS Ref NZ329488   Landranger Sheet 88
Nearest Town Durham   **Size of Reserve** 4.4 hectares (11 acres)
Managed by Durham Wildlife Trust (DWT)   **Access** Open all year

Joe's Pond is a deep freshwater pond surrounded by dense hawthorn shrubbery. The pond was an old brick pit. At the southern end of the reserve there are areas of damp meadow. The reserve is designated an SSSI.

Nature Trail A short waymarked trail provides access to part of the reserve. A Nature Trail leaflet is available from DWT.

There is a birdwatching hide overlooking the pond.

Plants Tufted Vetch, Cowslip, Pondweed, Water Mint, Reedmace.

Birds Little and Great Crested Grebes, Mute Swan, Lesser Whitethroat, Blackcap, wintering Ducks.

Insects Water insects, such as Water Scorpion, Agrion Nymph, Dragonflies, Damselflies.

Under Threat Pollution from a reclaimed pit heap nearby is affecting the pond.

Guide By prior arrangement with DWT **Disabled Access** Partial access for wheelchair users. Contact DWT for further details **School Parties** Yes. Contact DWT for details **Parking** On roadside, a short walk from the reserve **Toilets** No **Food** No

Further Information Contact DWT.

Durham

ROSA SHAFTO

OS Ref NZ245350   Landranger Sheet 93
Nearest Town Spennymoor   **Size of Reserve** 31 hectares (77 acres)
Managed by Durham Wildlife Trust (DWT)
Access Open all year

The Rosa Shafto Reserve consists of a series of unspoilt inter-connecting plantations on the Whitworth Estate. Habitats include varied woodland (deciduous, coniferous and mixed), together with scrub, grassland and two ponds.

Nature Trail There is no formal waymarked trail, but the reserve has a number of footpaths, many of which connect with paths outside the reserve.

Plants Wood Anemone, Wood Sorrel, Arum.

Trees Norway Spruce, Alder.

Birds Great Spotted Woodpecker, large population of Warblers.

Animals Wood Mouse, Wood Vole, Roe Deer, Badger, Fox, Pipistrelle Bat, Brown Long-eared Bat, Red Squirrel.

Insects Six-spot Burnet Moth.

Guide By prior arrangement with DWT **Disabled Access** No **School Parties** By prior arrangement with DWT **Parking** In car park **Toilets** No **Food** No

Further Information Reserve leaflets are available from DWT.

Durham
WITTON-LE-WEAR

OS Ref NZ160315   Landranger Sheet 92
Nearest Town Bishop Auckland   **Size of Reserve** 40 hectares (84 acres)
Managed by Durham Wildlife Trust (DWT)   **Access** Open access to Trust members
following the Nature Trail. Non-members must be accompanied by a guide

T he reserve covers an area that was once farmed and then worked for
gravel. When this ceased in 1964, the site was developed as a nature
reserve, including major landscaping of the central section. Features
include open land, scrub and mature alder wood. There are small streams,
three lakes and some shallow pools. The River Wear forms the southern
boundary. The reserve is designated an SSSI.

Nature Trail 1.2 km (¾ mile), marked with numbered posts corresponding to
information in a Nature Trail leaflet available from DWT.

There are several observation hides on the reserve.
Plants Vipers Bugloss, Butterbur, various Trefoils, Marsh Orchid hybrids,
Reedmace.
Birds Many woodland and hedgerow birds, resident Waterfowl and Waders, plus
winter visitors.
Animals Roe Deer, Badger.
Other Frogs, Toads and Smooth Newt.

Information Centre There is a laboratory on the reserve, which is open whenever a
warden is in attendance.

Guide By prior arrangement with DWT   **Disabled Access** Part of the trail is accessible
to wheelchair users   **School Parties** Yes. Contact DWT for details   **Parking** Near
farmhouse and laboratory   **Toilets** In laboratory when open   **Food** No

Further Information Contact DWT.

Humberside
SPURN

OS Ref TA417151   Landranger Sheet 113
Nearest Town Patrington   **Size of Reserve** 113. 3 hectares (280 acres)
above water mark; 193 hectares (477 acres) below water mark
Managed by The Yorkshire Wildlife Trust (YWT)   **Access** Open all year

S purn is a sand and shingle spit, 5.6 km (3½ miles) long, forming a
narrow peninsula stretching more than one third of the way across the
mouth of the Humber. It is the only unspoilt sand dune area of any size on

the Yorkshire coast. The spit is constantly growing as sand and shingle is washed from the eroding cliffs of Holderness and deposited in the more sheltered waters inside the mouth of the Humber. The reserve has become an important site for migrant birds.

Nature Trail There is no formal trail but paths provide access almost to the point. Access to the very tip of the spit is only possible via the beaches.

Plants Marram Grass, Cord Grass, Sea Buckthorn, Sea Bindweed, Sea Holly, Storksbill, Pyramidal Orchid, Restharrow, Common Centaury, Yellow-wort, Ragwort, Ploughman's Spikenard.
Birds Migrant birds include Wheatear, Whinchat, Redstart, Pied and Spotted Flycatchers, Black Redstart (sometimes), Fieldfare, Redwing, Dunlin, Knot, Redshank, Turnstone, Curlew, Oystercatcher, Mallard, Shelduck, Brent Goose and Terns. Breeding birds include Linnet, Reed Bunting and Dunnock.
Animals Seal, Fox, Rabbit.
Insects Six-spot Burnet Moth; Small Tortoiseshell, Wall Brown, Painted Lady and Red Admiral Butterflies.

Information Centre There is an Observatory with Information Centre and Sales Point.

Guide No   **Disabled Access** No   **School Parties** No   **Parking** Available near the lighthouse   **Toilets** No   **Food** No

Further Information Reserve leaflets are available from YWT.

Lancashire
HASKAYNE CUTTING

OS Ref SK358088   Landranger Sheet 108
Nearest Town Ormskirk   **Size of Reserve** 7.5 hectares (18½ acres)
Managed by Lancashire Trust for Nature Conservation (LTNC)
Access By permit available from LTNC

Haskayne Cutting Nature Reserve is a disused railway cutting with a wide variety of habitats, including scrub, grassland, marsh and rock outcrops. The main interest of the reserve is its plant life and many interesting and attractive wild plants occur, including spectacular orchid populations. The reserve is an isolated example of semi-natural vegetation in an area of intensively managed agricultural land.

Nature Trail The trail runs through the southern section of the reserve from Barton Station to Chisnall Brook, a distance of about 1.2 km (¾ mile). The trail is marked with numbered posts corresponding to information given in a Nature Trail Guide available from LTNC.

Plants Marsh Orchids, Cowslip, Kidney Vetch.
Birds Breeding Warblers.
Insects Good butterfly populations and other rare insects.

Guide Only occasionally. Contact LTNC for details   **Disabled Access** No
School Parties Only occasionally. Contact LTNC for details   **Parking** On roadside
Toilets No   **Food** No

Further Information Contact LTNC.

Lancashire
THE IRWELL VALLEY WAY

OS Ref SD804223   Landranger Sheet 109
Nearest Towns Radcliffe, Ramsbottom, Waterfoot and Weir
Managed by Rossendale Groundwork Trust (RGT)   **Access** Open all year

The Irwell Valley Way is a 48.2-km (30-mile) walk through the heritage of South East Lancashire. The route extends from Manchester through industrial towns and attractive countryside to the upland villages of Rossendale. The river corridor provides an excellent haven for wildlife.

Nature Trail The most attractive 5-km (3-mile) stretch of the Irwell Valley Way makes an ideal Nature Trail and runs from the headquarters of RGT, at Rawtenstall, southwards to the village of Stubbins. The route is described in the 'Ramsbottom to Waterfoot' leaflet, one of four covering the Irwell Valley Way.

Plants Butterbur, Bistort, Celandines, colourful marsh plants.
Birds Sand Martin, Kingfisher, Willow Warbler, Greenfinch, Goldfinch, Blue and Great Tits.
Butterflies Orange-tip, Green Veined White, Small Tortoiseshell, Small Copper.
Other The East Lancashire Light Railway runs along the trail route. The Nature Trail makes a natural walking link between stations.

Information Centre There is a Visitor Centre and a Farm Centre with information on farming and wildlife.

Guide By prior arrangement with RGT   **Disabled Access** Only to Visitor Centre
School Parties By prior arrangement with RGT   **Parking** Yes   **Toilets** At Visitor Centre, including for the disabled   **Food** Yes

Further Information Contact The Croal Irwell Valley Warden Service, Rock Hall, Farnworth (tel. 0204 71561), Rossendale Tourist Information Centre, Kay Street, Rawtenstall (tel. 0706 217777), or RGT.

Lancashire
MERE SANDS WOOD

OS Ref SD446157   Landranger Sheet 108
Nearest Town Rufford   **Size of Reserve** 42 hectares (105 acres)
Managed by Lancashire Trust for Nature Conservation (LTNC)
Access Open all year

Mere Sands Wood Nature Reserve consists of disused gravel workings that now form a collection of attractive lakes, heath and broadleaved and coniferous woodland. The creation of these new habitats has increased the range of wildlife present and has provided a refuge in an area otherwise dominated by intensive farming. The reserve is designated a geological SSSI.

Nature Trail A circular waymarked trail of 1.5 km (1 mile) can be extended to 3 km (2 miles). A Trail Guide is available at the reserve or from LTNC.

There are several birdwatching hides and an observation platform on the reserve.
Plants Plant life is not rich but is improving.
Birds Breeding Wildfowl, including Mallard, Tufted Duck, Ruddy Duck, Little Grebe, Great Crested Grebe, Little Ringed Plover.
Animals Red Squirrel population.

Information Centre There is an Educational Centre on the reserve.

Guide Yes. Contact LTNC for details   **Disabled Access** The birdwatching hide adjoining the car park is accessible to disabled visitors   **School Parties** Yes. Contact LTNC for details   **Parking** In car park   **Toilets** Yes   **Food** No

Further Information Contact LTNC.

Lancashire
PENWORTHAM RIVERSIDE NATURE TRAIL

OS Ref SD515294   Landranger Sheet 102
Nearest Town Preston   **Size of Reserve** 2.4 km (1½ miles) long
Managed by Lancashire Trust for Nature Conservation (LTNC)
Access Open all year

This Nature Trail follows the south bank of the River Ribble, opposite Preston Dock. It passes through marginal river/coastal vegetation and is important for coastal and passage birds.

Nature Trail About 2.4 km (1½ miles), unmarked. A Nature Trail leaflet is available from LTNC. The footpath is on top of the bank built to keep the river deep enough for ships to reach Preston Dock (now closed).

Plants Sand Leek, Soapwort, Sea Aster, Spiny Restharrow.
Birds Common Tern, Cormorant, Shelduck – all on passage.

Guide No   **Disabled Access** No   **School Parties** No   **Parking** Adjoining A59(T) alongside River Ribble   **Toilets** No   **Food** No

Further Information Contact LTNC.

Lancashire
ROSSENDALE NATURE'S WAYS TRAIL

OS Ref SD879164   Landranger Sheet 109
Nearest Town Whitworth   **Size of Reserve** 6.4 km (4 miles) long
Managed by Rossendale Groundwork Trust (RGT)   **Access** Open all year

The Nature's Ways Trail in Rossendale has been established by RGT as a means to study the natural environment and the way man has influenced it. The trail runs through the Spodden Valley, encompassing varying terrain from river valley and valley sides to moorland. Habitats also include oak, beech and birch woodland in the Spodden Valley, water habitats on former mill 'lodges' (ponds) and moorland.

Nature Trail 6.4 km (4 miles), waymarked. The walk follows statutory rights of way. Boots are recommended for the upland section. Detailed information about the trail is found in the booklet 'Nature's Ways', part of a series entitled *The Changing Faces of Rossendale*, available from RGT.

Plants Valerian, Ragged Robin, Wood Sorrel, Golden Saxifrage, Lesser Celandine, Bluebell, Tormentil, Water Horsetail, Water Plantain.
Birds Lapwing, Wheatear, Meadow Pipit, Warblers, Short-eared Owl, Moorhen, Kingfisher.
Animals Water Vole, Water Shrew.
Insects Sheltered former railway line is an ideal habitat for Bees, Small Copper and Meadow Brown Butterflies, Dragonflies, Damselflies and Moths.

Information Centre The Healey Dell Visitor Centre is nearby.

Guide By prior arrangement with RGT   **Disabled Access** No   **School Parties** By prior arrangement with RGT   **Parking** Car park at SD879164   **Toilets** No
Food No

Further Information Contact the local Tourist Information Centre on Rossendale (0706) 217777, or RGT.

Lancashire

WARTON CRAG

OS Ref SD495725 Landranger Sheet 97
Nearest Town Carnforth **Size of Reserve** 82 hectares (202½ acres)
Managed by Lancashire Trust for Nature Conservation (LTNC)
Access Open all year

W arton Crag Nature Reserve is designated a Local Nature Reserve (LNR) and is a nationally important area of limestone grassland, woodland and limestone pavement. Geologically, Warton Crag is the southern tip of a ridge of limestone running north to Yealand Redmayne. The south face of the Crag consists of a series of terraces.

Nature Trail A circular waymarked Nature Trail of about 1.5 km (1 mile) covers the LNR area. Strong footwear is desirable. The trail is described in detail in a leaflet available from LTNC.

Plants Rockrose, Cowslip, Early Purple Orchid, Wood Anemone, Primrose.
Birds Good breeding bird populations.
Animals Red Squirrel.
Butterflies High Brown Fritillary, amongst others.

Guide By prior arrangement with LTNC **Disabled Access** No
School Parties Occasionally. Contact LTNC for details **Parking** In old quarry car park immediately north of the Black Bull Hotel, Warton **Toilets** No **Food** No

Further Information Contact LTNC.

Manchester, North

ALKRINGTON WOODS

OS Ref SD862051 Landranger Sheet 109
Nearest Town Middleton **Size of Reserve** 37 hectares (91 acres)
Managed by The Oldham & Rochdale Groundwork Trust (ORGT)
Access Open all year

A lkrington Woods is designated a Local Nature Reserve (LNR) and consists of mature deciduous woodland, scrub and grassland surrounding Alkrington Hall, near Middleton Town Centre. The woodland is situated on the valley sides of the River Irk. Included in the reserve is a series of disused mill lodges, now open for fishing.

Nature Trail The 2.4–3.2-km (1½–2-mile) circular trail is waymarked. Parts of the trail can be muddy and quite steep.

Plants Great Willowherb, Marsh Woundwort, Reed Canary Grass, Butterbur, Wall Rue (uncommon in Rochdale), Purple Moor Grass, Bracken.

Trees Alder, Beech, Silver Birch, Rowan, Hawthorn, Pedunculate Oak, Sycamore, Black Poplar, Sweet Chestnut, Larch, Whitebeam, False Acacia, Red Oak.
Birds Great Crested and Little Grebes, Mallard, Coot, Moorhen.

Under Threat As a reserve situated in an urban area, Alkrington Woods is constantly under threat from industrial and urban development.

Guide By prior arrangement with ORGT **Disabled Access** No **School Parties** By prior arrangement with ORGT **Parking** Car park off Manchester Old Road **Toilets** No **Food** No

Further Information Contact ORGT.

Manchester, North
HEALEY DELL

OS Ref SD880158 Landranger Sheet 109
Nearest Town Rochdale **Size of Reserve** 62 hectares (153 acres)
Managed by Lancashire Trust for Nature Conservation (LTNC) and The Oldham & Rochdale Groundwork Trust (ORGT) **Owned by** Rochdale Metropolitan Borough Council and Rossendale Borough Council **Access** Open all year

Healey Dell Nature Reserve lies in the lower Spodden Valley. It is an extremely good example of clough woodland and is in sharp contrast to the surrounding Pennine moorland and urban areas. It is situated just 3 km (2 miles) to the north west of Rochdale town centre. As well as woodland, the reserve includes grassland and scrub alongside the River Spodden and part of the disused Rochdale to Bacup railway line.

Nature Trail About 3 km (2 miles), waymarked. The trail crosses a spectacular viaduct, providing an observation point for enjoying views of the surrounding woodlands. The main Nature Trail and a suggested detour are described in detail in the Healey Dell Guide Book available from LTNC or from ORGT. Paths are very steep in places.

Plants Hartstongue Fern, Bilberry, Wild Strawberry, Marsh Orchids, Bellflower.
Trees Oak, Birch, Sycamore, Beech.
Birds Rook, Nuthatch, breeding woodland birds and winter visitors.
Other Smooth and Palmate Newts, Frogs

Under Threat Many adjacent woodlands have suffered vandalism (current) or historic clear felling. The reserve is also under threat from urban and industrial development. Traditionally managed agricultural areas are in decline, especially hill and moorland farming, leading to loss of habitats.

Information Centre Yes

Guide By prior arrangement with LTNC or ORGT **Disabled Access** Not at present
School Parties Yes. Contact LTNC or ORGT for details **Parking** There are 2 car parks as well as street parking available. Coaches by arrangement **Toilets** In Information Centre **Food** No

Further Information Contact LTNC or ORGT.

Manchester, North
HOPWOOD WOODS

OS Ref SD875083   Landranger Sheet 109
Nearest Town Middleton   **Size of Reserve** 30 hectares (74 acres)
Managed by The Oldham & Rochdale Groundwork Trust (ORGT)
Access Open all year

T he Hopwood Woods Nature Reserve is an attractive series of small woodlands over fine acidic grasses and bracken. The woodlands lie in a narrow valley and around 16th-century Hopwood Hall. There are also ponds with well developed aquatic flora and fauna.

Nature Trail The 4-km (2½-mile) waymarked trail passes through old clay pits and coal mining areas as well as the woodlands. Expect soft muddy conditions in some areas. Trail leaflets are available from ORGT.

Plants Bracken, Wavy Hair Grass, Rosebay Willowherb, Greater Reedmace (Bulrush), Great (Hairy) Willowherb, Sweet Cicely, mosses, liverworts and ferns.
Trees A small area of woodland, known as Hopwood Clough, contains a number of exotic species, such as American Red Oak, Turkey Oak, Larch and Rhododendron. Also on the reserve are Alder, Birch, Beech, Oak, Yew, Field Maple and Lime.
Birds Redpoll, Goldfinch, Siskin, Blue Tit, Great Tit, Warblers, Goldcrest, Lapwing, Fieldfare, Redwing, Tawny Owl, Great Spotted Woodpecker, Yellow Bunting, Woodcock, Jack Snipe, Kingfisher, Sparrowhawk.
Other Good Fungi in Autumn.

Under Threat This is another reserve which, because of its position in the Greater Manchester area, is constantly under threat from urban and industrial development.

Guide By prior arrangement with ORGT   **Disabled Access** No
School Parties Contact ORGT   **Parking** Street parking only   **Toilets** No   **Food** No

Further Information Contact ORGT.

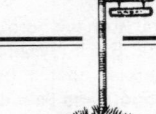

Manchester, North
JUBILEE TRAIL

OS Ref SD949104   Landranger Sheet 109
Nearest Town Shaw   **Size of Reserve** 0.5 hectares (1¼ acres)
Managed by The Oldham & Rochdale Groundwork Trust (ORGT)
Access Open all year

T he Jubilee Trail is based on the site of a former colliery which closed in the 1930s. Since then, natural regeneration has ensured that the area is now well wooded and supports a varied flora and fauna. A pond has been created and a number of plant and animal species now live there. The remains of the old colliery buildings provide added interest.

Nature Trail 500 metres (546 yards), unmarked. There are steps on some parts of the trail although the lower areas are quite flat. The route of the trail is shown on a map available from ORGT.

Plants Golden Rod, Figwort, mosses and lichens, and a large bank of Heather which is not common elsewhere in the area.
Birds A number of bird boxes have been constructed in the hope of attracting more birds to the site.

Guide By prior arrangement with ORGT   **Disabled Access** No
School Parties School parties have visited the park but there is no current programme of school visits. There are plans to promote the site for school use in the future
Parking Small car park adjacent to the start of the nature trail   **Toilets** No   **Food** No

Further Information Information leaflets are available from ORGT.

Manchester, North

PRINCESS PARK

OS Ref SD894033   Landranger Sheet 109
Nearest Town Chadderton   **Size of Reserve** 0.6 hectares (1½ acres)
Managed by The Oldham & Rochdale Groundwork Trust (ORGT)
Access By prior arrangement with ORGT

P rincess Park is situated on formerly waterlogged grassland adjacent to a residential area. A number of habitats have been created on the small site, including a pond, marsh area and woodland. There is good access to the park and a network of footpaths allows an easy approach to all points of interest.

Nature Trail 250 metres (275 yards), with points of interest marked. Paths are shown on a map on the Information Sheet provided by ORGT.

A derelict pavilion has been converted into a Countryside Study Centre for Environmental Education. Other features of the Park include a Tree Nursery, wild flower meadow and a Nature Club Garden.
Plants A number of species have been planted in the Park. In particular, many wetland species now survive in the pond and marsh areas, including Reedmace, Rushes, Gypsywort and Mint. The Wild flower Meadow also acts as home to Corn Cockle, Marigold, Cornflower and Poppy. The heathland area has Teasels and Orchids.
Birds Most garden birds, plus Goldfinch, Mallard and Kestrel.
Other At the moment, the pond provides the best feature of the Park with Frogs, Newts, Water Beetles, Dragonflies, Pond Skaters and a range of other creatures.

Under Threat In the next few years the Manchester Ring Road is to be built within a few hundred yards of the park. This will run across wasteland which currently supports a variety of trees and some orchids. The significance of the Princess Park habitats will thus increase.

Guide By prior arrangement with ORGT   **Disabled Access** The footpaths in the park are suitable for wheelchair users, and facilities for the disabled are planned for the new Study Centre   **School Parties** By prior arrangement with ORGT. A number of school worksheets have been developed for use at the park
Parking   Adjacent to the park   **Toilets** To be included in the new Study Centre – plus a toilet for disabled visitors   **Food** No

Further Information Information sheets and maps are available from ORGT.

Manchester, North

SUMMIT CIRCUIT

OS Ref SD948189   Landranger Sheet 109
Nearest Town Summit   **Size of Reserve** 8 km (5 miles) long
Managed by The Oldham & Rochdale Groundwork Trust (ORGT)
Access Open all year

T he Summit Circuit Trail utilises statutory rights of way and crosses the Pennine moorland fringe, river valleys, water catchments, open farmland and a length of the Rochdale Canal towpath.

Nature Trail The circular trail is about 8 km (5 miles) long and is waymarked. Interpretative information on industrial and natural history are given in material available from ORGT.

Birds Plover, Skylark, Wildfowl.

Guide By prior arrangement with ORGT   **Disabled Access** No
School Parties By prior arrangement with ORGT   **Parking** Yes   **Toilets** No
Food At cafés and restaurants on or close to the route

Further Information Contact ORGT.

Manchester, North

THORNHAM LANE TRAIL

OS Ref SD885086   Landranger Sheet 109
Nearest Town Middleton   **Size of Reserve** The walk is 3 km (2 miles) long
Managed by The Oldham & Rochdale Groundwork Trust (ORGT)
Access Open all year

This historical trail was developed initially by the staff, pupils and parents of Thornham St. Johns Primary School. It passes through lowland Rochdale farmland and explains the social and industrial history of the area. Apart from numerous wild flowers, the reserve has limited wildlife interest.

Nature Trail The trail is signposted entirely along public rights of way. Strong footwear is recommended. Please keep dogs on a lead as the trail crosses private farmland. Trail leaflets are available from ORGT.

Plants Tutsan, Red Hemp Nettle, Goose Grass, Woody Nightshade, Tufted Vetch, Pineapple Mayweed, Red Shank, Hawkweed, Shepherds Purse, Wild Parsley, Meadow Vetchling, Rose of Sharon, Fever Few, Ox Eye Daisy, Large Flowered Hemp Nettle, Sweet Cicely, Scentless Mayweed, Common Hemp Nettle, Himalayan Balsam, Yellow Loosestrife, Smooth Sow Thistle, Snowberry
Trees Silver Birch, Sycamore, Horse Chestnut, Ash, Oak, Holly, Lilac.

Guide No **Disabled Access** No **School Parties** No **Parking** Street parking only
Toilets No **Food** No

Further Information Contact ORGT.

Northumberland
INNER FARNE

OS Ref NU2437   Landranger Sheet 75
Nearest Town Bamburgh   **Size of Reserve** 6.5 hectares (15 acres)
Managed by The National Trust (NT)
Access Open April to September, weather permitting. Restricted access during breeding season (mid-May to mid-July). The island is reached by boat from Seahouses. Telephone in advance to check weather conditions. A landing fee is charged.

Inner Farne is one of only two Farne Islands, off the north Northumberland coast, that is open to the public. The Farne Islands form one of the most important nature reserves in the British Isles and their future is safeguarded by a management plan which not only ensures the well-being of the wildlife and the preservation of habitat, but also enables the public to enjoy fully these fascinating islands. Inner Farne is the largest island in the group, and the nearest to the mainland.

Nature Trail There is a nature trail on the island.

Plants Some 125 species have been recorded on the Farne Islands, the largest number being found on Inner Farne. They include *Amsinckia Lycopsoides*, Yorkshire Fog, Red Fescue, Sea Campion, Scurvy Grass, Silverweed, Hemlock, Ragwort, Thrift, Yellow Flag Iris, lichens.
Birds More than 250 species recorded on the Farne Islands, including Fulmar, Cormorant, Shag, Eider, Oystercatcher, Ringed Plover, Gulls, Kittiwake, Terns, Guillemot, Razorbill, Puffin and Rock Pipit. Migrants include Wheatear, Swallow,

Martin, Pipit, Wagtail, Warblers, Flycatcher, Finches, Bunting. (A list of the birds recorded each day is displayed on the noticeboard outside the chapel. Visitors should consult this list to discover what they may hope to see on a particular day.)
Animals Rabbit.

Information Centre At Seahouses, on the mainland.

Guide Contact NT for details   **Disabled Access** No   **School Parties** No
Parking On the mainland   **Toilets** Yes   **Food** No

Further Information Leaflets are available from the Information Centre at Seahouses or from NT Wardens on the island.

Tyne & Wear

SHIBDON POND

OS Ref NZ195628   Landranger Sheet 88
Nearest Town Blaydon   **Size of Reserve** 13.7 hectares (34 acres)
Managed by Durham Wildlife Trust (DWT) and the Countryside Management Team of Gateshead Metropolitan Borough Council (GMBC)   **Access** Open all year

S hibdon Pond is a large subsistence pond with adjacent reedswamp, scrub and damp pasture. The reserve is of great ornithological importance with over 160 species recorded. The pond is also one of the most important sites for wintering wildfowl in the north east. The reserve is classified as an SSSI and a Local Nature Reserve (LNR).

Nature Trail There is a waymarked nature trail on the reserve. Nature Trail Guides are available from GMBC at nearby Thornley Woodland Centre, near Rowlands Gill (tel. 0207 545212).

There is an observation hide which is open when a warden is on site, or keys can be purchased from Thornley Woodland Centre.
Plants Cottongrass, hybrid Marsh Orchids, Birdsfoot.
Birds Water Rail, Teal, Mallard, Shoveler, Wigeon, Gadwall, Garganey, Scaup, Goldeneye.
Animals Water Vole, Noctule and Pipistrelle Bats.
Other Waxcap Fungus, Morrel and other Liverworts. Perch and Eel in pond with other coarse fish.

Guide By prior arrangement with DWT   **Disabled Access** No   **School Parties** Yes. Contact DWT for details   **Parking** At Blaydon Swimming Baths on Shibdon Road
Toilets Adjacent to cemetery, 400 metres (¼ mile) towards Blaydon   **Food** No

Further Information Contact DWT.

Tyne & Wear
WASHINGTON WATERFOWL PARK

OS Ref NZ330565   Landranger Sheet 88
Nearest Town Washington   **Size of Reserve** 40 hectares (100 acres)
Managed by The Wildfowl Trust (WT)   **Access** Open daily 9.30–17.00 in summer or 1 hour before dusk in winter. Closed 24th and 25th December. There is an entrance charge for all visitors over 4 years of age, but there are group and educational concessions

This reserve is sited on a hillside above the River Wear. It consists of many large and small pools and some woodland. The reserve includes a 'wild' area as well as a 'collection' area where many rare species of wildfowl may be seen. There is a Visitor Centre and a Children's Play Area in the grounds.

Nature Trail 4 km (2½ miles), waymarked. WT Walkabout Guides are available (price 25p).

Birds Wild birds include Heron, Redshank, Common Sandpiper, Sparrowhawk and Great Spotted Woodpecker. There is also a flock of Chilean Flamingos.
Animals Water Vole, Hare, Rabbit, Stoat, Weasel, Mole.
Butterflies Small Tortoiseshell, Red Admiral, Peacock, Common Blue, Small Copper.

Guide No   **Disabled Access** Yes, there are ramps into some hides, and paths are level. The Visitor Centre, with picture windows, is on one level
School Parties Welcomed   **Parking** Yes   **Toilets** Yes   **Food** There is a Tea Room selling light refreshments and there are picnic facilities   **Shop** Selling books and gifts

Further Information Contact The Wildfowl Trust, Washington Waterfowl Park, District 15, Washington, Tyne & Wear NE38 8LE (tel. 091 4165454).

Yorkshire
BRIDESTONES MOOR

OS Ref SE880904   Landranger Sheet 94
Nearest Town Pickering   **Size of Reserve** 120 hectares (48½ acres)
Managed by The Yorkshire Wildlife Trust (YWT) and The National Trust (NT)
Access Open all year

Bridestones Moor Nature Reserve is situated in the North York Moors National Park on the edge of Dalby Forest. The reserve consists of heather, woodland and upland pasture and is drained by two becks. There are sandstone outcrops – the 'Bridestones'. The reserve is reached by way of the Forestry Commission Dalby Forest Drive.

Nature Trail 2.4 km (1½ miles), unmarked. The start of the walk is marked by a Forestry Commission board. A Nature Walk leaflet is available from the NT or YWT. Parts of the path are rather steep.

Plants Heather, Lichens, Water Mint, Water Forget-me-not, Rushes.
Trees Sessile Oak, Bilberry, Rowan, Birch, Aspen.
Birds Curlew, Meadow Pipit, Jay, Kestrel, Sparrowhawk, Sandpiper, Yellow Wagtail, Grouse.
Animals Roe Deer, Fox.
Insects Green Hairstreak Butterfly, Emperor Moth, Green Tiger-beetle.
Other In the streams can be seen Caddis Larvae and Freshwater Shrimp.

Guide By prior arrangement with YWT **Disabled Access** No **School Parties** Yes. Contact YWT for details **Parking** On either side of the Forest Drive **Toilets** No **Food** No

Further Information Contact The National Trust (32 Goodramgate, York YO1 2LG), or YWT.

Yorkshire
CAPHOUSE COLLIERY

OS Ref SE255166   Landranger Sheet 111
Nearest Town Wakefield   **Size of Reserve** 3 hectares (7½ acres)
Managed by Wakefield Groundwork Trust (WGT)
Access The Nature Trail is available to paying museum visitors only.

Caphouse Colliery is the home of the Yorkshire Mining Museum, providing visitors with a detailed historical insight into the county's coal mining industry by means of static displays, audio-visual presentations and a guided underground tour. The Mining Museum also includes the land surrounding the colliery buildings. Most of this is former colliery spoil upon which there is well established naturally regenerating woodland.

Nature Trail 650 metres (710 yards), waymarked. Trail leaflets, with maps, are available on site or from WGT.

The Nature Trail gives visitors an opportunity to see a fine example of succession of natural woodland regeneration, from almost barren colliery soil through to mature oak/birch woodland.

Guide By prior arrangement with the Yorkshire Mining Museum (see below)
Disabled Access No **School Parties** By prior arrangement with the Yorkshire Mining Museum (see below) **Parking** Ample **Toilets** Yes **Food** There is a restaurant/snack bar at the Museum.

Further Information Contact the Yorkshire Mining Museum, Caphouse Colliery, **New Road, Overton, Wakefield WE4 4RH (tel. 0924 848806)**, or WGT.

Yorkshire
GARBUTT WOOD

OS Ref SE514830   Landranger Sheet 100
Nearest Town Thirsk   **Size of Reserve** 24.2 hectares (60 acres)
Managed by The Yorkshire Wildlife Trust (YWT)   **Access** Open all year

G arbutt Wood is an area of mainly natural hardwood trees situated in the Hambleton Hills on the North Yorkshire Moors. The wood is reached along the Moors Path from Cooper Cross. The Moors Path provides a wonderful view across the Plain of York to the Pennines. Other features include Whitestone Cliff (sandstone) with scree below, scattered scrub, and views over Lake Gormire.

Nature Trail The circular trail is 3 km (2 miles) long and is waymarked. It involves some fairly rough walking, with steep slopes which may be slippery in wet weather, so suitable footwear is essential. A Nature Trail booklet is available from YWT.

The area is of interest for its geology as well as its wildlife.
Plants Bog Bean, Skullcap, Greater Spearwort, Tufted Looesestrife, Marsh Cinquefoil, Wood Sorrel, Orchids.
Trees Birch, Hazel, Sallow, Oak, Sycamore, Rowan.
Birds Great Spotted and Green Woodpeckers.
Animals Red, Roe and Fallow Deer, Fox, Badger.

Information Centre There is a Visitor Centre nearby at Sutton Bank.

Guide By prior arrangement with YWT   **Disabled Access** No   **School Parties** Yes.
Contact YWT for details   **Parking** At Sutton Bank Visitor Centre
Toilets At Visitor Centre   **Food** No

Further Information Contact YWT.

Yorkshire
MOORLANDS

OS Ref SE577590   Landranger Sheet 97
Nearest Town York   **Size of Reserve** 6.8 hectares (17 acres)
Managed by The Yorkshire Wildlife Trust (YWT)   **Access** Open all year

M oorlands Reserve is a woodland area with ponds and deep sandy soils. The vegetation has not developed naturally but has been planted with various kinds of trees to afford protection to the rhododendrons and azaleas which make the wood so colourful in spring and early summer.

Nature Trail About 1.5 km (1 mile), unmarked. This is not a formal trail but paths are clearly defined and marked on a map in the booklet available from YWT.

Plants Vegetation includes planted Daffodils, Narcissi, Azalea, Rhododendron and Lily of the Valley; naturally developed plants include Ferns, Bog Bean, Duckweed, Forget-me-not, Wood Sorrel and Foxglove.
Birds Great Spotted Woodpecker, Goldcrest, Tree Sparrow, Warblers, Spotted Flycatcher, Fieldfare, Chaffinch.
Trees Firs, Pines, Spruce, Larch, Oak, Beech, Lime, Chestnut, Rowan, Cherry, Hazel, Ash, Tulip Tree, Maidenhair Tree.

Guide By prior arrangement with YWT   **Disabled Access** No   **School Parties** Yes. Contact YWT for details   **Parking** On roadside near entrance   **Toilets** No   **Food** No

Further Information Reserve leaflets are available from YWT.

Yorkshire
POTTERIC CARR

OS Ref SE598010   Landranger Sheet 111
Nearest Town Doncaster   **Size of Reserve** 109.2 hectares (270 acres)
Managed by The Yorkshire Wildlife Trust (YWT)   **Access** Open all year

Potteric Carr Nature Reserve is in a shallow peaty basin containing reed fen and open water. It contains many species of marsh vegetation but is best known for its bird life – both resident and visiting.

Nature Trail There are 2 trails – Balby Carr and Bessacarr. Both are about 3 km (2 miles) long and are unmarked.

There are birdwatching hides overlooking open water.
Plants Marsh Stitchwort, Water Violet, Purple Small Reed, Yellow Iris, Marsh Marigold.
Birds Shoveler, Teal, Pochard, Wigeon, Grebes, Warblers, Owls, Woodpeckers; visiting species include Bittern, Marsh Harrier, Crane and Black Tern.

Under Threat The reserve has been threatened in the past by motorway, rail and drainage schemes but is now fairly secure.

Guide By prior arrangement with YWT   **Disabled Access** One of the observation hides is accessible to disabled visitors   **School Parties** By prior arrangement. Contact Mr. R. Tyler, 149 Sheffield Road, Warmsworth, Doncaster (tel. 0302 858375)   **Parking** There are 2 car parks   **Toilets** No   **Food** No

Further Information Contact YWT.

Yorkshire

SKIPWITH COMMON

OS Ref SE669378   Landranger Sheet 105
Nearest Town Ricall   **Size of Reserve** 242.8 hectares (600 acres)
Managed by The Yorkshire Wildlife Trust (YWT)   **Access** Open all year

T he Skipwith Common Reserve is on the site of an old airfield. Habitats include ponds, wet and dry heath, marsh and woodland.

Nature Trail 2.4 km (1½ miles) or 1.2 km (¾ mile), waymarked. The trails are confined to hard paths although some of these are liable to flood, especially in winter. Nature Trail leaflets are available from YWT.

Plants Bog Pimpernel, Sundew, Twayblade, Spotted Orchid and Broadleaved Helleborine.
Trees Birch, Oak, Scots Pine, Willow.
Birds Ducks – Wigeon and Teal, Nightjar.
Animals Fallow Deer.

Guide By prior arrangement with YWT   **Disabled Access** All paths are suitable for wheelchair users   **School Parties** Yes. Contact YWT for details   **Parking** On disused runway no. 2   **Toilets** No   **Food** No

Further Information Contact YWT.

Yorkshire

THORPE MARSH

OS Ref SE594093   Landranger Sheet 111
Nearest Town Doncaster   **Size of Reserve** 60.7 hectares (150 acres)
Managed by The Yorkshire Wildlife Trust (YWT)   **Access** By free permit only from
Mr. A. Mitchell, 79 Jossey Lane, Scawthorpe, Doncaster

T horpe Marsh Nature Reserve is situated on land beside Thorpe Marsh Power Station owned by the CEGB. It lies on flat land and consists of ancient pastures, a disused railway line, a pond and an excavated lake. The reserve is particularly noted for its birdlife and is a good example of the creation of a conservation area immediately adjacent to a major industrial site.

Nature Trail There is a waymarked 1.2-km (¾-mile) circular trail around one of the pasture areas, known as Reedholme.

There is a birdwatching hide overlooking the lake.
Plants Pepper Saxifrage, Sneezewort, Great Burnet, Water Dropwort, Orchids.
Birds Linnet, Redpoll, Whitethroat, Greenfinch. Also seen: Goldcrest, Long-tailed

Tit, Willow Warbler, Short-eared Owl. On lake: Swan, Heron, Sandpiper, Tufted Duck.
Butterflies 15 species recorded, including the uncommon Speckled Wood.

Information Centre A Field Centre has been established on the reserve to promote interest in the wildlife and in conservation in general. The Centre is equipped with displays and can be made available to those wishing to pursue more serious field studies.

Guide By prior arrangement with YWT. There is also a cassette tape guide **Disabled Access** With the help of the cassette tape and a sighted guide, the trail is accessible to visually handicapped visitors. In the Field Centre, a display of tactile material is available by arrangement **School Parties** Yes. Contact YWT for details **Parking** Car park nearby **Toilets** No **Food** No

Further Information Reserve leaflets and cassette tapes are available from YWT.

1 St. Abb's Head
2 Doune Ponds
3 Threave Wildfowl Refuge
4 Buchan Line Walkway
5 Crathes Estate
6 Balmacara Estate
7 Isle of Eigg
8 Loch Fleet
9 Ardmore
10 Brodick Country Park
11 The Falls of Clyde
12 Linn Park
13 Mugdock Country Park
14 Pollok Country Park
15 Arbroath Cliffs
16 The Hermitage
17 Linn of Tummel

SCOTLAND

GHLAND

Golspie

GRAMPIAN

Fraserburgh

4

Peterhead

Ellon •

Banchory • 5

Killiecrankie
17

AYSIDE

16 • Dunkeld   15 • Arbroath

FIFE

Doune
rling

avie   LOTHIAN   1 • Eyemouth

lasgow
Lanark
11 •

BORDERS

MFRIES &
LLOWAY

astle
ouglas

Borders

ST. ABB'S HEAD

OS Ref GR913674   Landranger Sheet 67
Nearest Town Eyemouth   **Size of Reserve** 77.7 hectares (192 acres)
Managed by The National Trust for Scotland (NTS) and Scottish Wildlife Trust (SWT)
Access Open all year

S t. Abb's Head National Nature Reserve (NNR) is a spectacular headland and is part of a larger SSSI which is of national importance for seabirds, geology and plant life. The densest populations of seabirds nest on the Head itself and a great range of coastal plants and invertebrates can be seen on the reserve.

Nature Trail About 5 km (3 miles), waymarked. The coastline consists of 91.4-metre (300-foot) cliffs topped by slippery turf. Visitors should take great care near the unfenced cliff edges. Suitable footwear is essential. The route of the footpath is marked on a map in the reserve booklet available from NTS and SWT.

A checklist of birds, plants and butterflies to be found on the reserve is included in the reserve booklet.
Birds March to June: nesting seabirds, including Guillemot, Razorbill, Kittiwake, Fulmar, Shag, Puffin. Spring and Autumn: migrants.
Animals Seals.

Information Centre There is a Visitor Centre, open all year round.

Guide By prior arrangement with the Ranger on Coldingham (08907) 71443
Disabled Access Yes. Contact NTS or SWT for details   **School Parties** By prior arrangement with the Ranger (as above)   **Parking** In free car parks   **Toilets** Yes, including for the disabled   **Food** The café is open during the summer months only

Further Information Reserve booklets are available from NTS or SWT.

Central

DOUNE PONDS

OS Ref NN723020   Landranger Sheet 57
Nearest Town Doune   **Size of Reserve** 16 hectares (40 acres)
Managed by Stirling District Council and Scottish Conservation Projects
Trust (SCPT)   **Owned by** Moray Estates   **Access** Open all year

D oune Ponds Reserve is on the site of an old sand and gravel pit which closed in the mid-1970s. It now consists of one large pond and two smaller ones, and a scrape pool, with surrounding woodland, birch scrub and osier.

Nature Trail 800 metres (½ mile), waymarked. A Nature Trail Guide is available from Stirling District Council Countryside Ranger Service, Directorate of Leisure and Recreation, Beechwood House, St. Ninian's Road, Stirling FK8 2AD (tel. 0786 79000), or from SCPT.

There are two observation hides on the route of the Nature Trail, making it an ideal walk for birdwatching.
Plants Marsh Orchids and a variety of wetland plants.
Birds 90 species recorded, mostly woodland, marshland or wetland.
Animals Fox, Rabbit, Shrew, etc.

Under Threat High quality wetland sites are scarce in lowland Stirling District and there are no major Country Parks. The area is under high pressure from tourism and development for housing and roads.

Information Centre Planned for the future. Contact Countryside Ranger Service (as above), or SCPT, for details.

Guide Yes. Contact Countryside Ranger Service (as above)   **Disabled Access** The eastern part of the trail is accessible to wheelchair users   **School Parties** Yes. Contact Countryside Ranger Service (as above) for details   **Parking** For 20 cars
Toilets Not at present but planned for the future   **Food** No, but village is only a short distance away

Further Information There is an information board at the entrance to the reserve. For more detailed information, contact the Countryside Ranger Service (as above), or contact SCPT.

Dumfries and Galloway
THREAVE WILDFOWL REFUGE

OS Ref GR742608   Landranger Sheet 84
Nearest Town Castle Douglas   **Size of Reserve** 607 hectares (1,500 acres)
Managed by The National Trust for Scotland (NTS)   **Access** Open all year

T he Refuge includes a stretch of the River Dee and associated farmland that is attractive to wintering wildfowl.

Nature Trail 1.5 km (1 mile), waymarked. The trail leads to several observation points from where the birds can be watched. Further details of these hides are given in a reserve booklet available from the Threave Garden Visitor Centre or from NTS. Maps showing the positions of the hides are also displayed on the tracks leading to the Refuge.

Plants Wetland species.
Birds Winter: Greylag Geese, Goldeneye, Goosander, Wigeon, Mallard, Teal, etc. All year: Kingfisher, Buzzard, Willow Tit, Barn Owl.
Animals Roe Deer, Otter.

Information Centre Threave Garden Visitor Centre is about 1.5 km (1 mile) away. **It is open throughout** the year but not staffed during the winter months (October to March).

Guide By prior arrangement with the Ranger on Castle Douglas (0556) 2575
Disabled Access No   **School Parties** By prior arrangement with the Ranger (as above).
A Young Naturalists' Club also operates   **Parking** Yes   **Toilets** In Threave Garden
Visitor Centre   **Food** At Threave Garden in the summer months

Further Information Contact the Ranger (as above) or NTS.

Grampian

BUCHAN LINE WALKWAY

OS Ref NJ9967   Landranger Sheet 30/38
Nearest Towns Fraserburgh, Mintlaw and Ellon
Size of Reserve The complete walkway is 64.3 km (40 miles) long
Managed by Buchan Countryside Group (BCG)   **Access** Open all year

T he Buchan Line Walkway follows the route of a disused single track
railway. Since its closure in 1979, the track has been reclaimed by
nature and now provides refuge for plants, animals and birds which have
been driven from the surrounding cultivated land. Parts of the line are
enclosed and sheltered, offering a habitat for small birds and mammals,
while other parts are open, revealing expansive views of the open Buchan
countryside.

Nature Trail There are several access points along the Walkway, eg. at Deer Abbey
(NJ9748) and Aden Country Park, Mintlaw, from where walks may be taken along
the line in either direction. Parts of the line have been re-surfaced to provide easier
walking, eg. a 2.4-km (1½-mile) stretch south of Auchnagatt (NJ9342). It is planned
eventually to provide a smooth walking surface the length of the Walkway. Trail
leaflets are available from BCG.

Plants Rosebay Willowherb, Ox-eye Daisy, Harebell, Pink Purslane, St. John's
Wort, Mullein, Yellow Rattle, Orange Hawkweed, Trefoils.
Trees Regenerating Birch, Willow, Alder, Ash, Rowan, Elder, Scots Pine,
Hawthorn, Beech, Sycamore, Aspen.
Birds Common species, plus Reed Bunting, Sedge Warbler, Yellowhammer, Linnet,
Geese, Swans, Snipe, Partridge.
Animals Badger, Fox, Roe Deer.
Butterflies Common Blue.

Guide No   **Disabled Access** In some areas, eg. near Aden Country Park, Mintlaw
School Parties No   **Parking** At various points along the line   **Toilets** In all villages
and towns along the way   **Food** From local pubs, cafés, etc.

Further Information Contact BCG.

Grampian

CRATHES ESTATE

OS Ref GR734968 Landranger Sheet 38
Nearest Town Banchory **Size of Reserve** 242.8 hectares (600 acres)
Managed by The National Trust for Scotland (NTS) **Access** Open all year

The Crathes Estate Reserve consists of woodland, plantation, pond and river habitats surrounding Crathes Castle. The wild habitats are complemented by a formal garden and wildlife garden.

Nature Trail There are 5 waymarked Woodland Trails of varying lengths from 2.4 km (1½ miles) to 9.6 km (6 miles). A sixth trail of 400 metres (¼ mile) is specially designed for use by disabled visitors. A Woodland Trails leaflet is available at the reserve or from NTS.

Plants Woodland and estate species.
Birds Woodland and estate species.
Animals Roe Deer, Red Squirrel, Rabbit.

Information Centre There is a Visitor Centre.

Guide By prior arrangement with the Ranger Service on Crathes (033 044) 651. A wide range of guided walks is available throughout the summer months
Disabled Access To Woodland Walk (see above) and Visitor Centre
School Parties By prior arrangement with the Ranger Service (as above)
Parking Yes **Toilets** Yes, including for the disabled **Food** The restaurant is open in season. There is also a picnic site

Further Information Contact NTS. A thriving Young Naturalists' Club is based at Crathes.

Highland

BALMACARA ESTATE

OS Ref GR798276 Landranger Sheet 33
Nearest Town Lochalsh **Size of Reserve** 2,272.7 hectares (5,616 acres)
Managed by The National Trust for Scotland (NTS) **Access** Open all year

The reserve comprises most of the Kyle/Plockton peninsula opposite the Isle of Skye and offers the typical highland variety of moorland, woodland, lochs and seashore.

Nature Trail There are several unmarked trails of varying lengths. Trails include excellent viewpoints.

Plants Full range of highland flora.
Birds Diver, Buzzard, etc.

Animals Otter, Red and Roe Deer, Badger, Wild Goat.

Information Centre There is a natural history display in the Coach House at Lochalsh House.

Guide By prior arrangement with the Ranger on Glenshiel (059 981) 219. A programme of guided walks is available in the summer months.
School Parties By prior arrangement with the Ranger (as above) **Parking** Yes
Toilets Yes **Food** In nearby hotels. There is a campsite on the estate run by the Forestry Commission

Further Information Contact NTS.

Highland
ISLE OF EIGG

OS Ref NM474875 Landranger Sheet 39
Nearest Town Arisaig **Size of Reserve** 1,518 hectares (3,750 acres)
Managed by Scottish Wildlife Trust (SWT)
Access By ferry from Arisaig or Mallaig. Cars may not be taken on to the island

The Isle of Eigg is an Inner Hebridean island about 19.3 km (12 miles) from the mainland. It is a naturalist's paradise and contains a number of SSSIs and three SWT reserves. Habitats represented on the island include woodland, flower-rich pasture, bog and heath.

Nature Trail There are 4 trails of various lengths and difficulty. The longest is 14.4 km (9 miles) long, the shortest is 5.6 km (3½ miles) long. A 'Walks' leaflet is available from SWT.

Plants Ramson, Primrose, Bluebell, Common Spotted Orchid, Lousewort, Rushes, Sedges, Grasses, Sundew, Butterwort, Water Forget-me-not.
Trees Oak, Ash.
Birds Woodland species, including Tits, Warblers, Finches, Spotted Flycatcher, Treecreeper, Buzzard, Kestrel, Meadow Pipit, Wheatear, Stonechat, Whinchat, Golden Eagle (occasionally).
Animals Otter.

Guide Contact SWT **Disabled Access** No **School Parties** Contact SWT
Parking On mainland **Toilets** On island **Food** No

Further Information Contact SWT.

Highland

Highland

LOCH FLEET

OS Ref NH794965   Landranger Sheet 21
Nearest Town Golspie   **Size of Reserve** 1,163 hectares (2,873 acres)
Managed by Scottish Wildlife Trust (SWT)   **Access** Open access all year to
Balblair Wood and Ferry Links. Permits are required for visiting the remainder
of the reserve

The reserve at Loch Fleet lies within the estuary of the River Fleet, the most northerly inlet on the east coast of Scotland. Within its boundaries are the contrasting habitats of estuary, pine woods and sand dunes. The loch is designated an SSSI.

Nature Trail There is no formal trail but footpaths provide access to Ferry Links and Balblair Wood.

Many of the birds that visit Loch Fleet can be watched from the road along the south shore, as can the Common Seals that haul out on the sandbanks to bask.
Plants One-flowered Wintergreen, Lesser Twayblade, Sea Milkwort, Sea Centaury.
Trees Scots Pine.
Birds Redstart, Siskin, Scottish Cross bill, Terns, Shelduck, Waders, Eider, Wigeon.
Animals Roe Deer, Wild Cat.
Other Salmon pool with spectacular sight of salmon leeping in summer.

Information Centre The SWT's summer warden provides information and help for visitors between April and August.

Guide A series of guided walks, during summer, explore the habitats of Balblair Pinewood and Ferry Links   **Disabled Access** Yes. Contact SWT for details
School Parties Contact SWT   **Parking** In car parks   **Toilets** No   **Food** No

Further Information Contact SWT. Boards with information about Loch Fleet and its wildlife are situated in the parking areas.

Strathclyde

ARDMORE

OS Ref NS319786   Landranger Sheet 63
Nearest Town Helensburgh   **Size of Reserve** 194 hectares (479 acres)
Managed by Scottish Wildlife Trust (SWT)   **Access** Open all year

The rocky promontory of Ardmore contains an unusual diversity of habitats for such a compact area – woodland, farmland, marsh, saltmarsh, shingle beach, rocky shore and mudflats. It is of interest not only for the wildlife associated with these different habitats, but also for its geology and landforms. It is designated an SSSI.

Nature Trail 3 km (1¾ miles) circular, waymarked. Wellington boots are strongly recommended as the path frequently floods after rain. A Nature Trail Guide is available from SWT.

Plants Thrift, Sea Aster, Sea Campion, Silverweed, Water Mint, Water Forget-me-not, Yellow Flag, Meadowsweet, Heather, Cross-leaved Heath, Sphagnum Moss, Purple Spotted Orchid, Bog Asphodel, Sundew, English Stonecrop.
Birds Redshank, Snipe, Lapwing, Reed Bunting, Gulls, Ducks (especially Shelduck), Heron, Curlew, Oystercatcher.
Insects Dragonfly.

Guide By prior arrangement with SWT   **Disabled Access** No   **School Parties** By prior arrangement with SWT   **Parking** Yes   **Toilets** No   **Food** No

Further Information Contact SWT.

Strathclyde
BRODICK COUNTRY PARK

OS Ref NR006380   Landranger Sheet 69
Nearest Town Brodick, Isle of Arran
Size of Reserve 202.3 hectares (500 acres)
Managed by The National Trust for Scotland (NTS)   **Access** Open all year

B rodick Country Park comprises the gardens and woodland surrounding Brodick Castle. While the gardens are internationally famous for their rhododendrons and floral display, the park and surrounding area provide a variety of wildlife habitats.

Nature Trail There are 3 circular waymarked trails of varying lengths (20 minutes, 1½ hours, 2 hours) running from the seashore through parkland, woodland and plantation to the lower slopes of Goatfell. Strong footwear is recommended for the two longer trails.

Plants Mosses, Ferns, Liverworts, Common Polypody, Foxglove, Tormentil, Ragwort.
Birds Blue, Great, Coal and Long-tailed Tits, Treecreeper, Spotted Flycatcher, Nightjar, Tawny Owl, Buzzard, Sparrowhawk, Golden Eagle, Raven.
Animals Red Squirrel, Red Deer.

Information Centre In the Nature Display Room, illustrated talks are given to visitors, including schools and other organised groups.

Guide By prior arrangement with the Ranger on Brodick (0770) 2462. A full programme of guided walks is available from May to September
Disabled Access Yes   **School Parties** By prior arrangement with the Ranger (as above)   **Parking** Yes   **Toilets** Yes   **Food** Available from April to October

Further Information Contact the Ranger (as above) or NTS. Country Park leaflets, with details of the Nature Trails, are available at the Park or from NTS.

Strathclyde

THE FALLS OF CLYDE

OS Ref NS882425   Landranger Sheet 71/72
Nearest Town Lanark   **Size of Reserve** 67 hectares (165½ acres)
Managed by Scottish Wildlife Trust (SWT)   **Access** Open all year

The reserve at the Falls of Clyde stretches along both sides of the Clyde gorge, from the historic village of New Lanark southwards to Bonnington Weir. As well as the spectacular falls from which it takes its name, the reserve contains fine examples of old woodland. It is designated an SSSI. An exciting and diverse range of wildlife lives around the Falls.

Nature Trail There is no formal trail, but there are miles of footpaths on both sides of the river.

Plants Bluebell, Wood Anemone, Wood Vetch, Common Cow-wheat.
Trees Oak, Ash, Birch, Beech, Douglas Fir.
Birds Great Spotted Woodpecker, Dipper, Spotted Flycatcher, 5 species of Tit.
Animals Red Squirrel, Badger, Mink, Roe Deer, Natterer's Bat.

Information Centre The Falls of Clyde Centre provides information and a shop.

Guide By prior arrangement with the Ranger at the Falls of Clyde Centre, The Dyeworks, New Lanark, Lanark ML11 9DB (tel. 0555 65262)   **Disabled Access** No **School Parties** By prior arrangement with the Ranger (as above)   **Parking** Yes **Toilets** Yes   **Food** No, but there is a picnic site

Further Information Contact the Ranger (as above), or SWT.

Strathclyde

LINN PARK

OS Ref NS583592   Landranger Sheet 64
Nearest Town In City of Glasgow   **Size of Reserve** 85 hectares (210 acres)
Managed by City of Glasgow District Council Parks and Recreation Department (an affiliated group member of Glasgow Urban Wildlife Group)   **Access** Open all year

Linn Park is a city park which has been designated countryside. The park is surprisingly wild in character and White Cart Water runs through it. It provides habitats such as deciduous woodland and established conifer plantation, with interesting riverside flora and fauna.

Nature Trail 3 km (2 miles), waymarked. A Wildlife Walkabout Trail Guide is available from the Information Centre in the Park or from City of Glasgow Parks and Recreation Department at 20 Trongate, Glasgow G1.

The interesting flora and fauna to be seen in the park are listed in the Walkabout Trail Guide.

Information Centre Open Saturday and Sunday afternoons.

Guide By prior arrangement with the Countryside Ranger on 041-637 1147
Disabled Access No **School Parties** Yes. Contact the Countryside Ranger (as above) for details **Parking** At the Simshill Road entrance **Toilets** Open office hours and Saturday and Sunday afternoons **Food** No

Further Information Contact Parks and Recreation Department on 041-227 5067, or the Countryside Ranger (as above).

Strathclyde
MUGDOCK COUNTRY PARK

OS Ref NS547780 Landranger Sheet 64
Nearest Town Milngavie **Size of Reserve** 202.3 hectares (500 acres)
Managed by Central Regional Council (an affiliated group member of Glasgow Urban Wildlife Group) **Access** Open all year

Mugdock Country Park contains a variety of parkland scenery, woodlands, marshes, lochs and pastures. The diversity of plant and animal species and the variety of habitats, together with the Park's proximity to Glasgow and its educational value, led to the designation of the area as an SSSI in the early 1970s.

Nature Trail There are several unmarked trails of varying lengths (1.5 km/1 mile to 5 km/3 miles). Contact the Countryside Ranger Service on 041-956 6100 for details.

Plants Common Spotted, Heath Spotted and Lesser Butterfly Orchids, Lesser Twayblade, Fairy Foxglove, Nettle-leaved Bellflower, Chickweed, Wintergreen, Amphibious Bistort.
Trees Oak, Hazel, Wild Cherry, Blackthorn.
Birds Tawny, Long-eared and Short-eared Owls, Whooper Swan, Heron, Buzzard, Sparrowhawk, Kestrel, Black Grouse, Red Grouse, Woodcock, Cuckoo, Green and Great Spotted Woodpeckers, Spotted Flycatcher, Reed Bunting.
Animals Roe Deer, Fox, Hare, Mole, Mink, Weasel, Stoat.
Insects *Phyllobrotica Quadrimaculata* (Beetle) is found in Mugdock Wood (only site in Scotland), Pearl-bordered Fritillary Butterfly.
Other Pipistrelle Bat, various fungi, water insects and freshwater fish.

Information Centre Yes.

Guide By prior arrangement with the Countryside Ranger on 041-956 6100
Disabled Access Yes. Contact the Countryside Ranger (as above) for details
School Parties Yes. Contact the Countryside Ranger (as above) for details
Parking Yes **Toilets** Yes **Food** No

Further Information For details of available leaflets, etc., contact the Countryside Ranger at Craigend Stables Visitor Centre, Mugdock Country Park, Craigallion Road, by Milngavie, Glasgow G62 8EL (tel. 041-956 6100).

Strathclyde

POLLOK COUNTRY PARK

OS Ref NS555625   Landranger Sheet 64
Nearest Town In City of Glasgow   **Size of Reserve** 146 hectares (361 acres)
Managed by City of Glasgow Parks and Recreation Department (an affiliated group
member of the Glasgow Urban Wildlife Group)   **Access** Open all year

The gently undulating landscape of Glasgow's first country park provides a range of wildlife-rich habitats within 5 km (3 miles) of the City Centre. The Park contains semi-natural ancient woodlands, 19th-century plantations, herb-rich grasslands, scrubby areas, ponds and a 3-km (2-mile) stretch of the White Cart Water. The value of the country park is enhanced by the fact that it is surrounded by another 283.2 hectares (700 acres) of golf course, woodlands and farmlands – the remainder of the former Pollok Estate.

Nature Trail 4.4 km (2¾ miles), waymarked. Wildlife Walkabout leaflets are available from the Countryside Rangers' Centre at Pollok House.

Plants About 200 species recorded, including some rarities, eg. Toothwort, Giant Bellflower, Broadleaved Helleborine. Bluebells provide a spectacular show in the woods in May.
Birds 85 species recorded and about 30 of these breed most years, including Sparrowhawk, Great Spotted Woodpecker, Kingfisher, Little Grebe.
Animals 20 mammal species recorded, including Rabbit, Grey Squirrel, Fox, Roe Deer (now rather scarce), Mink, Otter, Brown Hare, Bats.
Insects Dragonfly and damselfly on Pollok Fish Pond.
Other The Park is good for fungal foraging in the autumn.

Under Threat Important wetland areas in north-east Glasgow and adjoining districts are threatened by open cast coal mining, peat extraction and infilling proposals. The western fringe of the Pollok Estate (outside the Country Park) may be lost to road construction.

Information Centre Countryside Rangers' Interpretation Centre. Opening times can be obtained prior to visiting by contacting the Countryside Ranger on 041-632 9299.

Guide For organised groups, by prior arrangement with the Countryside Ranger on above telephone number. A programme of guided walks is organised for the general public. Telephone for details   **Disabled Access** Yes, but limited. Telephone the Countryside Ranger (as above) for details   **School Parties** Advance bookings essential. Contact the Countryside Ranger (as above)   **Parking** Yes   **Toilets** Yes, including for the disabled   **Food** Restaurant

Further Information Telephone the Countryside Ranger on the above number, or the Conservation Section, Parks and Recreation (041-227 5067). Various leaflets are available from the Park, the Greater Glasgow Tourist Board (35-39 St. Vincent Place, Glasgow G1) and Parks and Recreation (20 Trongate, Glasgow G1).

ARBROATH CLIFFS

OS Ref NO6440   Landranger Sheet 54
Nearest Town Arbroath   **Managed by** Scottish Wildlife Trust (SWT)
Access Open all year

F rom some distance out to sea, the Arbroath Cliffs appear like a gigantic wall of red. They are composed of Old Red Sandstone, the age of which is approximately 350 million years. Both maritime and non-maritime plant species flourish on the cliffs and a variety of interesting animals may also be found. A number of seabirds can be seen at any time of year.

Nature Trail 5 km (3 miles), waymarked. Most of the trail follows well-defined paths but it is steep in places. Great care must be exercised near the cliff edge. A Nature Trail booklet is available from SWT.

Plants Lime-loving plants, such as Clustered Bellflower and Carline Thistle; Early Purple Orchid, Red Campion, Wood Vetch, Birdsfoot Trefoil, Kidney Vetch.
Birds Herring Gull, Fulmar, Eider, Rock Dove, House Martin, Arctic Tern, Oystercatcher, Curlew, Snow Bunting.
Butterflies Green-veined White, Common Blue, Small Heath, Meadow Brown.

Guide Contact SWT in advance   **Disabled Access** No   **School Parties** Contact SWT in advance   **Parking** Along the Arbroath promenade   **Toilets** In Arbroath
Food In Arbroath

Further Information Contact SWT.

THE HERMITAGE

OS Ref GR013422   Landranger Sheet 52
Nearest Town Dunkeld   **Size of Reserve** 13.3 hectares (33 acres)
Managed by The National Trust for Scotland (NTS)   **Access** Open all year

T he Hermitage is an area of mixed coniferous and deciduous woodland in the Gorge of the River Braan.

Nature Trail 1.5 km (1 mile), waymarked. A Woodland Walk booklet is available from NTS.

Trees Possibly the tallest Douglas Fir in Britain.
Birds Woodland and river birds.
Animals Red Squirrel.

Guide By prior arrangement with the Ranger on Dunkeld (03502) 667. A programme of guided walks is available in the summer months   **Disabled Access** Cars can be driven into the woodland   **School Parties** By prior arrangement with the Ranger (as above)   **Parking** Yes   **Toilets** No   **Food** Mobile snack bar in season

Further Information Contact NTS.

Tayside

LINN OF TUMMEL

OS Ref GR913610   Landranger Sheet 43
Nearest Town Killiecrankie   **Size of Reserve** 19 hectares (47 acres)
Managed by The National Trust for Scotland (NTS)   **Access** Open all year

The Linn of Tummel is an area of mixed woodland on the banks of the Rivers Tummel and Garry. There are also clearings and streams in the wood, adding further woodland habitats.

Nature Trail 3 km (2 miles), waymarked with numbered posts corresponding to map and information in Woodland Walk leaflet available from Killiecrankie Visitor Centre, or from NTS.

Plants Woodland species.
Birds Woodland and river species, eg. Goosander, Oystercatcher.
Animals Red Squirrel, Otter.

Information Centre The Visitor Centre at Killiecrankie is about 1.5 km (1 mile) away.

Guide By prior arrangement with the Ranger on Pitlochry (0769) 3233
Disabled Access No   **School Parties** By prior arrangement with the Ranger (as above)   **Parking** Yes   **Toilets** At Killiecrankie   **Food** At Killiecrankie

Further Information Contact the Ranger (as above), or NTS.

NORTHERN IRELAND

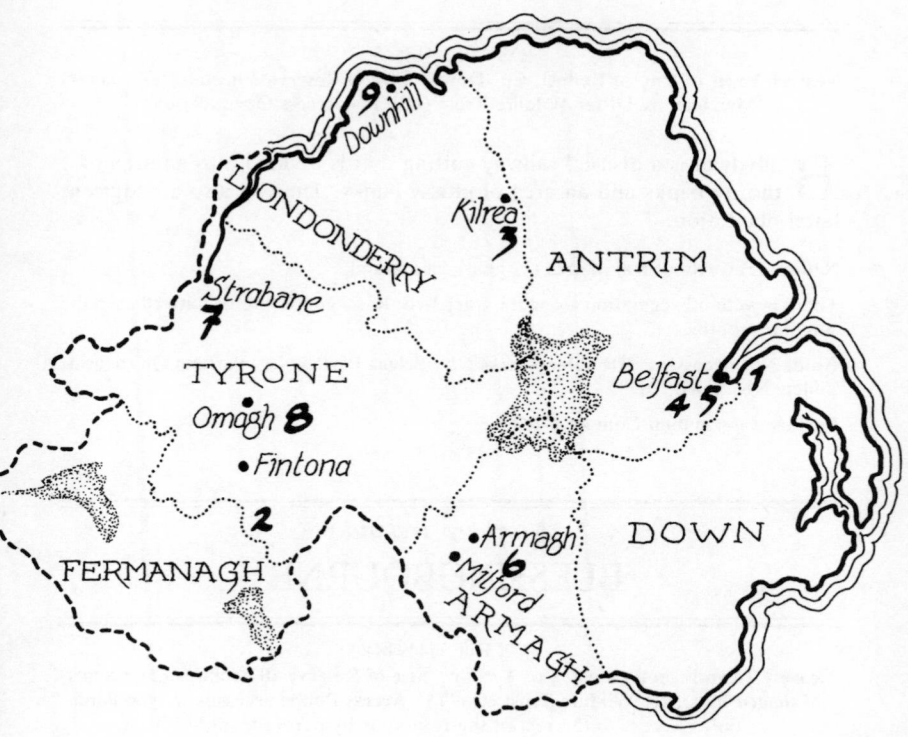

1 Ballydyan Cutting
2 Blessingbourne
3 Creighton's Wood
4 Knock Nature Trail
5 Lagan Meadows
6 Milford Cutting
7 Strabane Glen
8 Termon Glen
9 The Umbra

Northern Ireland
BALLYDYAN CUTTING

OS Ref J418545

Nearest Town In City of Belfast, Co. Down   **Size of Reserve** 3 hectares (7½ acres)
Managed by Ulster Wildlife Trust (UWT)   **Access** Open all year

B allydyan is a disused railway cutting that is divided into an area of thorny banks and an area of grassy banks. There is also an adjacent larch plantation.

Nature Trail About 800 metres (½ mile), unmarked.

There is wetland vegetation along the track bed. It is a good spot for butterflies in the summer months.

Guide Not necessary   **Disabled Access** No   **School Parties** No   **Parking** On roadside
Toilets No   **Food** No

Further Information Contact UWT.

Northern Ireland
BLESSINGBOURNE

OS Ref H449484

Nearest Town Fivemiletown, Co. Tyrone   **Size of Reserve** 10 hectares (24½ acres)
Managed by Ulster Wildlife Trust (UWT)   **Access** Public access is to woodland
only. Access to the rest of the reserve is by permit from UWT

B lessingbourne Nature Reserve consists of mixed estate woodland with many exotic specimens. There is also a large lake.

Nature Trail About 4 km (2½ miles), unmarked.

The main interest is the attractive lake and surrounding reedbeds.
Animals Otter.

Guide By prior arrangement with UWT   **Disabled Access** No   **School Parties** Yes.
Contact UWT for details   **Parking** No   **Toilets** No   **Food** No

Further Information Contact UWT.

Northern Ireland
CREIGHTON'S WOOD

OS Ref H927111
Nearest Town Kilrea, Co. Londonderry   **Size of Reserve** 32 hectares (79 acres)
Managed by Ulster Wildlife Trust (UWT)   **Access** Open all year to UWT members.
Public access is by prior arrangement with Trust

C reighton's Wood consists of a variety of habitats, including oak woodland, old coppice woodland, heather bog, wetland and a small lough. Both woods are situated on prominent ridges protruding from the south side of the Rough Hills.

Nature Trail About 3 km (2 miles), unmarked.

Plants Excellent woodland flora in spring time. Sparrowhawk nest in Hazel woodland.
Trees Interesting area of coppiced Hazel woodland, now being reworked.
Animals Active Badger sett.

Guide By prior arrangement with UWT   **Disabled Access** No   **School Parties** Yes.
Contact UWT for details   **Parking** At Kilrea Golf Club (difficult on Sundays)
Toilets No   **Food** No

Further Information Reserve leaflets and information are available from UWT.

Northern Ireland
KNOCK NATURE TRAIL

OS Ref J387735
Nearest Town In City of Belfast   **Size of Reserve** 0.3 hectares (¾ acre)
Managed by Ulster Wildlife Trust (UWT)   **Access** Open all year

K nock Nature Walk has been created along a short stretch of the old Belfast to Comber Railway. The area has recently been whip-planted and will not be fully developed for several years.

Nature Trail 300 metres (330 yards), signposted at each end. The path is surfaced and there are seats at intervals.

Numerous examples of berry-bearing native species.

Under Threat A further stretch of the same railway has been allotted for development into a new road. There is also pressure from housing developments along the line.

Guide No   **Disabled Access** No   **School Parties** No   **Parking** In nearby streets
Toilets No   **Food** No

Further Information Contact UWT.

Northern Ireland
LAGAN MEADOWS

OS Ref J335700
Nearest Town Belfast   **Size of Reserve** 13.2 hectares (32 acres)
Managed by Ulster Wildlife Trust (UWT)   **Access** Open all year

L agan Meadows Nature Reserve lies within the Lagan Valley Regional Park and is situated less than 3 km (2 miles) from Belfast City Centre. It is a large area of wet meadowland, part of the Lagan Valley Flood Plain, with views over the River Lagan, Belvoir Forest Park, etc. It is a good site for wetland plants, birds, frogs and butterflies.

Nature Trail About 3 km (2 miles), waymarked.

Plants Tussock Sedges, remnant hedges.
Trees Good examples of native Oak.
Birds Large number of Heron.

Guide By prior arrangement with UWT   **Disabled Access** No   **School Parties** Yes. Contact UWT for details   **Parking** On roadside   **Toilets** No   **Food** No

Further Information Reserve leaflets produced by Belfast City Council Parks Department are available from UWT.

Northern Ireland
MILFORD CUTTING

OS Ref H859429
Nearest Town Armagh   **Size of Reserve** 0.8 hectares (2 acres)
Managed by Ulster Wildlife Trust (UWT)   **Access** Open all year

M ilford Cutting is a section of disused railway line with grassy banks, thorny banks and a wet base.

Nature Trail About 400 metres (¼ mile), unmarked.

Plant life includes 2 species protected under 1985 legislation. The cutting is a good site for butterflies.

Guide Not necessary   **Disabled Access** No   **School Parties** No   **Parking** Off-road parking   **Toilets** No   **Food** No

Further Information Contact UWT.

STRABANE GLEN

OS Ref H358990
Nearest Town Strabane, Co. Tyrone   **Size of Reserve** 11 hectares (27 acres)
Managed by Ulster Wildlife Trust (UWT)   **Access** Open all year

S trabane Glen is within walking distance of Strabane Town Centre and is a wooded glen with dramatic cliff faces. A stream runs along the centre of the Glen and is surrounded by hazel woodland and marsh area.

Nature Trail About 4 km (2½ miles), unmarked. The trail runs along interesting paths with bridges, stepping stones, etc.

Trees Interesting area of old coppiced Hazel woodland.
Birds Peregrines have been known to nest on the cliff face.

Guide By prior arrangement with UWT   **Disabled Access** No   **School Parties** Yes. Contact UWT for details   **Parking** On roadside   **Toilets** No   **Food** No

Further Information Maps of the reserve, plus further information, are available from UWT.

TERMON GLEN

OS Ref H625715
Nearest Town Omagh, Co. Tyrone   **Size of Reserve** 12.1 hectares (30 acres)
Managed by Ulster Wildlife Trust (UWT)   **Access** Open all year

T ermon Glen is an area of old estate woodland with an attractive stream and infilling lough.

Nature Trail About 1.5 km (1 mile), unmarked. Paths are well-surfaced. The Nature Trail is now included as part of a Heritage Trail run by Omagh District Council.

Guide For groups only, by prior arrangement with UWT   **Disabled Access** No
School Parties By prior arrangement with UWT   **Parking** Yes   **Toilets** No   **Food** No

Further Information Contact UWT. Maps are available on request.

Northern Ireland
THE UMBRA

OS Ref C722355

Nearest Town Downhill, Co. Londonderry   **Size of Reserve** 43.7 hectares (108 acres)
Managed by Ulster Wildlife Trust (UWT)   **Access** Open all year to UWT members.
Public access is by prior arrangement with the Trust

The Umbra Nature Reserve forms part of the largest area of unspoilt sand-dune vegetation in Northern Ireland. It is an important botanical site and a good area for bird and insect spotting. It is also the site of experimental work on dune stabilisation and recreation. The Umbra Stream flows through a low wooded area on the inland margin of the reserve.

Nature Trail About 5 km (3 miles), unmarked.

Plants 7 species of Orchid, plus other examples of rare species.
Birds Good site for birdwatching. The reserve is backed by cliffs which are a nesting site for birds of prey (including Buzzard).

Guide By prior arrangement with UWT   **Disabled Access** No   **School Parties** Yes.
Contact UWT for details   **Parking** Off-road parking at entrance   **Toilets** No
Food No

Further Information A reserve leaflet is available from UWT.

THE WILDLIFE TRUSTS

The walks in this book have been compiled with the help of the various local wildlife trusts and other organisations who manage the nature reserves in which most of the walks are located. The information given for each walk is based on answers to questionnaires completed, in almost every case, by an Officer of the relevant organisation.

The Royal Society for Nature Conservation (RSNC) heads an active network of 48 associated local wildlife trusts and over 50 urban wildlife groups. RSNC and the trusts form the largest voluntary organisation concerned with all aspects of wildlife conservation in the UK. The regional trusts operate on a non-profit-making basis, relying on membership and other sources for funding. Their aims are primarily to look after the countryside and protect the wildlife on the nature reserves they own or lease. This involves general care of each reserve, including maintenance of visitor facilities, such as footpaths and observation hides, as well as management of habitats to promote the growth of certain rare plants or encourage additional wildlife to the reserve. On some reserves, it may even be necessary to create a completely new habitat, such as a pond or lake, or a cleared area of grassland, in order to make it more attractive to wildlife or to safeguard a particular endangered species.

The majority of trusts also provide trail guides, maps, leaflets, booklets or information sheets that are available to anyone wishing to visit a reserve. When writing to a trust for information, always enclose a stamped, addressed envelope. A number of walks on National Trust Reserves have been included in this book, but by no means all of them. For a list of NT Country Walks, send an s.a.e. to NT headquarters.

Not all trusts can allow open access to all their reserves. In some cases, access has to be limited in order to protect rare species. When membership or permits are required for any of the walks in this book, this has been stated in the relevant entries, along with information on how to obtain access. It is advisable to contact the trust headquarters or local office in advance whenever possible, especially when planning a group visit, or if a guide is required. The trusts can also provide further access details for disabled people who wish to visit a reserve, several of which have special facilities.

The following is a list of the wildlife organisations that have provided details for the walks in this book. It is worth remembering that the trusts do not operate in isolation; many are funded or supported in other ways by such organisations as the government's Nature Conservancy Council (NCC) or the World Wide Fund for Nature (WWF). Many of the trusts work in cooperation with their local council, and in Scotland the Association of Countryside Rangers provides a Ranger service.

Wardens or Rangers are always pleased to hear about species spotted on their reserves, so do make a note of anything unusual you see while walking.

Royal Society for Nature Conservation 164 Vauxhall Bridge Road, London SW1 (tel. 01-828 1657)

World Wide Fund for Nature Panda House, Weyside Park, Godalming, Surrey GU7 1XR (tel. 0483 426444)

Nature Conservancy Council Northminster House, Northminster, Peterborough PE1 1UA (tel. 0733 40345)

The National Trust 36 Queen Anne's Gate, London SW1H 9AS (tel. 01-222 9251)

The Wildfowl Trust The New Grounds, Slimbridge, Gloucestershire GL2 7BT (tel. 045 389 333)

Groundwork Foundation Bennetts Court, 6 Bennetts Hill, Birmingham B2 5ST (tel. 021 236 8565)

South-West England

Avon Wildlife Trust The Old Police Station, 32 Jacobs Wells Road, Bristol BS8 1DR (tel. 0272 268018/265490)

Cornwall Trust for Nature Conservation Five Acres, Allet, Truro, Cornwall TR4 9DJ (tel. 0872 73939)

Devon Wildlife Trust 35 New Bridge Street, Exeter, Devon EX4 3AH (tel. 0392 79244)

Dorset Trust for Nature Conservation 39 Christchurch Road, Bournemouth, Dorset BH1 3NS (tel. 0305 64620)

Plymouth Urban Wildlife Group 8 Cambridge Road, Ford, Plymouth PL2 1PU (tel. 0752 500468)

The Somerset Trust for Nature Conservation Fyne Court, Broomfield, Bridgwater, Somerset TA5 2EQ (tel. 0823 451587)

South-East England

Kent Trust for Nature Conservation PO Box 29, Maidstone, Kent
ME14 1YH (tel. 0622 53017)

London Wildlife Trust 80 York Way, London N1 9AG (tel. 01-278 6612)

Surrey Wildlife Trust The Old School, School Lane, Pirbright, Woking,
Surrey GU24 0JN (tel. 0483 797575)

Sussex Wildlife Trust Woods Mill, Henfield, West Sussex BN5 9SD
(tel. 0273 492630)

Trust for Urban Ecology PO Box 514, London SE16 1AS
(tel. 01-237 9165)

Wiltshire Trust for Nature Conservation 19 High Street, Devizes,
Wiltshire SN10 1AT (tel. 0380 5670)

Wales

Brecknock Wildlife Trust 7 Lion Street, Brecon, Powys LD3 9ED
(tel. 0874 5708)

Dyfed Wildlife Trust 7 Market Street, Haverfordwest, Dyfed
SA61 1NF (tel. 0437 5462)

Glamorgan Wildlife Trust The Glamorgan Nature Centre, Fountain
Road, Tondu, Bridgend, Glamorgan CF32 0EH (tel. 0656 724100)

Gwent Wildlife Trust 16 White Swan Court, Monmouth, Gwent
NP5 3NY (tel. 0600 5501)

Montgomeryshire Wildlife Trust 8 Severn Square, Newtown, Powys
SY16 2AG (tel. 0686 24751)

North Wales Wildlife Trust 376 High Street, Bangor, Gwynedd
LL57 1YE (tel. 0248 351541)

Radnorshire Wildlife Trust 1 Gwalia Annexe, Ithon Road, Llandrindod
Wells, Powys LD1 5DP (tel. 0597 3298)

Central England

Beds and Hunts Wildlife Trust Priory Country Park, Barkers Lane,
Bedford MK41 9SH (tel. 0234 64213)

Berkshire, Buckinghamshire and Oxfordshire Naturalists' Trust (BBONT)
3 Church Cowley Road, Rose Hill, Oxford OX4 3JR (tel. 0865 775476)

Cheshire Conservation Trust c/o Marbury Country Park, Northwich,
Cheshire CW9 6AT (tel. 0606 78168)

Derbyshire Wildlife Trust Elvaston Castle, Derby DE7 3EP
(tel. 0332 756610)

The Gloucestershire Trust for Nature Conservation Church House,
Standish, Stonehouse, Gloucestershire GL10 3EU (tel. 045382 2761)

The Herefordshire Nature Trust 25 Castle Street, Hereford
HR2 2NW (tel. 0432 56872)

Leicestershire and Rutland Trust for Nature Conservation 1 West Street,
Leicester LE1 6UU (0533 553904)

Lincolnshire and South Humberside Trust for Nature Conservation The
Manor House, Alford, Lincolnshire LN13 9DL (tel. 05212 3468)

Nottinghamshire Wildlife Trust 310 Sneinton Dale, Nottingham
NG3 7DN (tel. 0602 588242)

Shropshire Wildlife Trust Old St. George's School, New Street,
Shrewsbury, Shropshire SY3 8JP (tel. 0743 251691)

Staffordshire Nature Conservation Trust Coutts House, Sandon, Stafford
ST18 0DN (tel. 08897 534)

Warwickshire Nature Conservation Trust Montague Road, Warwick
CV34 5LW (tel. 0926 496848)

Worcestershire Nature Conservation Trust Hanbury Road, Droitwich,
Worcestershire WR9 7DU (tel. 0905 773031)

East Anglia and Regions

Beds and Hunts Wildlife Trust Priory Country Park, Barkers Lane,
Bedford MK41 9SH (tel. 0234 64213)

Broads Authority Thomas Harvey House, 18 Colegate, Norwich, Norfolk
NR1 4DF (tel. 0603 610734)

Cambridgeshire Wildlife Trust 5 Fulbourn Manor, Fulbourn, Cambridge
CB1 5BN (tel. 0223 880788)

The Essex Naturalists' Trust Fingringhoe Wick Nature Reserve, South
Green Road, Fingringhoe, Colchester, Essex CO5 7DN (tel. 020628 678)

Herts and Middlesex Wildlife Trust Grebe House, St. Michael's Street,
St. Albans, Hertfordshire (tel. 0727 58901)

The Norfolk Naturalists' Trust 72 Cathedral Close, Norwich
NR1 4DF (tel. 0603 25540)

Suffolk Wildlife Trust Park Cottage, Saxmundham, Suffolk IP17 1DQ
(tel. 0728 3765)

Northern England

Cleveland Wildlife Trust Old Town Hall, Mandale Road, Thornaby-on–Tees, Cleveland TS17 6AW (tel. 0642 608405)

The Cumbria Wildlife Trust Church Street, Ambleside, Cumbria LA22 0BU (tel. 05394 32476)

Durham Wildlife Trust 52 Old Elvet, Durham DH1 3HN (tel. 091 386 9797)

East Durham Groundwork Trust Ltd. Thornley Station Industrial Estate, Salters Lane, Shotton Colliery, Co. Durham DH6 2QA (tel. 0429 836533)

Lancashire Trust for Nature Conservation Cuerden Park Wildlife Centre, Shady Lane, Bamber Bridge, Preston, Lancashire PR5 6AU (tel. 0772 324129)

The Oldham & Rochdale Groundwork Trust Ltd. Bank House, 8 Chapel Street, Shaw, Oldham, Lancashire OL2 8AJ (0706 842212)

Rossendale Groundwork Trust Ltd. New Hall Hey Road, Rawtenstall BB4 6HR (tel. 0706 211421)

Wakefield Groundwork Trust Ltd. 18 Ferrybridge Road, Castleford, West Yorkshire WF10 4JJ (tel. 0977 603126)

The Yorkshire Wildlife Trust 10 Toft Green, York YO1 1JT (tel. 0904 59570)

Scotland

Buchan Countryside Group 53 High Street, Strichen, (tel. 07715 394)

Glasgow Urban Wildlife Group 27 Groveburn Avenue, Giffnock, Glasgow GA6 7DA (tel.   )

The National Trust for Scotland 5 Charlotte Square, Edinburgh EH2 4DU (tel. 031-226 5922)

Scottish Wildlife Trust 25 Johnston Terrace, Edinburgh EH1 2N (tel. 031-226 4602)

Scottish Conservation Projects Trust Balallan House, 24 Allen Park, Stirling FK8 2QG (tel. 0786 79697)

Northern Ireland

Ulster Wildlife Trust Barnett's Cottage, Barnett Demesne, Malone Road, Belfast BT9 5PB (tel. 0232 612235)

NOTES

WILDLIFE SUPPORTERS URGENTLY NEEDED

We like to think of our country as a land rich in wildlife and wild places. The lochs of Scotland. The Norfolk Broads. The beautiful pennine Dales. Above all, thousands of miles of rivers and shores on which wild animals and birds abound.

But sadly, it could be very different in a few years time.

For example, the wetlands of the west coast of Scotland are one of the otter's last strongholds in Europe. Destroy them and we take a sad step towards the extinction of the otter.

Already some of the Scottish lochs are so affected by acid rain that they are like vinegar. And many of our rivers and marshes are so heavily polluted by farm chemicals that fish and water plants can no longer survive.

WWF is working hard to save wildlife, in Britain and around the world.

This is your chance to play an important part in conserving wildlife. As a WWF member, for just £20 a year you'll also get these benefits:

* BBC Wildlife – Britain's finest nature magazine, delivered to you FREE four times a year * WWF News – our free quarterly newsletter which tells you what WWF is doing to save wildlife and its habitats * Your WWF member's car sticker.

JOIN OUR BATTLE FOR NATURE TODAY

YES, I would like to join WWF. Please send my membership pack, including my first issue of WWF News.

I enclose a cheque/postal order (made payable to WWF United Kingdom) for £20 OR please debit this amount from my Access/Visa card, please delete as appropriate.

Card No.

Signed _____ Date _____

Mr/Mrs/Miss/Ms _____

Address _____

_____

Postcode _____ Tel no _____
(incl STD code)

Ref 84K